HOMEWORK

HOMEWORK

Historical and Contemporary
Perspectives on Paid Labor
at Home

Edited by
Eileen Boris
and
Cynthia R. Daniels

UNIVERSITY OF ILLINOIS PRESS
Urbana and Chicago

Parts of three essays in this work appeared in slightly different form in previously published collections. The editors wish to acknowledge permission to include this material:

Julia Kirk Blackwelder, "Texas Homeworkers in the 1930s," from *Women of the Depression: Caste and Culture in San Antonio, 1929–1939*, pp. 92–107, originally published by Texas A&M Press;

Eileen Boris, "Homework and Women's Rights: The Case of the Vermont Knitters, 1980–85," from *Signs* 13 (1987): 98–120, © University of Chicago Press;

Cynthia B. Costello, "Home-based Clerical Employment," from *The New Era of Home-based Work*, edited by Kathleen Christensen, © Westview Press, 1988.

Library of Congress Cataloging-in-Publication Data

Homework : historical and contemporary perspectives on paid labor at home / edited by Eileen Boris and Cynthia R. Daniels.
    p.   cm.
  ISBN 0-252-01601-7 (cloth : alk. paper). ISBN 0-252-06054-7 (paper : alk. paper)
  1. Home labor—United States—History. 2. Women—Employment—United States—History. I. Boris, Eileen, 1948– .
II. Daniels, Cynthia R.
HD2336.U5H66 1989
331.4'0973—dc19   88-23232
                                                            CIP

For
Clara Mortenson Beyer,
in recognition
—E. B.

———————

For
my grandmother,
Anna Sekanics,
who worked sixty years in the textile mills,
and my mother,
Margaret Daniels,
who has always given me love and support
—C.D.

Contents

Acknowledgments

A number of years ago, when Eileen was just beginning her research on industrial homework, she heard Cyndi present a slide lecture on the tenement workers of New York. This project originated in our discovery of the similarities in our analysis of the meaning of such home-based labor for women and our mutual interest in its history and current politics. Considering our own juggling of paid and unpaid labor, work and motherhood, scholarship and politics, we managed to bridge the miles from Boston to Washington and the differences in the disciplines of political science and history to edit this book collectively and in the spirit of sisterhood. We would like to thank our authors, and those whose pieces could not be included in the final shape of the book, for their willingness to make revisions—and usually make deadlines. To Carole Appel, Cynthia Mitchell, and the rest of the staff of University of Illinois Press, we offer our appreciation. Eileen would like to acknowledge support from Radcliffe College for a Research Support Grant and from Howard University for a Department of History Research Grant and a Research Grant for the Humanities, Social Sciences, and Education. Cyndi also would like to acknowledge Radcliffe College for a Research Support Grant and the American Association of University Women and the Woodrow Wilson Foundation for support of her research.

This book also benefited from the support of our families. Daniel Lichtenstein-Boris taught Eileen what it is like to simultaneously work at home and care for a child under circumstances of relative freedom; she really doesn't mind his guitar, Civil War soldiers, and Legos taking up the front of her study. As always, she is indebted to Nelson Lichtenstein for his willingness to leave his own scholarship to offer love, criticism, and historical insight. Cyndi would like to thank her partner, Bob Higgins, for his encouragement and support while she simultaneously worked a full-time job, edited this book, and gave birth to a daughter, Katherine Rae Daniels, born March 27, 1988. Special thanks go to both Bob and Katie for reminding her that life is not *all* labor.

HOMEWORK

Introduction

EILEEN BORIS and
CYNTHIA R. DANIELS

As more women in the 1980s balanced their need for a wage with their desire to have children, we witnessed an increased interest in the home as a workplace. The media presented glowing portraits of entrepreneurial mothers who turned crafts skills into thriving businesses while watching their toddlers play. We read about companies who put out work to home clericals and allowed valued programmers to work at home. Meanwhile, the Reagan administration attempted to lift existing bans on industrial homework, and liberals and unions countered with predictions of "the return of the sweatshop."

As the opponents of homework recognize, paid labor in the home has a long history. Since the development of a market economy, some women have always worked at home, both as unwaged laborers for their families and as waged laborers for manufacturers and contractors. Where once scholars assumed that industrialization separated home from work and that industrial homework represented an outmoded stage of production, today we recognize that was true only for certain paid laborers, mostly men and single women. By turning homes into factories and offices, the homework system exposes the separation of home and work life as ideological. The issue posed by the current controversy is stark: will such labor encourage new forms of sweated industry which reinforce the existing sexual and racial divisions of labor and stymie worker self-organization, or can it serve as a basis for an alternative to mass production, a new organization of work which integrates home and workplace in a more organic, autonomous synthesis?

This anthology clarifies the past and present of home-based labor. Focused on gender, race, and class, these case studies present a rich portrait of homework, for they recognize that such categories are necessary to fully comprehend the meaning of homework, both in the lives of women and in the structure of the political economy. But just as policy makers disagree over the implications of homework, so scholars present divergent perspectives: on the legacy of homework regulation and the motivations of reformers; on the experiences of homeworkers; on whether homework is a "terrific option," "the best of a bad lot," or an exploitative system of work.

The Evolution of Homework

In the United States, industrial homework developed along with the factory system. In the eighteenth century, merchant manufacturers put out work to farm families and artisanal households, but the homework system that grew in the 1830s and 1840s increasingly derived from industrial capital and relied upon households becoming proletarianized or dependent on wage labor. As Betty A. Beach discusses in her essay on Maine shoemaking, the context for such outwork was gendered from the start, relying upon the sexual division of labor within the household and between the household and the larger community. Moreover, in the transitional economy that was undermining urban artisans, wives needed to add to their husband's earnings and had few other options to do so, especially while also engaging in child care and housework. As the demand for home seamstresses developed, single women and the still married joined widows and deserted wives as garment homeworkers. From the birth of the homework system, then, capitalism and patriarchy reinforced each other.

According to Hilary Silver, in her overview of the demand for homework, deployment of homeworkers varied considerably by industry, depending on particular interplays of technology, labor supply, product demand, and capitalization. The sewing machine neither eased the burden of the seamstress nor compelled any special change. But at the turn of the century, new technologies in another consumer handicraft industry—cigar making—helped to reverse that industry's movement into home tenements. Moreover, as Susan Porter Benson makes clear in her analysis of Rhode Island textile and lace firms, homework employers could save on overhead and meet variable consumer desires. Even though some homeworkers were highly skilled, employers enjoyed a high degree of control over their work through subdividing the labor process. Still, as a number of the case studies here imply, the homework system constrains not only workers but also employers, who resort to homework when they can obtain a preferred labor force in no other way or as a response to market conditions beyond their individual control.

Cynthia R. Daniels, in her analysis of New York City immigrants, reports on the flourishing of homework in the early twentieth century, not only in the finishing of clothing but in other labor-intensive industries in the secondary market of the economy. Although mothers and daughters continued to take in outwork in rural regions, industrial homework grew in urban tenements with the massive immigration from southern and eastern Europe. Most homeworkers were married women with children whose husbands brought in inadequate wages and whose cultural traditions or family responsibilities kept them home. These general patterns persisted later into the century, though as Eileen Boris suggests in her analysis of African-American women in Chicago during the 1920s, homework appeared as a less restrictive option than many other forms of work available to women of color. Homework promised freedom from supervision, which could be as important as the seeming flexibility it offered working mothers.

Homework was a crucial component of the family economy, not one that can be dismissed merely as exploitative labor. Susan Porter Benson and Julia Kirk Blackwelder demonstrate how homework was interwoven in the lives of Providence's Italians and San Antonio's Mexicans. It belonged to a continuous web of family, neighborhood, and community among ethnic and racial women on the margins of industrial life. The portrait of the homeworker as isolated thus hardly reflects the actual experiences of those in the past, as also illustrated in our photographic essay, or, as Beach and Cynthia B. Costello indicate, in the present. Even if the amount of homework declined and its piece rates seemingly worsened with the general economic collapse during the 1930s, homeworking families continued to rely on such earnings. Living close to the margin, even when able to obtain relief, wives and mothers eagerly sought homework to counter the unemployment of other family members.

Forms of Homework

Contemporary studies expose the wide range of industries in which homework has persisted. From the shoe industry in Maine to the assembly of garments in Miami, homework remains a dynamic system of production. Homework also has adapted to meet the needs of new sectors of the economy, like the assembly of high-tech electronic components or manufacture of computer chips. While immigrant urban centers dominated homework at the turn of the century, today homework has dispersed: we find working-class women in rural settings reported in Jamie Faricellia Dangler's study of electronics; clerical workers in suburbs, in Kathleen Christiansen's overview of clerical homework; and first- and second-generation immigrants in "new" urban garment centers, in M. Patricia Fernández-Kelly and Anna M. García's comparison of Miami and Los Angeles.

While the shift of the United States economy from an industrial to a service base is changing the face of homework, the nature of the work done at home has not necessarily been transformed. Silver points out that homework has maintained a constant presence in older industrial occupations, but it also has expanded into newer sectors of the "service" economy. Still, homeworkers tend to be employed in the "secondary" sector, where wages are low, jobs have been segmented and deskilled, and workers are neither unionized nor protected from economic downturns.

At the same time, the development of workplace technologies has led to the growth of new forms of clerical and computer work at home. As studies by Christensen and Costello illustrate, clerical homework has taken on some of the same characteristics as industrial homework: women work for piece rates and the quality and quantity of work performed is controlled by the invisible hand of the contractor. At the other end of the economic spectrum, Margrethe H. Olson has shown how new technologies have led to the extension of the workday for professionals, who may literally bring the office home. While taking on different meanings for both professional and clerical workers, homework blurs the distinction between home and work life for both. The future of computer-based homework remains to be seen. Though such work grew in the 1970s, Olson's study of business attitudes toward homework demonstrates managerial reluctance to let more highly paid employees out of their sight. This may mean that homework will continue only in occupations and industries in which control can be maintained over workers at home or supervision is less significant than overhead savings.

Despite similarities between old and new forms of work at home, recent debates over the regulation of homework demand that we develop more sophisticated definitions. Are home-based businesswomen, for instance, to be categorized as homeworkers, along with women who earn piece rates at home? How do we distinguish between "independent contractors" and homeworkers as "employees"? The case studies here clearly show that homeworkers cover a wide spectrum of the labor market, with important distinctions in wage, skill level, and control over work. We must distinguish not only *who* works at home

but also *why* they work there. Scholars have not yet agreed on terminology; some referring to home-based workers mean *entrepreneurs,*
those who truly control their labor and their market, and others mean
employees, those who depend on an employer to work. To evaluate
homework as a labor system, we must clearly distinguish between
employer, independent contractor, and employee.

Our focus in this collection is on homeworkers as employees, and
we follow the historical terminology that considers the homeworker a
wage laborer, usually paid by the piece, dependent on the employer
or contractor for the opportunity to work. We have included case
studies of telecommuters, of salaried professionals, and of the self-
employed "independent contractor," not only to suggest the range of
home-based laborers but also to place "traditional" homeworkers in
context. The lines between the old homeworkers and some seemingly
more independent forms of home-based labor may be blurring.

These studies show that men and women enter the homework system
in different ways and for different reasons, raising important issues
regarding the gender segmentation of the labor market. More highly
paid forms of homework tend to be the preserve of professional male
employees who may bargain for work at home from a position of
strength in the job market, as Olson records. On the other hand, women
tend to turn to the homework system in an attempt to find a solution
to the conflict between work and family demands. Some, like the group
of Maine shoeworkers, find a balance between family and work. But
it is a solution that has many costs, with women bearing the burden
of trying to juggle work and child care in the same space and time, as
Costello's interviews with insurance clerks emphasize.

From this perspective, homework both reflects and reinforces the
traditional gender division of labor in *and* out of the home. Reflecting
broader economic patterns, female homeworkers are concentrated in
secondary "women's" jobs, while male homeworkers are in more highly
paid primary-sector occupations. And inside the home, homework
reinforces women's primary identification with motherhood and secondary economic position. In an era of political reaction, the call for
women to remain at home appears at least in part a return to traditional
patriarchal values, as Boris suggests in her discussion of the debate
over the Vermont knitters. But many homeworkers share these traditional values.

Given these considerations, why do many women "choose" to work
at home? We must look to homeworkers themselves for the answers.
Working mothers face an economic imperative to work but suffer from
the inadequacy of dependent care and a gender-segregated labor mar-

ket. As such, social and political structures constrain the "choice" of many homeworking women. That homework presents itself as a more flexible and attractive option for working mothers is itself a commentary on the structure of our political economy, which provides working mothers with so few options. Yet throughout these studies we hear the voices of women who gain a sense of self-worth and independence by earning wages at home. In exchange for low wages, many experience a greater sense of autonomy and control over both their work and family lives—a freedom from direct supervision of bosses and an increased flexibility in the structure of the workday. From this perspective, then, homework represents not exploited labor but the attempts of women to find more humane alternatives to a labor market alien to the needs of working parents. In this context, working at home challenges the division between family and work life. The links between factory and home are very real: some women work at home for shops or offices where they formerly worked inside; others rely upon relatives to bring work home from places of employment for them.

Different cultural contexts also affect the experience of homework for women. As Fernández-Kelly and García's study of Cuban and Mexican immigrant women shows, the intersection of class and race deeply shapes the meaning of homework in women's lives. Where women are not destitute and where they can rely on a stable family income, homework provides a source of independence from the economic power of husbands. Yet homework becomes much more exploitative for women who are first-generation immigrants, who have little income and fewer opportunities to earn wages.

The Politics of Regulation

Whether or not the 1980s witnessed an absolute growth in home-based labor, homework has stood on the political centerstage. As a number of authors in this volume (Christensen, Olson, Boris on the Vermont knitters, Virginia duRivage and David Jacobs) testify, the attempt by the Reagan administration to deregulate industrial homework highlighted both the changing political economy—especially the growth of a contingent workforce—and its articulation with the gender economy—the increased employment of mothers of small children. Conservative champions of free enterprise and New Right defenders of the patriarchal family called for the lifting of homework bans under the Fair Labor Standards Act for seven garment-related trades. Meanwhile, the AFL-CIO and some of its constituent unions asked for extending prohibition to cover clerical and other forms of white-collar employee homework. Feminists continue to question whether home-based labor can actually satisfy women's needs for quality child care, economic independence, and self-esteem.

Though regulation of homework began as a crusade against "sweated labor" and its contaminated products, from the start its opponents emphasized the demoralizing environment of the home factory in ways that suggested that the home should remain separate from the factory. Yet, as Daniels suggests here, tenement homework laws "protected" the consumer at the expense of homeworking mothers who remained hidden in the home. Regulation of homework, as Silver, Benson, and Boris (in her article on the knitters) recount, consisted of weakly enforced laws until federal action during the New Deal, when the Fair Labor Standards Act of 1938 led to the prohibition of homework in knitted outerwear, women's apparel, belts and buckles, gloves and mittens, handkerchiefs, embroidery, and jewelry—the bans called into question during the 1980s.

Key arguments of the past—that homework allows mothers to work and care for children at the same time, that it interferes with proper mothering—persist today. Yet, as Boris contends, feminist rhetoric has entered the discourse over homework; now some of its defenders link "women's rights" to "the right to work," while opponents promote mothers working outside of the home, with their children attending day-care centers. As the case studies in section two of this book remind us, the experiences of homeworkers are more diverse than the political stereotypes would lead us to believe. Neither unregulated homework nor outright prohibition may meet the needs of homeworkers; either might be the appropriate policy for certain kinds of homework, depending on the extent of exploitation, the impact on social relations within the household and its relation to the larger political economy, and the viable options that working mothers face.

The Future of Homework

Homework presents us with a corollary to the truism "Women have always worked," because it is equally true that "women have always worked at home." As in the past, homework will continue to form a significant part of the modern economy. But as this collection demonstrates, unless we shed old assumptions about women, work, and family life, homeworkers will continue to remain an invisible part of the labor force. The research presented here points to the need to restructure conceptions of work and home life for women. As Sheila Allen points out, assumptions regarding the division between work and home, public and private life in industrialized societies, have led to the invisibility of homework as well as the undervaluation of women's labor in and out of the home. By its very nature, the study of homework itself provides an opportunity for us to rethink the tools we use to understand women's historic relation to the production and reproduction of the social order.

To what extent will homework provide a positive alternative to factory or office work in the future? As Allen discusses, the answer will lie partly in the levels of control and choice homeworkers have over their work, especially how work in the home intersects with labor outside of it. One key aspect will be the freedom to control one's domestic work in the home, with expanded options for shared child rearing and a restructured sexual division of labor; the other key factor will be the freedom to control one's paid work at home, through new forms of organization and collectivization.

A positive vision of homework requires a re-visioning of the relationship between home and work life and a restructuring of the class, race, and gender relations which help to constitute both home and workplace. As Allen illustrates through a discussion of homeworkers' organizations in India, women in "developed" countries may well have much to learn from the alternative organizations established by homeworkers in less developed nations. In contrast to some of the U.S. unions discussed by duRivage and Jacobs, her example of the relationship between British labor and homeworkers suggests that a deeper understanding of why women work at home can generate new alliances in the interests of all workers, whether or not they are in the home.

On a macroeconomic level, homework represents the "devolution" of industry into new "underground" and informal economies where immigrant workers once again work for subminimum wages. The growth of this informal sector, with its disregard of legal regulations, in advanced capitalist economies appears as a response to larger international trends in which Third World nations have sought to improve their stagnant economies through export of cheap goods. Moreover, as custom services and small batch production of luxury items find a niche with one segment of consumers and economic dislocation leaves an abundant labor supply, homework has moved from the periphery back into the core of the global economy. Fernández-Kelly and García place their discussion of homework in the context of the development of this informal sector. Does the reemergence of homework reflect a long-range restructuring of the organization of worklife? Will small-scale and labor-intensive production mark the end of "Fordism," as Silver asks us to consider? We do not know yet how much the growth of homework will substantially increase the number of men and women employed as marginalized temporary or part-time workers who are neither unionized nor have the power to bargain for better working conditions or wages. Neither do we know to what extent work at home will exacerbate a growing polarization of the labor market by class, race, and gender. However, we do know that homework belongs to the decentralization of production that seems to be a central strategy of some sectors and firms for coping with the international restructuring of production, consumption, and capital accumulation.

Assessments of the future of homework—whether it is a good, an evil, or a mixed blessing—depend on our understanding the complexity of the issue. We must view homework not only from the perspective of the individual homeworker but also from the vantage point of the international political economy. Because the same forces that shape all women's experiences in the home and the marketplace shape homework, what we learn from our study casts new light on women's larger struggle for survival and justice. The solution to the homework problem will not be simple: like the achievement of gender equality, it will require the transformation of both the workplace and the home and an end to the devaluation of "women's work." Until we redefine the terms of the debate on homework, there will be no easy answers.

SECTION ONE

Historical Perspectives

1

Between Home and Factory: Homeworkers and the State

CYNTHIA R. DANIELS

Debates over homework—specifically the employment of women to do piecework at home—have involved a complex web of questions about class relations, gender relations, and the nature of state power. In this study of New York homeworkers at the turn of the century, I will explore the role of the state in establishing homework policies that reinforce women's primary association with the home and secondary standing in the public labor market. This will entail an examination not only of the homework system but of the way in which struggles over homework reflected deeper concerns over the stability of the gender order in a period of social, political, and economic turmoil. That is, the development of homework policy illustrates the ways in which state policies reproduce gender inequality by reinforcing dominant assumptions about women and work and by circumscribing the real choices available to women for paid labor.

While state policy is informed by a dominant gender ideology, state policymakers are also subject to conflicting pressures from a variety of sources. Because of this conflict, state policy only *partially* reflects the interest of those at the top of the social order. Rather than simply expressing the interests of a dominant class or gender, state policy often represents an attempt to resolve conflict while maintaining basic structures of privilege. Struggles over homework policy in particular have reflected competing assumptions about women's "proper" relation to home and work life.

In the early twentieth century, in a climate of massive social transformation, debates over homework represented divergent attitudes toward the nature of motherhood, women's proper place in the workforce, and the role of the state in regulating relations in both the public and private spheres. Beyond the kitchens of homeworking women, negotiations over homework policy reflected the different interests brought to bear on the state over the issue of women's work at home. In opposition to homework, social reformers sought to reinforce the division between the public and private spheres by banning homework entirely: they believed women—mothers—should not work at all. Joining them, labor unions opposed homework on the grounds that homeworkers posed unfair competition to unionized, male factory workers. On the other side of the debate, manufacturers who sought to exploit working mothers for their cheap labor defended the rights of women to work and argued that the state lacked the authority to interfere in the 'privacy' of the home. An analysis of these different political pressures will illustrate the ways in which the homework debate mirrored larger concerns over the changing nature of public/private relations.

History shows that attempts to prohibit homework entirely do not address the reasons why women engage in homework in the first place. Now, as in the past, homeworkers often side with the conservative manufacturers and legislators who defend their right to remain at home.[1] Social advocates and union organizers meet with hostility from homeworkers whose options are limited by a workplace incompatible with the needs of working mothers.

Understanding the history of the homework debate will help to unravel this complex of issues and suggest a resolution of the homework question in a way that prevents the exploitation of women and yet addresses the difficult choices confronting working-class women who face the limited choices offered to mothers who must work.

This study concentrates on New York City at the turn of the century, then the center of homework production. As the heart of urban industrialization, an entry point for millions of immigrants, and a hotbed of political activity around the homework question, New York reflected in microcosm the struggles that would later develop nationally over the legality of paid work at home.

Characteristics of the Homework System— New York City, 1910

Although homeworkers were employed by a great variety of industries, a number of characteristics were common to all forms of homework. First, homeworkers were typically found in industries adapting a highly specialized division of labor, and most homeworkers performed only a fraction of the total labor on each item. Second, homeworkers were always paid by the piece, and their piece rates were systematically lower than those paid in the factory, often for the same work. Third, home-workers were most common in seasonal industries, so that the rates of employment fluctuated tremendously over the course of a year.[2] Sewing pants and coats, making artificial flowers and feathers, sorting coffee beans or shelling nuts, embroidering, making human-hair wigs, cigar-rolling, hat-making, and lace work—these represent some of the more than 100 homework occupations found in New York tenements.[3]

While exact figures are difficult to establish, census data and figures from the homework licensing system suggest that as many as 250,000 women may have been engaged in homework in New York City in 1910.[4] During this time homeworkers constituted a very large and undocumented sector of the labor force—one that formed the foundation of many industries. Most homeworkers were married women between twenty-five and forty-five years old with young children and husbands who lived with them in the home.[5]

Immigrant men faced a labor market in which competition was heavy and work was scarce; during the best of times these men could earn a subsistence wage as day laborers on city construction sites, railroads, and other casual, seasonal jobs. As the husband of one home-worker stated, "When the weather is not too cold, or the sun too hot, or the rain too wet, then there is work."[6] On the average, these men were unemployed for at least one-third of the year. As a result, immigrant women and children often worked to maintain basic economic survival.

The Garment Industry

By far the largest number of homeworkers were found in the men's ready-made clothing industry. The garment industry itself employed one-fourth of all industrial workers in New York City in 1905 and was one of the largest employers of women.[7] While factory workers operated machines and basted and pressed garments, homeworkers engaged in the more labor-intensive process of hand finishing.

Although Jewish and Italian workers dominated the garment industry in the factory, Italian women monopolized the finishing of garments at home. One U.S. Senate investigation reported that Italian homeworkers and their children finished 98 percent of all garments.[8] In addition, a New York state study reported that "the Italian home finisher works for about two-thirds the price which other nationalities formerly received for the same work."[9]

The garment industry had both ethnic and sexual divisions of labor, with Jewish men as foremen in the factory, single Jewish and Italian women workers in the factory, and married Italian women working at home. As one investigator stated, despite the prevailing tendency "for the employees to be recruited from the same race as the foremen," Jewish foremen tended to hire Italian women exclusively for homework. One study reports that "no matter how great the poverty, the Hebrew men seldom allow the women of their family to do the [clothing] work at home, even though they may have been shop workers before marriage."[10] While Jewish women were employed in garment homework before 1900 (due to the extreme pressures of poverty associated with recent immigration at that time), the immigration of Italians at the turn of the century combined with lower wages to change the homeworking population.

Because of the seasonal nature of the industry, garment finishers worked an average of 220 days per year, keeping up a frantic pace during the seven months when work could be found. Between preparing meals, caring for children, and cleaning the house, these women worked between eight and ten hours a day sewing garments. Their housework extended their homework well into the night, so that, as the *Report on Women and Child Wage-Earners* of 1911 noted, "part of the work is generally performed after the point of fatigue has been reached."[11]

In addition to the tremendous burden of this double day, these women paid a price in wages. As in all forms of homework, wages differed dramatically between those working at home and those in the factory. On the average, women in the garment industry earned $6.00 per week, while homeworkers could earn only $3.60. And this figure represented the work of more than one laborer, for many children worked with their mothers at home.[12]

Feathers and Flowers

Another large group of immigrants, 98 percent of them Italians, found work making artificial flowers for manufacturers who used the flowers to decorate ladies' hats and Easter bonnets. The starching, dying, cutting, and the final process of branching the artificial flowers was done in the factory. Flower homeworkers produced over 75 percent of all the artificial flowers made in the U.S. in 1910.[13] The flower makers pulled the precut rose, violet, or poppy petals apart, slipped them up the stem, and pinched them into place around the "bud." Sometimes they also pasted leaves onto the stem.

One investigator found the Rapallo family at work on artificial flowers in their two-room apartment. Their rate of work and pay represent the average for a flower-making family. In one week, the Rapallos made an incredible 18,000 violets, for which they were paid $4.50. Mrs. Rapallo, a 30-year-old southern Italian woman with seven children, told an investigator: "We get 15 cents a bunch for this kind of flowers and we can make five bunches a day if they [her children] all work. But 75 cents a day's not much, with rent $11.00 a month, and seven children who always want to eat." Her husband, she said, "had no work for two years."[14]

As another homeworker said, "We all must work if we want to earn anything."[15] The rate of work and the "flexibility" of wages paid in this industry are well illustrated by the remarks of one experienced homeworker: "You can't count homework by the day, for a day is really two days sometimes, because people often work half the night. When the boss asks me how many flowers I can make in a day I say I cannot tell, but I know how many I can do in an hour. Some girls are so foolish. I've heard them praising themselves and telling the boss that they did the work in a day. They're ashamed to say they worked half the night too. But they only hurt themselves, for the boss says if they earn that much in a day he can cut the price."[16] On the average, flower makers could earn between sixty cents and one dollar per day—for a woman working with the help of at least three children.[17]

As with other homework, the demand for artificial flowers was seasonal. From April to October there was no work. In the busy season, a family with more than three workers could earn $4.90 a week, which was approximately 60 percent of what a factory worker doing exactly the same work could earn.[18]

Milliners used feathers as well as flowers to decorate ladies' hats. The sweeping artificial ostrich feathers that were the fashion around 1910 were made in tenements in the Italian districts of the upper East Side. The feather maker was employed at "willowing"—tying to every flue or filmy strand of a good ostrich feather two strands stripped from inferior ostrich feathers.[19] One homeworker reported that she had to work one and a half days to earn 72 cents for one finished plume, which might sell at retail for up to $25.00.[20]

The life/work cycle of these immigrant women forms a distinctive pattern. Children contributed to family income through homework, while sixteen-to-twenty-year-old women engaged in better-paying factory jobs. Then, as these young women approached marital age, their rates of labor-force participation outside the home dropped dramatically. As the *Report on Woman and Child Wage-Earners* indicated, "Between 18 and 22 the changes in the labor force are so rapid that less than half of the number of females employed at the age of 18 are found employed at 22."[21] Presumably, at marriage these women would drop out of public view as wage-earners and continue to earn a wage as homeworkers. Thus the peak wage-earning power of most women was concentrated in the few short years from age sixteen to twenty. Once married, the new-found social status of these women as mothers and wives served to drive down their earning power because they became homeworkers.

Though the wages of homeworkers were small, it would be wrong to think of their income as simply "supplementary" to their husbands' income. Wages from homework provided income essential to family survival—especially during winter months when bad weather meant little work for immigrant men. On the average, husbands could earn only ten to twelve dollars a week, and they were usually unemployed for one-third of the year. During a husband's unemployment, home-workers could earn income by bringing in work. As one homeworker answered when asked why she did the work, "The children need bread, shoes." For these women, the distinction between mothering and breadwinning simply did not exist.

Invariably, children did homework with their mothers, primarily because the low rate of pay required many busy hands and the tasks were simple enough. In almost every form of homework, boys worked with their mothers until they were eleven or twelve; then they would get jobs as errand or newpaper boys on the streets. Girls, on the other hand, continued doing homework until they could find work in a fac-tory, usually when they turned sixteen or seventeen. Many of these older daughters, once employed outside the home, would help with the homework when they got home or would bring additional home-work with them when they returned at night. In this way, employers could avoid prosecution for working girls overtime in the factory, for work done in the home was exempt from labor regulations. This form of overtime work occurred in any trade adapted to homework.

A Factory in Every Kitchen

Industrialists clearly recognized the exploitative value of maintaining married women at home as a "surplus" labor pool of homeworkers and employing primarily young single women in the factory. As one manufacturer stated, "I want no experienced girls [to work in my shop], they know the pay to get . . . but these greenhorns . . . they cannot speak English and they don't know where to go and they just come from the old country and I let them work hard, like the devil, for less wages."[22]

Older women in the factories might demand fair wages; older women at home could not. Scattered throughout the tenements of New York, hired on a day-to-day basis, and caught between the need to earn a living and the demands of childcare, these women had little option but to accept whatever wage was offered. As the journalist and feminist Rheta Childe Dorr stated in 1912, homework "exists because the manufacturer finds it economical to spread his finishing processes through thousands of kitchens. . . . They get their work done for practically nothing. That is why homework exists."[23]

While women in the factory were paid less than men, homeworkers systematically earned less than their factory sisters. Homeworkers were subject to the most exploitative effects of women's secondary status in the marketplace. Manufacturers made use of dominant ideological prescriptions to justify their exploitative rates of pay. Homeworkers, they argued, worked for mere "pin money" and as such did not "need" to earn a living wage.[24] Such self-serving logic allowed manufacturers to sidestep the blame for incredibly low wages and guaranteed them high rates of return from homeworkers.

In addition, competition from homeworkers could help drive down wages inside the factory. One can hardly imagine a more profitable arrangement for manufacturers. While paying homeworkers only 60 percent of factory wages, manufacturers could also save the expense of renting, heating, and lighting a workplace. The expense of direct supervision of workers was easily replaced by the discipline enforced by circumstance. Competition for homework was enough to insure high rates of return for manufacturers.

In addition, factory owners could subvert almost every form of labor protection through the use of homeworkers. When shopworkers went on strike, homeworkers could be employed to make up the slack. While labor regulations prohibited the employment of children under fourteen and the overtime work of women, homework could be given out at unregulated rates. During the busy season, homeworkers could be employed by the thousands, only to be dismissed at the slightest downturn in trade.

The insecurity fostered by irregular work compelled the homeworker to produce at a rate that tested the limits of human endurance. In essence, the homework system created a sweatshop in every kitchen, where there were no limits to the pace or price of work.

Organized Labor and Homework

By the turn of the century, organized labor had good reason to oppose homework. Homeworkers, they argued, were "unorganizable," cut the price of labor, and undermined striking factory workers.[25]

Beginning in 1874, the Cigar Makers International Union waged a public campaign against the homework system, stressing the unsanitary quality of cigars rolled in "TB-ridden" tenements and condemning the wide-spread use of child labor in homework.[26] This campaign resulted in the passage of the first piece of legislation prohibiting homework in 1884. But the law was challenged by cigar manufacturers in the courts and within four months ruled unconstitutional in the Jacobs Decision of the New York Court of Appeals.[27] The court ruled that because "the health of the tenement population is not jeopardized by the manufacture of cigars in those houses," the act exceeded the police powers of the state.[28] The legislation and the court decision were significant, for they marked the beginning of a fifty-year period in which no legislation directly prohibiting homework would be judicially upheld. Instead, legal restrictions on homework were clothed in the form of sanitary and health regulations.[29]

Frustrated by the courts, the cigar makers turned to direct economic action as their strategy. First, they continued their public campaign against "infectious" homemade cigars and instituted the first union label campaign to distinguish homemade from factory-made cigars. Playing on the fear of tuberculosis, the cigar makers greatly reduced the number of cigar homeworkers employed by the industry. Second, the union made the abolition of homework a demand in their strikes and boycotts. As a result of all of these efforts, by 1912 almost all home-based cigar making was gone.

The United Garment Workers of America soon joined the fight against homework. Like the cigar workers, their first line of attack was to institute the union label and to incorporate the abolition of homework into strike demands. But partly because of the highly specialized division of labor in the industry, the garment workers met with little success. It was easy to identify cigars made at home, since the entire production process took place at one site. But a garment sewn in the factory could be shipped out to homeworkers for finishing and then brought back into the factory to be labeled "union-made." Indeed, investigators of the time found workers at home sewing pants which contained a union label.[30]

In the end, abolition of homework in a particular industry generally reflected the level of organization and militancy of its unionized workers. The only effective way of limiting homework was through direct action: strike demands. The first union to successfully demand the elimination of homework was the United Cloth and Hat and Capmakers Union. After a thirteen-week strike in the winter of 1904–5 in New York, the union won an agreement to eliminate all trade with sweatshops and homeworkers. The International Ladies' Garment Workers, after a 1910 strike in New York, were able to greatly reduce the amount of homework in the women's clothing industry. This provision was then incorporated into every subsequent strike settlement.[31] By contrast, in the men's readymade clothing industry, where the Amalgamated Clothing Workers were not organized until 1914, homework continued to flourish.

Except for restrictions imposed in those few strongly unionized industries, homework remained largely unregulated. Union strength again would be indicated by the 1938 federal bans on homework, which eliminated homework in only seven of the best-organized trades.[32]

At the turn of the century, Progressive social reformers joined organized labor to make homework a cause célèbre. But, as we shall see, reformers opposed homework on very different grounds.

Social Reformers and the Home/Work Split

Social reformers based their pleas for the elimination or regulation of homework on the claim that such work polluted the home and degraded the act of mothering. Certainly the nature of the homework system itself posed serious hazards to the health of women and their children. Lack of sleep, lack of play, inadequate access to fresh air and sufficient light, the tedious concentration on repetitive and boring tasks—all of these posed threats to the physical well-being of women and their families. The insecurity engendered by irregular homework must also have posed high costs to family life. Yet such concerns with the ways in which homework degraded family life also belie, at a deeper level, the commitment of social reformers to a very particular "ideology of motherhood"—one that did not often mesh with the reality of immigrant life. This dominant ideology drew a sharp distinction between home and work, between mothering and breadwinning. What impact did these cultural prescripts have on attempts to reform the homework system?

In large part, the ideological distinction between public work and private family was based on real material transformations in the nature of social production. In precapitalist agrarian society, the home was the site of production. Entire families farmed, raised livestock, spun and wove, and produced the goods the family needed for daily use. In addition, families often produced goods for exchange at the market. With the rise of the factory and wage labor system, home production gradually declined. While some controversy continues over the extent to which the family and home was emptied of its economic functions, it is clear that in important ways the home did lose its status as the *center* of production.[33]

As the wage labor system developed outside of the home, the domestic labor of women came to be defined as separate from, and qualitatively different than, "outside" labor done for a wage. Women's household tasks were systematically undervalued as the idea of "work" was defined in terms of wage labor done in the public sphere, physically and ideologically separate from home.

But while the ideological distinction between home and work *reflected* real transformations in the nature of production, it also *mystified* the economic importance of women's work at home, paid or unpaid. Homework, as such, was rendered invisible by this ideology. When recognized at all, it was considered a historical anomoly—a vestige of less advanced systems of production that would gradually disappear.

Concurrent with the loss of family-centered production came a middle-class "ideology of motherhood" which filled the functional void left by the loss of production inside the home. Rather sharp ideological distinctions were drawn between women's and men's work and between private familial relations of nurturance and public market relations of competition. From the point of view of this new ideology, women were *all* mothers at heart and motherhood stood as the antithesis—indeed, the antidote—to market relations. In this context the home took on new meaning. Home life—specifically the guidance provided by mothers—established the very foundations of the social and moral order, it was argued. If social reformers were to combat the degradation wrought by the industrial system, what better place to start than in the homes of immigrant women?

It is in the context of this ideology that one must understand the attempts of social reformers to abolish the homework system. The elimination of homework, they argued, would protect home life from the worst vicissitudes of urban industrialization—from child labor, disease, and exploitative working conditions. In every homework investigation made during this time period social reformers expressed two main concerns: opposition to child labor and fear of spreading infectious disease. Both concerns, while worthy in and of themselves, demonstrate an essential blindness to the condition of homeworkers and a level of analysis that failed to reach the true causes of these conditions.

Homeworkers lived in the crowded tenement districts near the factories and workshops on which they depended for a livelihood. In 1894 New York's East Side included thirty-two acres on which 32,000 people lived.[34] It is estimated that 95 percent of the immigrant families lived with more than three people in a room; six in one room was not uncommon. In New York City there were at least 100,000 tenement rooms with no window, even onto an air shaft or an adjoining room; only one in four had any direct sunlight; the rest had windows which opened onto an alley or stagnant air shaft.[35]

Infectious diseases spread easily under these conditions, and ordinary childhood diseases often brought death. Italian children had a death rate from measels almost five times that of the city as a whole, and the highest mortality rate from scarlet fever and whooping cough.[36] Overall, the death rate of children under five years of age in tenements ran up as high as 204 per thousand.[37] Homeworkers living in the Italian district of New York City were fourteen times more likely to die from tuberculosis as people living in the upper-income neighborhoods across from Central Park.[38]

In addition to garment finishing, homeworkers also often earned a wage picking through coffee beans and shelling and cleaning nuts for fancy restaurants in Manhattan. Members of the Consumers' League of New York were appalled to find homeworkers with infectious diseases sorting coffee beans, cracking nuts with their teeth, or using coats sent home for finishing as bed covering at night.[39] Eye-witness accounts by horrified investigators pivoted on reports of "disease-ridden" homeworkers: "One home finisher had a little boy suffering from whooping cough," one investigator reported. "When he had a coughing spell the mother thrust her finger down his throat in an effort to relieve him ... the mother wiped her fingers, covered with mucus, on the pants on which she was at work."[40]

While social reformers documented the unhealthy conditions under which homeworkers lived, they did so from the point of view of consumers. Rarely did reports recognize the hazards to homeworkers themselves from such work. Instead, reformers expressed concern over the unsanitary nature of the "work room" where the goods were produced, without any recognition of the fact that these same places were the *homes* of workers.

Under pressure from both social reformers and organized labor, New York State established the homework licensing system. In an attempt to control health and sanitary standards in tenement buildings, the New York Tenement House Homework Law required licensing in tenements where homeworkers were employed. Any building that housed tenants with infectious or contagious diseases could not be issued a license.[41] Because it applied to buildings rather than to individual homeworkers, the licensing system often worked to the detriment of homeworking families. If a homeworker was found to have a contagious disease, landlords could simply evict the family and maintain their good standing with the state. The licensing system was almost completely ineffective, in any case, because so few inspectors were assigned to the 13,000 buildings licensed for homework. Such laws could be selectively enforced only when social reformers brought cases to the attention of city officials.

Both the national and state branches of the Child Labor Committee joined with the Consumers' League in attempts to eliminate homework. These organizations characterized Italian homeworkers as the worst offenders of child labor laws. The social reformer Rheta Childe Dorr, in a 1912 article entitled "The Child Who Toils at Home," typically leveled sweeping criticism at homeworking parents: "The police power of the law is invoked to protect children against a parent who is so cruel, so greedy, or so ignorant as to be willing to sacrifice their health and lives for gain. But a parent may claim the services of his children from the day their baby hands are capable of performing a task. He may work them until they drop asleep from exhaustion. He may put them at work injurious to health, in surroundings actually conducive to physical and mental destruction. *Provided the work is done at home.*"[42]

The National Child Labor Committee tried to control homework by having child labor laws and restrictions on women's work extended to include homeworkers. Two tactics were used: enforcement of compulsory education and extention of labor laws to cover homework. Compulsory education laws, which required the attendance of children at school between the ages of six and fourteen, often came into conflict with the need of homeworkers to employ their children during school hours.[43] But this tactic failed because such laws were nearly impossible to enforce and could do nothing about the employment of children at home under the age of six or over fourteen.

Ironically, parents who complied with the compulsory education laws were often forced by necessity to violate child labor laws by having their children work before 8 A.M. or after 5 P.M. in order to make up for time "lost" during school.[44] Similarly, with the approval of the fifty-four-hour work week for women in 1912, women could not legally be employed for more than nine hours a day, before 6 A.M. or after 9 P.M., or for more than six days a week. Homeworkers inevitably violated all of these protective measures. But again, these efforts were ineffective. Since parents never paid a wage to children, they could not be said to be formally employed, and as a result, state labor inspectors resisted bringing cases against homeworking families.

Reformers failed to see that children were employed because their families could not survive on such low wages without them. Furthermore, the point of view expressed by many of these reformers demonstrates an ethnocentrism common among social workers of the time. American social workers accustomed to a middle-class conception of childhood could hold no sympathy for those who believed that children were responsible for contributing to the economic survival of the family under *any* circumstance. Such an idea was common among rural southern Italian immigrants and was reinforced by necessity once they had settled in New York.[45]

Social reformers fought for the elimination of homework in opposition to homeworkers themselves, who viewed this as one of their few options for work. Homeworkers shunned encounters with reformers and inspectors (hiding their work when investigators came to call) and viewed efforts to eliminate homework as yet one more attempt to limit their options for paid work.

Homeworkers and the State

Under pressure from social reformers to purify the home, from organized labor to prevent unfair labor competition, and from manufacturers to protect their freedom to contract, New York state legislators were faced with three options: They could prohibit homework entirely; they could regulate work at home; or they could do nothing at all. On the grounds that homeworkers were not real employees and that the state lacked the power to regulate the private relations of the home, state policy makers chose the third option, exempting homework from all forms of labor regulation.

While homework restrictions clearly would have presented some problems of enforcement, the real difficulty lay in the ideological distinction between home and factory and the state's unwillingness to recognize these women as employees. While policy makers argued that the state had an obligation to regulate the wages and conditions of those who worked outside the home, these same rights did not extend, they argued, to the work mothers did inside the home. The key to the argument lay in the crucial distinction between home and factory.

If indeed the home constituted a factory, or place of employment, then the state would be obligated to hold employers of homeworkers to the same standards used for workers in the public marketplace. The debates over this issue demonstrate a simple refusal to recognize these women as workers. Witness the following exchange as three members of the New York Factory Investigating Commission argue over whether the home in this instance was indeed a factory:

> MR. ELKUS: It is a factory if one person is employed for hire, isn't it, am I right?
>
> COMM. DREIER: Yes, if employed for hire, yes sir.
>
> MR. ELKUS: Now the father or the mother, somebody makes a garment for the manufacturer, by which for a certain sum of money he or she agrees to do a certain amount of work?
>
> COMM. DREIER: No, you are not right because she goes elsewhere to work.
>
> MR. ELKUS: That does not make any difference; a factory is a place where one or more persons are employed at labor.
>
> COMM. PHILLIPS: Must be a manufacturing or business establishment.
>
> MR. ELKUS: Any mill, workshop, or other manufacturing or business establishment.
>
> COMM. PHILLIPS: Business establishment must be the predominating idea of the thing.
>
> MR. ELKUS: No, it is not . . .[46]

To recognize homework as wage labor would be to legitimize the state's authority to regulate relations inside the private sphere of the home—a recognition that legislators were not prepared to make. Rheta Childe Dorr aptly characterized this attitude as "the old sentimental theory of the innate sacredness of The Home. There probably exists in the human mind no stronger tradition than that The Home is an institution which does not change and which ought not to be invaded or interfered with. The tradition is strongest in strong men. It sways legislatures and the courts, which, being composed entirely of men, allow me humbly to remark, have no more than a theoretical knowledge of Home."[47]

Reluctance to regulate homework was not simply due to an abstract commitment on the part of legislators to principles of freedom from state interference in the private sphere. During this same period, the state clearly stepped in to regulate and supervise the private lives of poor mothers on relief. Among the provisions in various mothers' pension laws—the first widely adopted state-aid programs for mothers with dependent children—there were stipulations, for instance, as to how many days a mother might be absent from home for work and for what kind of work she might do.[48] Mothers' pensions regulations forbade male boarders and insisted that English be spoken in the home. The enforcement of these laws could not have posed less difficult problems than enforcing minimally decent conditions for homeworkers. At least such regulations suggest that state officials did not feel constrained by principles of citizens' privacy when their concern centered around the protection of motherhood.

These very same legislators eagerly regulated the work of women in the public workplace, explicitly prohibiting women entirely from more lucrative male-dominated industries when such exclusions could be justified on grounds of risks to women's capacity to bear children.[49] When it came to women, freedom from state regulation was clearly not absolute. The state's fragile commitment to this principle, therefore, cannot adequately explain the tenacity of state reluctance to regulate homework.

More compelling were arguments about the effect of regulations on the structure of the patriarchal family. Legislators viewed the cure to the homework problem as worse than the disease. Many of them sympathized with manufacturers, such as Joshua L. Ambers, who argued that "to take away this work would be a hardship on the women in our industry . . . and would take away from them their means of earning a livelihood. There are many women who have to take care of children, or perhaps to prepare lunch for a boy or girl at school, and for a hundred and one reasons they may have to work at home, in order to make a living."[50] Legislators were swayed by those who painted scenarios of women—mothers—who would be pushed out into the public marketplace and forced to abandon children and husbands. Better to allow women to work at home, even under the worst of circumstances, legislators argued, than to force them into the workplace. Social reformers responded only by arguing that the husbands of homeworkers might be forced to be more "regular" breadwinners if their wives or children could not work—an attitude which clearly demonstrated a lack of sensitivity to the circumstances under which poor immigrant men worked.

In the end, the state deflected all efforts to further regulate homework and by doing so tacitly approved the homework system. Legislators were less concerned with upholding ideal standards about the separation of home and work than they were in making sure women stayed at home. And by exempting homeworkers from all forms of regulation, they could also avoid the public recognition that the traditional patriarchal family was not functioning as it ideally should. In the end, this failure to act evinced the deeper commitment of legislators to the mystification of the sexual division of labor—one that guaranteed that homeworkers would continue to labor under the most exploitative working conditions.

Homeworkers and the Structure of Family Life

Today, as in New York City at the turn of the century, homeworkers continue to side with the conservative manufacturers who defend their right to work at home. Given limited options for work, homeworkers have consistently resisted attempts by organized labor to abolish the homework system.

At least in part, this reluctance to give up homework must be understood in relation to women's valuation of the kind of work done in the private sphere of the home—the necessity to care for children and to create a culture of work and family life that is to a limited extent free from the strict work ethic enforced on working-class men and women in the factory. In addition, for immigrant women working at the turn of the century, financial survival depended very much on the stability of family relations. While single women might survive on the wages of industry, women who had children depended on their central position in the family for survival. Their responsibility for care of young children placed them at a distinct disadvantage in a marketplace structured to absorb only workers without primary childrearing responsibilities.

In addition, many women may have preferred to return home after marriage in order to maintain strong family ties both between and across generations. As Virginia Yans-McLaughlin has pointed out, the Italian family has been described as "father-dominated, but mother-centered."[51] Immigrant women may well have viewed their predominance within the family, their care of children and husband, as an important source of power. Their hesitancy to relinquish this central position in the family by going out to work may reflect a realistic assessment of their situation. After all, in the labor market women could barely earn a living wage and were under the constant scrutiny of bosses or foremen. Moveover, the possibilities of earning an independent wage were limited even at the peak of their wage-earning years and steadily declined as they passed marital age. Retaining the stability of the family represented a kind of long-term security that, however tenuous, was more than the market could ever provide. Children who were taught at an early age that they were responsible for the economic survival of the family could be expected to (and did) support parents in old age.

In addition, women at home often worked together with neighbors or relatives.[52] Homework provided a way to establish and maintain extended family ties that must certainly have been important for the survival of individual family members.[53] Going out to work might have disrupted or threatened these extended networks, either through a violation of cultural norms or simply by absence from the home for long periods of time. This need to maintain reciprocal social relationships with friends and family may have played a significant role in keeping women at home.

But despite the value of women's presence in the home, the conditions which lie at the root of the exploitation of homeworkers remain the same today. The devaluation of women's work, whether in or out of the home, paid or unpaid labor, is the source of the exploitation of working women. When homeworkers refuse other options of work and continue to work at home, even where homework is illegal, they make a statement about the value of the services women perform at home and their willingness to trade off wages for the right to care for their children. In this society that is an unfortunate choice that all mothers must face.

Dominant assumptions about women's relationship to home and factory not only color our perceptions of history but also inform and underlie the development of state policies—policies which can powerfully shape the kinds of work options open (or closed) to women. It is crucial, therefore, to understand the ways in which political struggles over homework reflect conflicting attempts to shape women's historic relationship to home and work life. Most important, such struggles over homework can provide women with an arena through which to raise new questions about the structure of the gendered division of labor.

NOTES

I would like to thank the Woodrow Wilson Foundation and the American Association of University Women for their support of my dissertation research, which provided the basis for this essay. Also, portions of the original research for this essay grew out of joint research conducted at the University of Massachusetts with Susan Nurenberg, with whom I developed a slide and lecture presentation on homeworkers in New York City at the turn of the century.

1. See Eileen Boris, "Regulating Industrial Homework: The Triumph of 'Sacred Motherhood,'" *Journal of American History* 71, no. 4 (March 1985): 45–63 for a history of federal bans on homework.

2. For a more detailed discussion of homework during this period see my dissertation, "Working Mothers and the State" (University of Massachusetts, Amherst, 1983).

3. Elizabeth C. Watson, "Homework in the Tenements," *Survey* 25 (February 4, 1911): 772–73

4. New York State, *Second Report of the Factory Investigating Commission,* 1913, 2: 677, 691, 729.

5. Ibid.: 691.

6. Ibid.: 696.

7. Thomas Kessner, *The Golden Door: Italian and Jewish Immigrant Mobility in New York City, 1880–1915* (Oxford University Press, 1977), p. 63; U.S. Bureau of Labor, *Report on the Condition of Woman and Child Wage-Earners in the U.S.,* 61st Senate report, document no. 645, 1: 14 (G.P.O., 1911), hereafter cited as *Woman and Child Wage-Earners.*

8. *Woman and Child Wage-Earners,* 1: 221.

9. Mary Van Kleek, "Child Labor in New York City Tenements," *Survey/Charities,* 19 (January 18, 1908): 1414.

10. Kessner, *The Golden Door,* p. 77.

11. *Woman and Child Wage-Earners,* 2: 241–42.

12. Ibid., 2: 139.

13. Mary Van Kleek, *Artificial Flower Makers* (New York: Survey Associates, 1913), pp. v, 90.

14. Elizabeth Shepley Sergeant, "Toilers of the Tenements, Where the Beautiful Things of the Great Shops are Made," *McClure's Magazine,* July 1910, pp. 239–41.

15. Van Kleek, *Artificial Flower Makers,* p. 95.

16. Ibid., pp. 97–98.

17. Louise C. Odencrantz, *Italian Women in Industry* (New York: Russell Sage Foundation, 1919), p. 183.

18. Van Kleek, *Artificial Flower Makers,* pp. 107–8.

19. Sergeant, "Toilers of the Tenements," pp. 241–42.

20. Watson, "Homework in the Tenements," p. 778.

21. *Woman and Child Wage-Earners,* 1: 40.

22. Ruth Enalda Shallcross, *Industrial Homework: An Analysis of Homework Regulations, Here and Abroad* (New York: Industrial Affairs Publishing Co., 1939), p. 26.

23. Rheta Childe Dorr, "The Child Who Toils at Home," *Hampton Magazine,* April 1912, p. 186.

24. *Second Report of the Factory Investigating Commission,* 1913, 3: 1508, 1511.

25. For a detailed discussion of attempts by organized labor to abolish homework, see Frieda S. Miller, "Industrial Homework in the United States," *International Labor Review* 43, no. 1 (January 1941): 1–50.

26. See Edith Abbott, "Employment of Women in Industries: Cigar-Making, Its History and Present Tendencies," *Journal of Political Economy,* 15 (January 1907): 1–25, for a more complete discussion of the role of homework in the cigar-making industry. Cigar homeworkers differed from other homeworkers in that most cigar-makers at home were men and were considered to be skilled laborers. This had an effect on attempts by organzied labor to bring homeworkers in this industry into the factory.

27. New York State, *Preliminary Report of the Factory Investigating Commission,* 1: 83, and Miller, "Industrial Home Work in the U.S.": 13.

28. New York State, *Fourth Report of the Factory Investigating Commission,* 1915, 1: 382.

29. Miller, "Industrial Home Work in the U.S.": 17–18.

30. Henry White, "Perils of the Home Factory," *Harper's Weekly* February 11, 1911, p. 10.

31. Miller, "Industrial Home Work in the U.S.": 12–16, 20, 26–31.

32. The industries in which homework was banned included knitted outerwear, women's apparel, jewelry, gloves and mittens, buttons and buckles, handkerchiefs and embroidery. In 1981 the Reagan administration successfully deregulated homework in the knitted outerwear industry. For a more popular discussion of contemporary homework, see my article in *Dollars and Sense,* December 1986, p. 16.

33. For further discussion of the separation of home and work life, see Elizabeth Pleck, "Two Worlds in One: Work and Family," *Journal of Social History* 10 (Winter 1976): 178–95.

34. Harvey Wasserman, *History of the United States* (New York: Harper and Row, 1972), p. 35.

35. Sergeant, "Toilers of the Tenements," p. 232.

36. White, "Perils of the Home Factory," p. 10.

37. Robert Hunter, *Poverty* (New York: MacMillan, 1904), p. 150.

38. Dr. William H. Guifoe of the New York health department, figures cited by White, "Perils of the Home Factory," p. 10.

39. Dorr, "The Child Who Toils at Home," p. 187.

40. Ibid.

41. The items covered under the law included coats, vests, kneepants, trousers, overalls, cloaks, hats, caps, suspenders, jerseys, blouses, dresses, waists, waistbands, underwear, neckwear, furs, fur trimmings, fur garments, skirts, shirts, aprons, purses, pocketbooks, slippers, paper boxes, paper bags, feathers, artificial flowers, macaroni, spaghetti, ice cream, ices, candy, confectionary nuts, and preservatives. *Second Report of the Factory Investigating Commission,* 2:725.

42. Dorr, "The Child Who Toils at Home," p. 183.

43. *Second Report of the Factory Investigating Commission,* 1:106–7.

44. *Preliminary Report of the Factory Investigating Commission,* 1912, 1:105 and *Second Report of the Factory Investigating Commission,* 1:107.

45. For further discussion of immigrant culture in the Italian community, see Elizabeth Pleck, "A Mother's Wage: Income Earning among Married Italian and Black Women, 1896–1911," in *A Heritage of Her Own,* ed. Nancy F. Cott and Elizabeth Pleck (New York: Simon and Schuster, 1979).

46. *Second Report of the Factory Investigating Commission,* 3:40–41.

47. Dorr, "The Child Who Toils at Home," p. 183.

48. For an excellent discussion of mother's pensions programs see Elizabeth Moore, "Mother's Pensions: The Origins of the Relationship between Women and the Welfare State" (Ph.D. diss., University of Massachusetts, Amherst, 1985).

49. A more complete analysis of protective labor legislation for women in New York in this period can be found in my dissertation, "Working Mothers and the State."

50. *Second Report of the Factory Investigating Commission,* 2:2210.

51. Virginia Yans-McLaughlin, "A Flexible Tradition: Southern Italian Immigrants Confront a New Work Experience," *Journal of Social History,* 7, no. 4 (Summer 1974): 429–45.

52. See Odencrantz, *Italian Women in Industry,* p. 13, where she notes that "the social character of the Italian soon induces the woman from Naples to take her home work into the rooms of her Sicilian neighbor." Also, many of the photographs that accompanied reports and articles on homework showed large groups of women working together.

53. For an extensive discussion of the importance of extended family networks in a poor black community, see Carol B. Stack's *All Our Kin,* (New York: Harper and Row, 1974).

2

Black Women and Paid Labor in the Home: Industrial Homework in Chicago in the 1920s

EILEEN BORIS

Writing to the National Women's Trade Union League in 1926, the chief labor researcher of the Illinois State Department of Labor noted that "most of the home workers [in Chicago] are women or children in the Polish, Jewish, Italian and Negro districts." Associated with southern and eastern European immigrants since their massive arrival at the turn of the century, industrial homework remained an economic and social problem in the mid-1920s. By then, with the cutting off of European immigration and the advent of the "Great Migration" of African-Americans from the South, homework had reached Chicago's "southside." While investigators reported less than 2 percent home-workers as African-American women and 3 percent as Spanish-speaking Puerto Rican "Negroes" in New York, they found hundreds of African-American women in Chicago making artificial flowers, assembling lamp shades, and working in twelve other garment-related trades.[1]

Neither scholars nor policy makers have associated such labor with the income-generating activities of black women. The tenement-house photographs of Lewis Hine and the muckraking reports of reform organizations have taught us to see the homeworker as an immigrant mother with her children.[2] Since most black women labored in the less industrialized South, they appeared invisible to urban reformers; because they were expected to labor, especially at "dirty" work, their home-based activities never appeared deviant to reformers who condemned white ethnic homeworking mothers. Yet perhaps even a higher proportion of African-American women labored for wages in their homes, in the North as well as in the South, as laundresses, seamstresses, and industrial homeworkers.[3]

The conditions under which African-American women engaged in industrial homework thus illuminate both the circumstances under which *all* women have found themselves working for wages and the nature of homework as an organization of production. From the perspective of African-American women's history, however, homework belongs to a larger tradition among black women in the post-Emancipation period of using the home as a place for paid labor and thus removing themselves from the daily supervision of whites.[4] The location of homework—a social space controlled by the black woman or her family—was its greatest attraction. To understand why some black women were homeworkers in Chicago during the 1920s, we need to compare homework both with other forms of home-based labor and with domestic service. Then we will have a better understanding of the place of homework in the African-American experience.

The Home as Workplace: Seamstresses and Laundresses

Homework belongs to a significant, though often neglected, pattern of black women's paid labor: work in the home, sometimes as small entrepreneurs (as with beauty parlor operators), other times as part of a family labor system (as with sharecroppers). The home-based occupations of seamstress, dressmaker, and laundress or washerwomen existed as alternatives to domestic service and agricultural labor for free women of color from the antebellum period. The persistence of such home-based work into the twentieth century suggests that not all African-American women left their children and homes to earn wages. Work outside the home did not necessarily signify the independence of black women—as popular stereotypes suggest—nor did it mean that they had solved the problem of combining wage labor with child care. Black women and their families may have wished to stay home and have chosen homework, like other homeworking women, because they could earn money while meeting family responsibilities. That larger numbers of black women historically have worked outside of the home than women from other groups may indicate a lesser, rather than greater, choice in the place of their wage-earning.[5]

The history of Rebecca Bellinger Garvin exemplifies the use of home-based labor as a protection from white supervision. Remembering life in Charleston nearly a century ago, her daughter, Mamie Garvin Fields, recalled: "Mother didn't go out to work. Although he didn't have much money, my father put it down: she would be a housewife; his wife would *never* go out to work for white people." However, Rebecca Bellinger Garvin was a dressmaker. "She sewed at home and sometimes worked on projects of her friend Harriet . . . [who] had a 'sewing room,' a little business, at her home. . . . If Harriet had an overflow of work, my mother helped." Not only did Rebecca Garvin sew and crochet for her own family but she "got plenty of orders from all around Charleston to make . . . beautiful [handmade] pinafores for other little girls." She earned wages while working in the home and, in so doing, maintained family integrity.

Such homework took advantage of sewing skills that African-American women had handed down since slavery. Here too the Garvin-Fields family appears typical. During slavery Aunt Harriet had been a "manshee maker," or seamstress, who taught her owner's daughters the arts and crafts of needlework. She also instructed Rebecca Bellinger Garvin, who gained further training from Northern teachers at the Wesley Church School and at the Claflin Normal School. She, in turn, passed on her skills to her daughters, who also learned the needle trade from Aunt Harriet and the Claflin School. Thus, as a school girl, Mamie made money by embroidery and other forms of fancy work. To earn money for her trousseau, she left South Carolina for Boston to sew sleeves in a sweatshop, alongside Italians and Poles. By night she opened "a sewing room at home" to provide other black women with the latest fashions.[6]

Mamie Garvin Fields followed in the steps of earlier generations of black women. During the antebellum period, while both Irish and native-born white homeworkers in New York City sewed rough clothes and New England mothers bound shoes for the Southern trade, slave women had major responsibility for the sewing done on plantations. They spun, wove, and fashioned homespun clothes, quilted coverlets, and—for those who showed talent—engaged in numerous delicate, decorative tasks, like hand-embroidering petticoats and tatting lace. Adept with the needle, these slave women, it has been claimed, "easily adapted themselves to the sewing machine."[7] They also passed on their skills to their daughters. The noted modiste Elizabeth Keckley remembered, "As mother had so much work to do in making clothes, etc., for the family, besides the slaves, I determined to render her all the assistance in my power." Keckley's reputation as a dressmaker and seamstress "kept bread in the mouths of seventeen persons for two years and five months" and allowed her in the 1850s to buy freedom for herself and her son.[8] While Keckley established a separate dressmaking shop in Washington, D.C., Eliza Ann Gardner of Boston more typically combined home and shop (which also, in her case, served as a station on the underground railroad.) This combination of home and workplace persisted among countless "unknown" black women. For example, a successful New York dressmaking and ladies tailoring establishment in 1912 used the front room of the family's apartment for business quarters.[9]

As industrial homework developed in the mid-nineteenth century as part of the industrialization process, free black women in the North already were sewing dresses in their homes, as well as washing and ironing laundry. According to one estimate, the majority of day workers in Northern cities were laundresses who worked out of their own homes. Perhaps 15 percent of black women workers were either dressmakers or hairdressers, another home-based entrepreneurial activity that continues into the twentieth century. Some women combined needlecrafts with other occupations. Rosetta Douglass, for one, in 1862 taught school and made "a few cents at spare times by knitting[,] edging and doing embroidery."[10]

While Southern black women attempted to withdraw from fieldwork after emancipation, the seamstress, dressmaker, and laundress continued working for wages in her home. Each occupation allowed married women to provide for their families and care for their children at the same time. Opportunities for such work existed in Southern as well as Northern cities, where widowed, deserted, and never-married female heads of households fled from rural areas which offered them little chance for employment. As a consequence, the recorded numbers of black women as dressmakers and seamstresses exploded: in New York City the number quadrupled between 1890 and 1900, increasing more dramatically than among white women.[11]

Both seamstresses and laundresses were self-employed. They legally could be classified as "independent contractors," unlike the garment homeworkers who depended on contractors to obtain work. Yet all three types of home-based labor shared features that stretched out the working day and limited a woman's control over her labor. Laundresses usually would pick up at the house of their client/employer bundles of clothes to wash and press. Although they worked out of their own homes, laundresses still entered personalistic relations with employers. From such relations, they could gain material goods, like clothes and food, or protection from other whites. But they also had to meet the schedules of their client/employers to receive future work. Similarly, seamstresses and dressmakers usually went to the houses of whites, though some customers (probably black or of lower-class standing) came to their homes. There they took measurements to produce dresses at home. They then delivered finished goods—a pattern similar to that of the industrial homeworker who had to pick up and deliver goods without additional compensation. Laundresses and seamstresses, as with homeworkers, lost time waiting around for their work; seamstresses, like homeworkers, suffered from seasonal employment more than laundresses, although when clients went on vacation, there was no work and thus no pay. Paid labor in the home was more easily controlled by seamstress or laundress than by the immigrant garment homeworker, but they too worked under conditions not of their own making: client demands, pressures of labor supply and demand, the wealth of the black community, and the amount and willingness of the white community to pay.[12]

The numbers of dressmakers and seamstresses remained small compared to those of domestic servants and agricultural laborers. But black women dominated washing to such an extent that they dared to organize for higher wages: in Jackson, Mississippi, in 1866; Galveston, Texas, in 1877; and Atlanta, Georgia, in 1881.[13] By 1900 in Washington, D.C., more women over age thirty-five engaged in this work than in domestic service. Of 731 black women in a 1908 study, 57 percent were laundresses and 34 percent, cooks and domestic servants. Only 3 percent were dressmakers or seamstresses.[14] As Carter Woodson pointed out in 1930, the "Negro Washerwoman" "was the all but beast of burden of the aristocratic slave holder and in freedom she continued at this hand labor as a bread winner of the family." Her efforts not only supplemented the low wages earned by men, when men were present and employed, but also supported community institutions such as schools and churches. Her savings allowed black families to purchase property and educate their children.[15] But by 1920, under competition from mechanized steam laundries and home appliances, home laundry was a declining occupation for black women. While laundresses (not in laundry) in 1920 composed 19.5 percent of all black women over sixteen in gainful occupations, their numbers had decreased 20.9 percent since 1910, from 356,275 to 281,761 women. This reduction in hand washerwomen led to an overall drop in black female employment, despite the holdover from World War I of increased numbers in the manufacturing sector.[16]

Joseph A. Hill of the Census Bureau attributed some of this drop in black female employment to the desire of black women to care for their children while working, which became more difficult with the decline in home laundry jobs. He noted, "Many of the Negro women who would be ready to take in washing if they had the opportunity . . . are not qualified for regular employment in other occupations, or are not in a position to accept employment outside the home."[17] Mary White Ovington, a social worker and cofounder of the NAACP, earlier had confirmed this reason for work in the home in her 1911 study,

Half a Man: "Laundry work is an important home industry, and one may watch many mothers at their tubs or ironing boards from Monday morning until Saturday night. This makes the tenement rooms, tiny enough at best, sadly cluttered, but it does not deprive the children of the presence of their mother, who accepts a smaller income to remain at home with them." While some contemporary reports emphasized the dirt, disease, and social disorganization of laundry homework to suggest that such mothers, like Italian homeworkers, could not possibly care for their children properly, Ovington emphasized how black women strove to feed, clothe, and educate their children. "The tenement dwelling becomes a home, and the boys and girls pass a happy childhood in it," she claimed.[18]

Before the full impact of the African-American migration to the North, then, black women in urban areas worked at home in two traditional women's occupations: dressmaking and laundry. Preference, as much as lack of other options, guided them. Like other homeworking women, they desired to combine child care and wage earning. They could pretty much determine their own hours and work free from white presence. But not all black women were pleased with laundry, sewing, or hair work in their homes as a substitute for teaching and other better-paying jobs from which they were excluded. The Chicago School of Civics and Philanthropy noted in 1910, "Day work is almost universally prefered." As long as they could live out, domestic service appealed to many and probably offered steadier, if not higher, wages.[19] Still, overall figures suggest that married women with children just as often took in wash than went out to service and even some single women turned to home sewing or laundry instead of domestic service when denied industrial or professional employment.[20]

Women in the Clothing Trades

During the time that black women were working at home as laundresses and seamstresses, Northern-financed vocational schools in the South and special trade schools and the public schools in the North provided them with the generalized skills necessary for the garment industry. In New York City alone between 1907 and 1911, one public night school instructed "hundreds of women in sewing, dressmaking, millinery, and artificial flower making." Met with racism in the garment shops from working women and their employers, some black women certainly tried to obtain home piecework in these fields. But Mary White Ovington reported that "race prejudice has even gone so far as to prevent a colored woman from receiving home work when it entailed her waiting in the same sitting room with white women," which suggests that women who did not have to wait in such rooms obtained homework.[21] Clothing manufacturers hired black women mainly as strikebreakers, as during the major New York walkout of 1909–10.[22]

With the opening up of the Northern clothing industry to African-Americans during World War I, black women gained an opportunity to apply their sewing skills. One local report noted that the owner of a factory with 300 black women was "inspired by [his] colored maid . . . the maid did beautiful hand work and made all of her clothes. This owner watche[d] her and thought that if one girl could do so well there were probably many other Negro girls." By 1930 the clothing industry employed the largest percentage (16 percent) of black women in any Northern manufacturing pursuit. In addition, uncounted black women, mostly immigrants from the Caribbean, "passed" for white in the garment shops. Still, in 1930 nearly one-fifth of all black women were classified as home dressmakers, the manufacturing category that held the largest numbers of black women workers in the North.[23]

Yet, from the start African-American women found themselves in the less-skilled sections of the clothing industry. In Chicago during the teens, they began to sew automobile cushions and lampshades when the manufacturers "found them to be efficient workers." During World War I, they gained an opportunity to engage in more skilled labor, with about a fifth operating machines, and they worked in the entire range of the industry, including ladies' silk dresses, underwear, men's shirts, and cheap lingerie. Some entered flower factories for pasting and branching parts of flowers and feathers. Nonetheless, as the Women's Bureau reported in 1922, "Frequently managers discriminated in favor of Negro women as pressers, because they felt that their work was more satisfactory," associating black women with hot, heavy, manual labor. They also worked as examiners, forewomen of cleaning groups, and as cleaners or bushers ("who cut and pick threads from finished garments.") But in the early 1920s they gradually returned to less-skilled work or cheaper sections of the trade (like aprons and overalls), if they retained employment in the industry at all.[24]

Black Women as Homeworkers in Chicago, 1926–27

Like African-American women throughout the nation, those in Chicago gained a permanent place as semiskilled workers in the garment factories during the war years. Those years also intensified the unionization and economic rationalization that by the mid-1920s would transform both the men's and women's clothing industry in Chicago, decreasing the amount of homework but not eliminating it. Despite this overall trend, African-Americans found themselves in the less-organized and newer branches of the garment trade—areas that exhibited characteristics conducive to homework: undercapitalization, hand labor, seasonality, and frequent changes in style. Black women engaged in homework in children's and women's dresses, aprons, caps, underwear, millinery, tags, paper flowers, china painting, furs, beading, and embroidery, though most worked on lamp shades and artificial flowers.[25]

While artificial flowers long had been a homework industry, lamp-shade homework was a relatively new phenomenon, having come about 1921 to Chicago's "black belt," where labor was cheap and plentiful and alternatives to domestic service, especially the non-live-in variety called day work, sparse. Manufacturers established "branch factories" under a black worker who acted as a contractor, training her neighbors in the process of covering a parchelite shade with muslin or placing a lining in a silk shade, pleating, and sewing the entire product. This contractor would also give out work to be done in the home. Other black women, who worked in factories by day, took home additional shades at night. In this way, the number of workers increased so that by 1926 piece rates were about half of what they formerly had been.[26]

This portrait of homework among black women in Chicago relies upon the survey research that Myra Hill Colson undertook for a master's thesis in the School of Social Service Administration at the University of Chicago in 1926. A black YWCA field secretary at the time, Colson went on to teach at Tuskegee Institute. Her thesis, "Home Work Among Negro Women in Chicago," for which she interviewed 100 homeworkers and surveyed another 100, provides the clearest description of black industrial homeworkers and one of the most precise pictures of any homeworkers during the 1920s.[27] Analysis of her findings further suggests that artificial flower making and other sewing crafts represent an extension of a strategy to earn wages without the immediate supervision of whites. Home-based labor belongs to the African-American women's quest for freedom but also relates to the discrimination that they and their men faced in labor and housing markets. As a unique local study, these findings can only suggest conditions in other cities, which exhibited different histories of black migration and industrial development. But they clearly show how one major Northern city developed the national picture of black women in the garment industry suggested earlier in this essay.

Inadequate economic resources, especially the casual and ill-paid labor of their husbands, pushed married women to homework, despite its low returns for hours spent on stitching pants, shelling nuts, or assembling flowers. African-American women were no exception; they and their families also faced the high costs of segregated housing and limited job markets in Chicago following the first World War. The 1910 Senate report on *Immigrants in Cities* had listed no black home laborers there, but between 1910 and 1920, the black population of Chicago increased 148.2 percent. Most homeworkers came from the major states of the Great Migration during its early phase—Mississippi, Alabama, Georgia, and Arkansas. Only a third of the 100 interviewed had lived less than five years in the city, and half of these had been in Chicago for four years when interviewed. Thus, like immigrant homeworkers a decade before, African-Americans were migrants; like immigrants, many also were long term homeworkers, with about half at such labor for three years or more. Though homework was a short-term strategy for some, for many it was becoming an integral part of the family economy.[28] With the closing of mass immigration during the war and through federal statute, with increased labor opportunities for second-generation white ethnics and restrictions on *where* African-Americans could work, these internal migrants offered employers a new source of homework labor.[29]

The majority of interviewed women previously had worked in the garment trades but at less-skilled and unorganized sections, with over a third in factories or shops and nearly a half in home dressmaking—an indication of skill transference. About one sixth had labored in lampshade factories. One woman, a milliner, had spent six years at the same factory until layoffs of blacks forced her out. Another woman also turned to homework after all blacks working inside the factory were forced out. Three former mail-order clerks could not retain their jobs after the war and so found themselves doing homework. A few former schoolteachers and at least one new normal school graduate took up artificial flower making and lamp shade sewing. Some could not find work in Chicago's segregated system, some perhaps lacked educational qualification, but others preferred "the freedom and glamour of city life and industrial employment" to the more circumscribed life of the small town and rural South. Still other homeworkers came from the farm, whose daily grind made making lamp shades seem easy. "What did I do?" a woman from Pecan Point, Arkansas, answered; "Lawd, I chopped and picked cotton."[30]

With about two-thirds of the sample married, Colson's homeworkers resemble those in other studies; however, they had fewer children and lived in relatively high-cost, well-kept-up housing. Though these women were in the prime child bearing and rearing years, from twenty to thirty-five, in over half of the families there were no children, only two had as many as four children, and about 40 percent had children below working age. Such a profile suggests decreased childbearing among the first black migrants and further contrasts sharply with Italian home-workers, who tended to have more children than the norm. Perhaps these demographics account in part for the almost nonexistence of child labor (long considered a major evil of the system) among African-American homeworkers. The reason that other homeworkers have given—to stay home with one's children—would only hold for the few mothers of small children, widows, and other female heads of house-holds. Only one woman, with three small children, presented the tra-ditional explanation for homework. Colson, however, did not system-atically ask her interviewees why they do homework, so it is impossible to be definitive on this issue.[31] But the lack of small children does suggest that family responsibilities by themselves fail to explain home-work among Chicago black women in the mid-twenties.

One of Colson's interviewees, the wife of an ice and coal seller who desired to buy their house, offered another explanation: "She wants to help him all she can." Hope for a higher standard of living, along with kin-based obligations, compelled some women to homework. Some were sending money back to the South to support elderly parents. Mrs. Z. spoke of working "so they can have some savings" but also noted how "the piece work system and the loose organization of the lamp shade industry allow her to leave home after her little girl is off for school and to return when she is out of school in the afternoon, bringing a few shades with her." Historically, homework has appealed to women because of such flexibility.[32]

These women took in homework because they needed the money. Like other homeworking women, they helped their men who lacked regular employment and thus earned wages inadequate to maintain the family. One-third of them were common laborers, but even those who were not and worked in the building trades, stock yards, and steel mills—still a small proportion of Chicago's black male laborers in the twenties—experienced seasonal work and daily fluctuations. One plumber, barred from joining the union on account of his race, never could predict when he would be turned away from a job reserved for union men. Expensive train fares to work and the high rents in Chi-cago's black areas further eroded men's wages. Some families re-sponded by pooling resources and sharing housing as well as having their women do homework—common working-class strategies among immigrants as well.[33]

Why homework instead of the better-paying labor of domestic service? Since emancipation, black families had attempted to keep wives and daughters out of white kitchens, to end any suggestion of continuing servitude, to better use their labor for the family, or to protect them from sexual harrassment. By the twenties, black women in the North, as previously in the South, were rejecting live-in service for day work, so they could live with their kin.[34] This group of homeworking families may have had a larger male wage than on average and thus could afford to keep their wives from domestic service, still the labor of two-thirds of the city's African-American women. Twenty-five dollars a week was a common wage for black men in industry; two-thirds of the estimated wages of husbands from homeworking families were at this level or higher.[35] Thus they may not have needed the wages of service badly enough to put up with its humiliations. They could take advantage of the greater flexibility of homework, when available, and still fall back upon day work when they needed additional income.

Among the unmarried, the few homeworkers who lived with their parents or their adult children were not expected to fully support themselves. A few others combined homework with taking in boarders, another home-based strategy to generate income common to married women in all racial/ethnic groups. A few others combined homework with factory or day work. The combination of day work and nighttime needlecraft homework perhaps was not unusual; one history of day workers in Washington, D.C., also found women beading in the evening to earn additional money.[36] Still others with children relied on charity, a mothers' pension, parents, or other forms of labor to supplement their meager homework earnings of between $3.50 and $12.00 a week.

A small number of single women preferred homework. Miss Lelia Smith, a thirty-two-year-old former schoolteacher from Mississippi, was making $13 a week, more than her former salary of $37.50 a month, and saving carfare and time. Mary Miller felt that she could work faster at home than in the factory, where inspectors and lack of materials delayed her. During the slack season, she tried working in a laundry factory but discovered the hours to be too long and the piece rate too low. She made only $2 a day for all that hard work, compared to $17 to $28 a week during the lamp shade busy season. She told Colson "she 'sure likes to make shades' and she expects to continue unless she finds something that fascinates her more." Another woman rejected laundry work for artificial flower making. Others did homework while they were studying to become teachers and one continued while she was waiting for an appointment to teach.[37]

But what was the nature of this "chosen" labor? The pay was low, given the hours worked. "You know they pay as little as they can," reported one beader of dresses who earned in two eight-hour days between $5.50 to $6 a dress. Embroiderers could do better, earning $9 for completing three dresses during a 9 A.M.-to-4 P.M. day. But the experience of Mrs. S. was more typical: earning between $6 and $6.50 a week for beading georgette dresses at rates varying from $2.25 to $4.50 per dress, she stopped after four months and took up day work for $5.00 a day. Lamp shade makers also found problems with their piece rates, which would decline as the season wore on, especially after retailers had chosen the styles for the year. Constant change in style and variation in orders received made it impossible to develop speed to increase piece-rate earnings. Simple shades could pay as much as complicated ones that took longer and required greater skill. With artificial flowers there also existed no relation between payment and work involved, even though the organization of the industry was more uniform than either beading, embroidery, or lamp shades. Larger sizes, which could sell for more, often paid more, even if smaller flowers were harder to assemble. All of these industries were seasonal, especially for homeworkers. Thus wages were both irregular and unpredictable; women reported cuts in the rates over the last few years, a common occurence once enough workers were tied into the system.[38]

African-American women in Chicago faced a homework system that hardly differed from the one Italians in New York experienced a decade before or would work under during the Great Depression in Connecticut and Rhode Island. Colson's interviewees described rush seasons in terms that resonate with those provided to Women's Bureau investigators a decade later. One woman who had worked "about sixty hours a week" on flowers since 1923 and who also commissioned work out to her roomer admitted, "It was 'getting on her nerves.'" Another woman confessed: "When I work hard on shades, I do not want to see any one when I am through. I prepare some cold food and begin to work. I work a little and eat a little. I do most of my work at night. I am a nervous wreck and cannot sleep anyhow. Frequently I work all night until the work is done. I pack the work up, then I sleep a few hours and when I awake it is all ready to take to the factory. Once last winter I made $42 in seven days. Another time I made $36 in three days. I only slept about two hours a day in those three days." But unlike other homeworkers, these women seemed to quit when prices went down too low. One flower maker of five years explained that when ribbon rosettes dropped from twenty-five-to-fifteen cents a gross, she gave up. "Only 3 or 4 foreign women would accept such work," she noted.[39] Unlike immigrant women, African-American women had domestic service, a race- and sex-segmentated occupation that they could still fall back upon, and so they did not have to accept rate cuts that would lower their customary wage.

Like other homeworkers, African-American women could move up the homework system by becoming a contractor or running a branch factory.[40] Employers redirected the leadership abilities of trouble makers who questioned discrimination in the workplace, removing them from the factory to run a lamp shade branch in the black section of the city. Female contractor and female homeworker shared social circumstances and cultural values, yet not without tensions. Mrs. A., a contractor, explained, "It was very difficult to make colored girls understand that a colored woman could be fair to them." Indeed, she told Colson that she acted in the interest of the workers against the company. She timed the rate given to new shades to insure that rate was fair and kept a shade from being made if it was unfair "until the factory agreed to raise the rate even if it were no more than five or ten cents. She would say, 'You'll have to send for these shades. I'll not be guilty of giving them to the girls.'" And when the manager would remind her that she received her commission (ten to thirty cents a shade) anyhow, she "would rejoin: 'I can't be guilty of taking bread out of children's mouths.'" This woman kept a list on the wall with the rates per shade for workers to consult, an unusual practice for any contractor, and claimed to pay the same as the factory. Other contractors seemed more concerned "to get [their] own" as manufacturers slashed rates and thus contractors took on more and cheaper shades and a larger commission out of each when conditions in the industry deteriorated during the decade.[41]

Colson described homework and homeworkers without fully analyzing the underlying circumstances that opened up the system to African-American women in Chicago. However, the perceptions that she offered were sympathetic and insightful. She concluded her thesis by noting that "the Negro woman home worker . . . is not a type such as the picture of the early 'sweater' recalls. She does not live in filth. Her surroundings are fairly comfortable. She does not work incessantly. She is conscious of a need of relaxation and rest. Home work for her is a means of aiding her to attain a slightly higher standard of living or of freeing her from the routine of factory work." Colson was concerned, as were other students of the Great Migration, with whether

Southern blacks could adapt themselves to industrial, urban life. She wondered whether homework could function as "a stepping stone to a more stable place in factory industries," which she judged superior to work in the home.[42] Like her teacher, Edith Abbott, and other women reformers, Colson condemned industrial homework for its exploitative conditions and applauded factory labor for women who had to work.[43] If she pointed out social problems associated with urban migration, she also portrayed African-Americans in a positive light.

Factory labor certainly paid better and lent itself more readily to unionization. But black women in Chicago were taking in homework even though they were not burdened by large families, in part because they were unable to obtain decent factory jobs, in part because their husbands faced similar discrimination, but also because they viewed labor under their own direction as preferable to labor under white supervisors. Day work, after all, still meant working in a white home. The Chicago case study reminds us that only in the context of the labor market, social conditions, and family demographics can we evaluate why women turn to home-based labor, whether such work is choosen freely or thrust upon them as the best of a set of bad options.

Concluding Questions

To fully understand the meaning of home-based labor in the lives of African-American women, we need to compare this case not only with the history of seamstresses and laundresses but with other experiences of industrial homework, especially those of racial/ethnic groups like Mexicans, Puerto Ricans, and Chinese.[44] Moreover, we need to know more about rural African-American homeworkers, like those who made candlewick bedspreads during the Great Depression, when white neighbors shared their homework, or those in the early 1960s in South Carolina, whose homework became legal when the National Consumers' League and the National Council of Negro Women organized them into a craft cooperative.[45] We need to know more precisely how large the practice of home-based labor was among African-Americans (for how many is almost impossible to uncover for such hidden labor) and among which groups in the community.

Rebecca Garvin sewed at home; her daughter Mamie was a schoolteacher. Why both were deemed respectable reminds us that black women and men saw in domestic service the legacy of slavery and sought to protect their daughters and wives from possible sexual harrassment from white men and other abuse from white women. To understand "why homework?" we have to keep our eyes open to a counter movement in the history of the paid labor of African-American women: one that values staying in the home rather than going out of it. This counter theme could derive from the patriarchal desires of men to care for their women even when they barely could meet economic needs of their families or from women's own desires to care for their children under circumstances that demanded that they contribute to the family economy. But we must recognize it to understand it, not to celebrate black women as a role model for white women who have become disillusioned with the burden of the double day or to justify as more natural the return of work to the home but to more fully understand the African-American experience.[46]

NOTES

Research for this paper was supported by grants from the National Endowment for the Humanities, a Radcliffe College Research Support Fellowship, and a Department of History, Howard University, Research Grant. I would like to thank Jacquelyn Dowd Hall, James O. Horton, Nelson Lichtenstein, and Leslie Rowland for their comments on an earlier version of this essay.

1. Letter to NWTUL from chief of Bureau of Industrial Accident and Labor Research, Illinois State Department of Labor, May 5, 1926, in Papers of the National Women's Trade Union League of America, 1904–1950, folder 15, Scheslinger Library, Radcliffe; Nelle Swartz, *Some Social and Economic Aspects of Homework,* State of New York, Department of Labor, Bureau of Women in Industry, Special Bulletin no. 158, 1929, p. 10.

2. For Lewis Hine, see his "Tenement House Scrapbook," prints and photographs division, Library of Congress; see also Boris and Daniels, "Images of Homework," this volume, plates 3, 4, 5. For the portrait of homeworkers and the attitudes of reformers, see my "Tenement Homework and the Reorganization of Immigrant Life" (Paper presented at the National American Studies Association Meeting, San Diego, November 1985). See also Cynthia R. Daniels, "Between Home and Family," in pp. 13–32.

3. For the home-based labor of black women compared to immigrants, U.S. Senate, 61st Congress, 2nd sess., Reports of the Immigration Commission, *Immigrants in Cities,* 2 vol. (Washington, D.C.: GPO, 1911), 1:464 (table 387) 1:293–98 (table 290); see also Elizabeth Pleck, "A Mother's Wages: Income Earning among Married Italian and Black Women, 1896–1911," in *A Heritage of Her Own,* ed. Nancy F. Cott and Elizabeth H. Pleck (New York: Simon and Schuster, 1979), pp. 367–92, especially table 2, p. 376. Pleck comes to conclusions similar to my own, though she is poking at another "truism," the exclusive home-based paid labor force participation of Italian women.

4. For discussions of the withdrawal of women from field labor, see Jacqueline Jones, *Labor of Love, Labor of Sorrow: Black Women, Work, and the*

Family from Slavery to the Present (New York: Basic Books, 1985), pp. 36–70; Herbert Gutman, *The Black Family in Slavery and Freedom, 1750–1925* (New York: Pantheon, 1976), pp. 163–64.

5. For women's labor force participation, see Claudia D. Goldin, "Female Labor Force Participation: The Origin of Black and White Differences, 1870–1880, "*Journal of Economic History* 16 (Summer 1983): 39–48; Barbara Klaczynaska, "Why Women Work: A Comparison of Various Groups—Philadelphia, 1910–1930, "*Labor History* 17 (Winter 1976): 73–87; Jilia Kirk Blackwelder, "Women in the Workforce: Atlanta, New Orleans, and San Antonio, 1930 to 1940," *Journal of Urban History* 4 (May 1978): 331–58; Susan M. Hartmann, *The Home Front and Beyond: American Women in the 1940s* (Boston: G. K. Hall, 1982), 78–79; Joseph A. Hill, *Women in Gainful Occupations, 1870–1920,* United States Department of Commerce, Bureau of Census Monograph (Washington, D.C.: GPO, 1929); Cynthia Taeuber and Victor Valdisera, *Women in the American Economy,* United States Department of Commerce, Current Population Report Special Studies Series P-23, no. 146 (Washington, D.C.: GPO, November 1986).

6. Mamie Garvin Fields with Karen Fields, *Lemon Swamp and Other Places: A Carolina Memoir* (New York: The Free Press, 1983), pp. 9, 8, 37; also pp. 33, 55, 62, 63, 87–90, 148–54.

7. For homework during the antebellum period, see Christine Stansell, "The Origins of the Sweatshop: Women and Early Industrialization in New York City," in *Working-Class America: Essays on Labor, Community and American Society* ed. Michael Frisch and Daniel Walkowitz (Urbana: University of Illinois Press, 1983), pp. 78–103; Mary Blewitt, "Work, Gender and the Artisan Tradition in New England Shoemaking, 1780–1860," *Journal of Social History,* 17 (Winter 1983): 221–48; for the work of slave women, see Deborah G. White, *Ai'n't I a Woman? Female Slaves in the Plantation South* (New York: Norton, 1985); for the needlework of slave women, see Judith Wragg Chase, *Afro-American Art and Craft* (New York: Van Nostrand Reinhold Co., 1971), pp. 87–90; *Craftsmanship: A Tradition in Black America* (New York: RCA Corporation, n.d.), p. 15.

8. Elizabeth Keckley, *Behind the Scenes: Thirty Years a Slave and Four Years in the White House* (New York: New York Printing Co. 1868), pp. 21, 45–85; see also Dorothy Sterling, ed. *We Are Your Sisters: Black Women in the Nineteenth Century* (New York: Norton, 1984), pp. 245, 248–52, 459–60.

9. *Craftsmanship: A Tradition in Black America,* p. 15; George Edmund Haynes, *The Negro at Work in New York City: A Study in Economic Progress,* Studies in History, Economics, and Public Law, vol. 49, no. 3, whole no. 124 (New York: Columbia University, 1912), pp. 98–99, 110, 131.

10. Sterling, *We Are Your Sisters,* pp. 97–98, 141, 215–18, 248–51; see also pp. 91, 96, for other examples of home-based business. See also James Horton and Lois Horton, *Black Bostonians* (New York: Holmes and Meier, 1979), pp. 15–20, for the work of antebellum free black women.

11. Jones, *Labor of Love,* pp. 71–135, especially 104–7; Orville Vernon Burton, *In My Father's House Are Many Mansions: Family and Community*

in Edgefield, South Carolina (Chapel Hill: University of North Carolina Press, 1985), pp. 300–306; Dolores Janiewski, *Sisterhood Denied: Race, Gender, and Class in a New South Community* (Philadelphia: Temple University Press, 1985), pp. 42–49, for rural life; Haynes, *The Negro at Work*, pp. 67–76.

12. Jones, *Labor of Love*, p. 127. See also note 11.

13. Sterling, *We Are Your Sisters*, pp. 357–59.

14. G. H. Weaver, "Sociological Study of 1,251 Families," in George M. Kober, *Report of Committee on Social Betterment* (Washington, D.C.: The President's Homes Commission, 1908), 226–27.

15. Carter Woodson, "The Negro Washerwoman, A Vanishing Figure," *The Journal of Negro History* 15 (July 1930): 269–77.

16. Woodson, "The Negro Washerwoman," pp. 269–70; Hill, *Women in Gainful Occupations*, pp. 109–21, especially 112–13, and 116 (table 85).

17. Hill, *Women in Gainful Occupations*, p. 119.

18. Mary White Ovington, *Half a Man: The Status of the Negro in New York* (1911; rpt. New York: Hill and Wang, 1969), pp. 20, 34–35, 77–79. See also Ovington, "The Negro Home in New York," *Charities* 15 (October 7, 1905): 25–30. For a contrasting view, which presents children "growing up in the streets and the schools, without the home training" of mothers, see Helena Titus Emerson, "Children of the Circle," ibid.: 82. For another contrast that paints the home of the laundress as diseased and dirty as that of the Italian homeworker, Ruth Reed, "The Negro Women of Gainesville, Ga.," *Bulletin of the University of Georgia* (Phelps-Stokes Fellowship Studies, no. 6) 22 (December 1921): 16–18.

19. "Employment of Colored Women in Chicago from a Study Made by the Chicago School of Civics and Philanthropy," *The Crisis* 1 (January 1911): 24–25.

20. Hill, *Women in Gainful Employment*, passim; Ovington, *Half a Man*, p. 79.

21. See, for example, Fields, *Lemon Swamp and Other Places*, pp. 87–90; Ovington, *Half a Man*, pp. 88–89. See also Rosalyn Terborg-Penn, "Survival Strategies among African-American Women Workers: A Continuing Process," in *Women, Work and Protest: A Century of U.S. Women's Labor History,* ed. Ruth Milkman (Boston: Routledge and Kegan Paul, 1985), p. 148.

22. The Chicago Commission on Race Relations, *The Negro in Chicago: A Study of Race Relations and a Race Riot* (Chicago: The University of Chicago Press, 1922), pp. 414–15; Ovington, *Half a Man*, p. 89; Meredith Tax, *The Rising of the Women* (New York: Monthly Review Press, 1980), pp. 223–26.

23. Jones, *Labor of Love*, p. 150; for passing, Terborg-Penn, "Survival Strategies among African-American Women Workers," pp. 150–51. For one local example, Phyllis Wheatley Branch YWCA, *Negro Women in the Industries of Indianapolis, Indiana: A Survey and Report* (Indianapolis: Phyllis Wheatley Branch YWCA, 1929), p. 13. For numbers in one city, see Allan Spear, *Black Chicago: The Making of a Negro Ghetto, 1890–1920* (Chicago: University of Chicago Press, 1967), p. 33 (table 7); p. 154 (table 12).

24. The Chicago Commission on Race Relations, *The Negro in Chicago,* pp. 367, 380–84; U.S. Department of Labor, U.S. Women's Bureau, *Negro Women in Industry,* Bulletin of the Women's Bureau, no. 20 (Washington, D.C.: GPO, 1922), pp. 12–13, 34; Nellie Swartz, Mary E. Jackson, Eva Bowles, et al., *A New Deal for the Colored Woman Worker: A Study of Colored Women in Industry in New York City* (New York: Charles P. Young, March 1, 1919), pp. 8, 14–17; Helen B. Sayre, "Negro Women in Industry," *Opportunity* 2 (August 1924): pp. 242–44. For a 1940 assessment of where black women were working in the clothing industry, Ruth Paul Porter, "Negro Women in the Clothing, Cigar and Laundry Industries of Philadelphia, 1940," *Journal of Negro Education* 12 (Winter 1943): 21–23.

25. St. Clair Drake and Horace R. Cayton, *Black Metropolis: A Study of Negro Life in a Northern City* 2 vol. (New York: Harcourt Brace and World, 1945), 2:222–23; Myra Hill Colson, "Home Work among Negro Women in Chicago" (Master's thesis, University of Chicago, 1928), pp. 2, 25–28; for the nature of the homework system, see my essay, "Homework in the Past: Its Meaning for the Future" in *The New Era of Homework,* ed. Kathleen Christensen, (Boulder: Westview Press, 1988): 15–29.

26. Colson, "Home Work among Negro Women in Chicago"; see also, Colson, "Negro Home Workers in Chicago," a shortened version of her thesis, in *Social Service Review* 11 (September 1928): 385–413. Subsequent references will be to the thesis.

27. Colson, "Home Work among Negro Women in Chicago," p. 2, 32–52. For Colson's biography, see *Who's Who in Colored America: A Biographical Dictionary of Notable Living Persons of Negro Descent in America,* ed. Joseph J. Boris (New York: Who's Who in Colored America Publishing Corp., 1927), 1:45. For the prevalence of day work as a black women's occupation in the city, see Spear, *Black Chicago,* p. 155.

28. *Immigrants in Cites,* p. 464 (table 387); Colson, "Home Work among Negro Women in Chicago," p. 29, 54, 57, 60–64, 70. For the general conditions in Chicago, see Spear, *Black Chicago,* and the Chicago Commission on Race Relations, *The Negro in Chicago,* passim.

29. For the end of mass immigration and immigrant restriction in the 1920s, see William E. Leuchtenburg, *The Perils of Prosperity, 1914–32* (Chicago: University of Chicago Press, 1958), pp. 205–8. See also "Negro Migration and the Immigration Quota," *Opportunity* 1 (April 1923): 18–19.

30. Colson, "Home Work among Negro Women in Chicago," pp. 64–68, 84.

31. Ibid., pp. 70, 90–91, 98, 110. In contrast, the 1929 New York report cites 56 percent of women giving "care of children" as reason for homework, with another 20 percent saying "care of home." The average number of children was 3.1, with 64 percent of them school age and 21 percent preschool. Swartz, *Some Social and Economic Aspects of Homework,* p. 6. My research on New Haven and Bridgeport in 1931, however, shows homeworking families considerably above average. See my "Homeworkers on Homework: Self-Per-

ceptions from Depression America" (Paper presented to the Social Science History Association, October 1986).

32. Colson, "Home Work among Negro Women in Chicago," pp. 96–97.

33. Ibid., pp. 91–92, 94, 95; Spear, *Black Chicago,* pp. 151, 155–57.

34. Spear, *Black Chicago,* pp. 151, 157; Drake and Cayton, *Black Metropolis,* p. 229.

35. Colson, "Home Work among Negro Women in Chicago," pp. 100–109; Elizabeth Clark-Lewis, " 'This Work Had A' End": The Transition from Live-In to Day Work," Working Paper no. 2, (Southern Women: The Intersection of Race, Class and Gender, Center for Research on Women), Memphis State University, July 1985, p. 31.

36. Colson, "Home Work among Negro Women in Chicago," pp. 104–8.

37. Ibid., pp. 72–73, 74–84, 86–87.

38. Ibid., pp. 94, 86–87, 78; for interviews recorded by the Women's Bureau, see my "Homeworkers on Homework." See also Susan Porter Benson, "Women, Work, and the Family Economy," and Julia Kirk Blackwelder, "Texas Homeworkers in the 1930s," in this volume.

39. On women as contractors, see "Homeworkers on Homework," in which I more fully explore this point.

40. Colson, "Home Work among Negro Women in Chicago," pp. 43–52, especially 44, 46.

41. Ibid., pp. 118–19.

42. On these women reformers, see my article, "Quest for Labor Standards in the Era of Eleanor Roosevelt: The Case of Industrial Homework," *Wisconsin Women's Law Journal* 2 (1986): 53–74; on the Abbotts, see Lea B. Costin, *Two Sisters for Social Justice: A Biography of Grace and Edith Abbott* (Urbana: University of Illinois Press, 1983).

43. For Mexicans, see Julia Kirk Blackwelder, *Women of the Depression: Caste and Culture in San Antonio, 1929–1939* (College Station: Texas A&M Press, 1984), pp. 90–103. Also see the original survey material of the U.S. Department of Labor, Women's Bureau (RG86), materials relating to Bulletin no. 126, National Archives, Washington, D.C. For Puerto Ricans, see Virginia Sanchez Korral, "The Other Side of the Ocean," *Carribean Review* 8 (January–March 1979): 22–29. For Chinese and other Asians, see U.S. Department of Labor, Bureau of Labor Statistics, "Report of Committee on Industrial Homework," in *Proceedings of the Fourteenth Annual Convention of the Association of Governmental Labor Officials of the United States and Canada,* Bulletin No. 455 (Washington, D.C.: GPO, 1927), pp. 77–78.

44. For Georgia in the 1930s, see fieldnotes relating to U.S. Department of Labor, Women's Bureau, "Potential Earning Power of Southern Mountaineer Handicraft," Bulletin no. 128 National Archives; for the 1960s, testimony of Ruth Jordan, U.S. Department of Labor, "In the Matter of: A Public Hearing to Commerce Labor Department Review of 'Homeworker Rules,' " February 18, 1981, Washington, D.C., p. 240, typescript on file in Office of Special Minimum Wage, Division of Labor Standards, U.S. Department of Labor, Washington, D.C.

45. Bonnie Thorton Dill, "The Dialectics of Black Womanhood," *Signs: A Journal of Women in Culture and Society* 4 (Spring 1979): 543–55; Thorton Dill, "Race, Class, and Gender: Prospects for an All-inclusive Sisterhood," *Feminist Studies* 9 (Spring 1983): 131–50; Phyllis Palmer, "White Women/ Black Women: The Dualism of Female Identity and Experience," ibid.: 151–70.

3

Women, Work, and the Family Economy: Industrial Homework in Rhode Island in 1934

SUSAN PORTER BENSON

On December 14, 1978, "Action Line," the *Providence Journal*'s problem-solving column, printed the following complaint: "I'm confused. I'd like to make some extra money at home, so I inquired about doing some piecework for a jewelry company. To my surprise, every place I call tells me it's illegal to give out piecework to do at home. That can't be. I know several people who have been doing this for years." The writer of this letter inadvertently pointed to the paradoxical nature of industrial homework in the United States since the turn of the twentieth century: increasingly illegal but stubbornly persistent. This paradox grew out of the peculiar conditions of this latest phase of production in the home.

Most observers agreed that by the late nineteenth century, a time-honored pattern of work—manufacturing in the home—had been transformed by industrialization into a social problem. Early twentieth-century investigations by reformers and feminists branded industrial homework a social problem for three reasons. First, it exploited women and children, intensifying the oppression of the least powerless through low wages, long hours, cheating by employers, and truancy. Second, it depressed the wage rates paid in factories and undid unions' gains. Finally, it imperiled public health because its products were manufactured beyond the reach of sanitary controls.[1]

These arguments reflected the convergence of three powerful forces in the mounting crusade against industrial homework: social feminists concerned with the welfare of women and children; public health and housing reformers; and trade unionists in the needle trades, an industry riddled with home manufacture. All accepted as axiomatic the notion that home and work should be separated, arguing like most of their contemporaries that social and economic progress rested on the rigidification of the boundaries between private life and work life.[2]

By 1919, reformers' efforts had secured the passage of laws regulating or prohibiting industrial homework in thirteen states, mostly in the Northeast. A few labor unions in the needle trades had negotiated contractual bans on industrial homework. After briefly banning homework in war-related production during World War I, the federal government joined the crusade against industrial homework with the National Industrial Recovery Act of 1933 (NRA).[3] The actual effect of the NRA was limited: five codes (including those for the notorious lace and pecan-shelling industries) allowed homework to continue essentially unabated, eighteen industries relying heavily on homework never settled on codes, and the 144 industry codes restricting or prohibiting industrial homework lapsed when the NRA was declared unconstitutional.[4] Nonetheless, the NRA marked a turning point in Washington's policy toward industrial homework, and the Fair Labor Standards Act of 1938 included broad provisions against the practice.

Efforts to regulate industrial homework sought in the final analysis to abolish it; typical was the Rhode Island Homework Law of 1936, which declared as its aim the "strict control and the gradual elimination of industrial homework."[5] The unstated assumption was that industrial rationalization would eliminate the need for this shadow labor market and accomplish the final and irrevocable separation of home and workplace. The persistence of industrial homework into the late twentieth century mocks the faith of these early reformers; it is not an archaism but a flourishing, if outlaw, feature of the economy, often entrenched in the most advanced sectors.

Industrial homeworkers remain phantom figures in the background of the antihomework campaigns. We see them primarily through reformers' eyes, hear their voices as the reformers wanted them to be heard. They appear as victims rendered powerless by desperation: destitute women, often immigrants, who worked long hours alongside their children in squalid tenement hovels. Reformers often sympathized with homeworkers, understanding their dependence on their meager wages and the likelihood that the prohibition of homework would impoverish them even further, but nevertheless regarded them as anachronisms locked into poverty by their immigrant status and their children's haphazard schooling. Just as they assumed that the demand side of the industrial homework labor market would shrink through the rationalization of industry, so too they believed that the supply side would wither as immigrants assimilated to American ways and children attended school more regularly.

The flaws in the reformers' Progressive optimism are readily apparent; we can now see that the separation of home and workplace, no less of family and work, is relatively recent and its implementation incomplete. The reformers, understandably eager to condemn industrial homework, saw it as a category of activity to be proscribed; historians, without excusing its abuses or arguing away its oppression, need to understand it instead as a varied and evolving experience. A practice which was from reformers' perspective a social problem was from other perspectives a social solution, however imperfect. By shifting the focus to the experiences and consciousness of the employers and the homeworkers—even while necessarily relying on evidence collected by reformers—we can frame a new view of homework combining an abiding awareness of its exploitative aspects with newer scholarly perspectives: of women's history, which views women not merely as objects but as subjects who marshalled resources to accomplish their ends; of labor history, which emphasizes workplace interactions and the social context of work; and, finally, of social history, which stresses the centrality of everyday life and the specificity of local situations.

During the 1930s, a unique context for industrial homework emerged: regulatory pressures increased and the movement for industrial efficiency intensified, while the economic crisis threw many back on the least advantageous forms of wage earning. The raw data collected in 1934 by Harriet A. Byrne and Bertha Blair for the Women's Bureau's report *Industrial Home Work in Rhode Island, with Special Reference to the Lace Industry* offer an unusually vivid picture of the competing agendas of reformers, industrialists, and homeworkers during this critical period.[6] This material includes the reports of interviews with homeworkers and their employers as well as assorted memoranda and working notes. The forms for homeworkers provide information about the workers and their families, wages and conditions of homework, the sources and amount of other family income, and the house, along with stray homeworkers' comments and interviewers' observations. The industry schedules focus on wages and methods of distributing the goods to homeworkers.

Elaborate statistical analysis of these data would not be appropriate for three reasons. First, the sample of interviewees was not systematic. Byrne and Blair obtained from payroll and school lists the names of 331 lace homeworkers and 69 working on other articles. They interviewed just over half of the former, but 58 of the latter, choosing interviewees with no apparent method. Second, the interview forms are rarely completed in full; the blank spaces could indicate the investigator's haste, the homeworker's reticence, or a negative response. Finally, the Bureau intended the report as a response to the failure of the lace industry's NRA code to outlaw homework.[7] In four of the other industries covered in the report, NRA codes had banned homework: in artificial flowers, tags, and garters, the prohibition had not yet taken effect when the interviews were conducted, but it had in jewelry. Although the raw data contain interviews with ten jewelry homeworkers, Byrne and Blair maintained in the published report that they had found no jewelry homework and ignored that industry—whether to highlight the lace industry, to protect the homeworkers, or to give the impression that homework could be successfully outlawed.[8] Margaret Ackroyd and Anna Tucker, who administered the state regulation of homework after the NRA was declared unconstitutional, affirmed that jewelry homework thrived despite its extralegal status, so that the focus on the lace industry and the omission of the jewelry industry seriously distorts the overall picture of homework in Rhode Island.[9] Given these limitations, any but the simplest statistical analysis would build on a shaky foundation indeed.

Homework in Depression Rhode Island was almost exclusively handwork. Work on clothing, a staple of industrial homework elsewhere, was virtually nonexistent in the state, apparently limited to a few women who embroidered (probably by hand) children's clothing in Pawtucket and Central Falls.[10] Rhode Island homeworkers instead pulled lace, mended worsted cloth, strung tags, and manufactured garters, jewelry, artificial flowers, and fishing tackle. Lace work was concentrated in the Providence metropolitan area, chiefly in Pawtucket; in West Warwick, the center of the Pawtuxet Valley textile industry; and to a lesser degree in the rural areas of southwestern Rhode Island. The 177 women in this group pulled out the threads connecting the strips of lace as they came off the loom. The twenty nine women who worked for the Wanskuck Mill in Providence mended—in effect, rewove—imperfections in worsted goods. Tag workers threaded strings through tags, tied a knot, and counted and bundled the tags; these thirteen women lived in Pawtucket and Central Falls. Twelve Providence jewelry workers performed varied operations such as bead stringing, linking, and stone setting. Ten women, again all in Providence, made artificial flowers for the California Artificial Flower Company. Finally, three Pawtucket women sewed or assembled garters, and three from Ashaway sewed and tied fishing tackle. In all seven industries, the tasks done by homeworkers were also performed by workers inside the factory. However, three of the eleven lace firms, employing about one-fifth of the lace homeworkers interviewed, relied entirely on homework for lace pulling.

These operations were performed outside the factory neither by chance nor by tradition; homework played a key part in manufacturers' long-run rationalization plans as well as in their tactics for coping with the Depression. First, manufacturers used homework to keep peace within the factory: they tended to put out "bad work"—that which was less desirable or more difficult. Byrne and Blair recorded comments by more than one in ten lace pullers that the fabric was too tightly woven, too starchy, or linked by weak threads that broke instead of pulling out smoothly. Evengelina Cordeiro, a puller in West Warwick, expressed her despair: "Hard to pull, goes to your heart."[11] Flora Santos was angry instead: Blair noted that she was "very much incensed that those in the mill get better lace."[12] The variations in the time required to pull a given amount tell the tale of "bad lace." Tina Teixeira, for example, reported that she would spend from five minutes to a full hour pulling one band of lace, depending upon its quality.[13] Worsted menders dreaded black fabric, which strained the eyes and was difficult to mend invisibly. Home menders for the Wanskuck Mill complained that they were given a disproportionate amount of black.[14]

Homeworkers on both lace and worsteds performed more tasks than comparable workers inside the factories. While factory pullers merely let the lace fall into baskets, home pullers had to fold and bundle it, unpaid work taking as much as half the time it took to pull the lace.[15] Homeworkers had to remove "slubs"—knots or thick places—on worsteds without an increase in rates, while special workers did this work in the mill.[16] By foisting off the bad work onto the relatively isolated homeworkers, manufacturers could placate inside workers by relieving them of distasteful tasks. The exasperation of a lace puller inside the factory could lead to collective action, disruptive behavior, or quiet sabotage; when a homeworker quit in despair or anger, her defection did not disturb factory discipline.

Homework as a management strategy had a more specific application in the Depression context. Manufacturers intensified the pace of factory work and introduced efficiency schemes to increase productivity and offset higher payrolls caused by NRA code provisions for a minimum wage. The Wanskuck Mill, with a brash anti-union tradition including gun-point threats to workers, inaugurated a point system. Those who failed to produce enough points were first disciplined and eventually laid off, sometimes to do the same work at home: three of the worsted menders were refugees from the efficiency expert, having been fired for not making their points.[17] The women who made garters inside the Moore Fabrics Company factory were forced to produce sixteen gross of garters per day; a pace nearly three times that of Mrs. Davenport, a reasonably skilled homeworker.[18] Both jewelry and lace firms required that women who did not meet their quotas take the unfinished work home to complete it.[19]

As manufacturers tightened discipline and pursued the speedup in their factories, they incorporated homework into their new management strategies. Outside work allowed them to take advantage of skilled and experienced, though perhaps not swift, workers. Inside the factory high production compensated for higher wages, while in the home lower rates offset a less intense pace of work. Factory workers sometimes challenged productivity drives; for example, when a group of outraged workers at the Wanskuck Mill barred the efficiency expert from their room, the superintendent interceded.[20] In such an unstable situation, employers found homework a useful fallback. Moreover, manufacturers developed a crude efficiency system for homework, calling on the most rapid workers for rush jobs and the slower ones for more difficult "bad lace." One firm, Bancroft Lace, tried to rationalize homework more directly, timing a few of the most adept homeworkers in order to set homework piece rates.[21] Finally, bosses could always make wildly unreasonable and arbitrary demands on homeworkers, even as they ran their factories more systematically: Richmond Lace Works, for example, often distributed lace at 6:00 P.M. and required that it be returned by 9:00 A.M.[22]

The Depression and government intervention shaped the organization of homework as well as that of the factory. Rhode Island homeworkers had long dealt with factories directly, but as the government required employers to impose certain conditions on homeworkers and to police their compliance, manufacturers turned to contractors as intermediaries. Acordinging to Tucker and Ackroyd, jewelry homework was outlawed, the principal manufacturers contracted out work to middlemen at specified rates; the unwritten rule was that the principal would ask no questions about how the work was done and what rates were paid for it.[23] Contracting emerged in the lace industry as well: Mrs. Tavares, who pulled lace for a West Warwick firm, reported that she had been fired by her former employer, the Bancroft Lace Company, when she had refused to yield to pressure to become a contractor.[24]

In practice, contracting varied enormously. Dennis O'Neil, the contractor for the Rhode Island Lace Works, made an art of exploitation. He posed to Byrne as the protector of his Italian clients, but investigation revealed that he richly merited his local reputation as a "swindler." Even though the company paid him for delivering and collecting the lace, he charged the workers 10 percent of their homework earnings—a practice which he hid from Byrne, who learned of it from the workers. In addition, he sold them coal at inflated rates, conspired with the town relief officer to give the lace to families who would otherwise apply for relief, and organized the homeworkers to write to the NRA opposing a ban on homework.[25] In the Depression context, contracting could add legal and political dimensions to long-standing economic exploitation and help to close the doors of the expanding social welfare system to those who needed it most. But in the hands of more scrupulous people, contracting could assure access to a scarce wage-earning resource. A man in rural Hopkinton drove his horse and wagon to the Richmond Lace Works to collect lace. His wife, Mary Hewitt, distributed the lace to neighbors, using an elaborate system of inventory control and bookkeeping and receiving for each band one-half cent of the three- or four-and-a-half-cent rates paid by the factory. This service made homework available to those who could not otherwise have secured it; the agent interviewing Hewitt noted that "she isn't doing the work just for the love of humanity" but that she was not "getting an excessive amount for what she does."[26] At the opposite end of the scale from O'Neil was Joseph Lemieux, who drove his truck several times a day to the Bestwick Lace Works to fetch lace for his wife, his daughter, and daughter-in-law. Not a contractor in the strict sense of the word, he nonetheless performed a service both for the company, which relied on his predictable appearances, and for his female kin, to whom he made no charge for his time or the cost of running his truck.[27]

Homeworkers found homework as flexible a strategy as did manufacturers. Although the median ages of the homeworkers clustered in the late thirties and forties for all occupations except jewelry work, the experience of homework was actually far more varied than these figures would suggest. In every occupational group the age range of the homeworkers was broad (see table 1). The ages at which women began to do homework similarly dispersed. Industrial groups do differ—jewelry workers were notably younger than the others and the four non-lace groups had begun work about a decade later than the lace workers— but all types of homework were accessible to women at all stages of adult life.[28] Both the homeworkers' present ages and the ages at which they started homework clustered in the child-rearing years, but a sub-

Table 1. Homeworkers' Ages in 1934 and on Beginning Homework

	Age, 1934		Age homework begun	
	Median	Range	Median	Range
Bancroft Lace, West Warwick				
n=34	40.5	26–65	25.5	6–52
Valley Lace, West Warwick				
n=20	36.5	26–68	31.5	6–68
Riverpoint Lace, West Warwick				
n=19	44.0	17–76	33.0	15–53
Richmond Lace, Alton				
n=20	50.5	20–74	35.5	5–64
Linwood Lace, Washington				
n=29	41.0	22–66	39.5	21–63
American Textile, Pawtucket				
n=30 (lace)	43.0	21–79	24.0	8–63
Miscellaneous lace*				
n=25	45.0	22–61	32.5	9–55
Wanskuck Mill, Providence				
n=29 (worsteds)	39.0	20–61	36.0	16–52
Tags, Pawtucket-Central Falls				
n=13	40.0	33–60	38.0	26–48
Jewelry, Providence				
n=12	19.0	14–52	14.0	9–50
California Artificial Flower, Providence				
n=10	46.0	18–56	39.5	17–50
Moore Fabrics, Pawtucket				
n=3 (garters)	45.0	38–51	44.0	32–51
Ashaway Line & Twine, Ashaway				
n=3 (fishing tackle)	32.0	30–46	28.0	26–46

*Includes New England Lace and Seekonk Lace of Pawtucket, United Net of Central Falls, Rhode Island Lace of West Barrington, and Bestwick Lace of Washington.

stantial number of older and younger women also did wage work in the home.

Although diverse in age, homeworkers were united by several other factors. A dense web of gender, kin, ethnic, and geographic ties linked them, providing channels for mutual assistance and the exchange of services and information. In all industries but worsteds, where the highly skilled nature of the work precluded the recruitment of children or occasional workers, the vast majority (76.8 percent, excluding worsted menders) of homeworkers worked alongside another member of their households (see table 2). In fact, many more probably shared the

Table 2. Homeworkers per Household, Number, and Median

	Households with each number of homeworkers*								
	8	7	6	5	4	3	2	1	Median
Bancroft Lace	0	1	2	2	6	8	12	3	3
Valley Lace	0	1	1	0	1	6	7	4	2
Riverpoint Lace	0	0	2	1	2	2	5	7	2
Richmond Lace	0	0	0	0	1	0	8	11	1
Linwood Lace	1	0	1	1	2	8	11	5	2
American Textile	0	0	2	0	2	10	12	4	2
Miscellaneous lace	0	0	0	1	2	3	9	10	3
Wanskuck Mill	0	0	0	0	0	0	1	28	1
Tags	1	0	0	2	3	4	2	1	3
Jewelry	0	0	0	0	1	4	1	0	3
California Artificial Flower	1	0	0	2	2	3	1	0	4
Moore Fabrics	0	0	0	0	0	2	0	1	3
Ashaway Line & Twine	0	0	0	0	0	0	0	3	3

*This information was not available for some homeworkers' households, and so the total number of households in this table is less than the total number of workers in each group, as listed in table 1.

homework but told the investigators otherwise because they had signed the lace manufacturers' agreement pledging to do the work themselves; Helen Jackson told Blair that she had signed the agreement rather than lose the lace, although she shared it with her husband.[29] The image of the isolated homeworker does not fit; these women worked at least part of the time alongside their kin. Sometimes, in fact, women took homework primarily for the sake of others. Angela Tremonti, for example, took in lace so that her unemployed sixteen-year-old daughter could earn some money.[30]

Although unemployment during the Depression led an unusual number of Rhode Island men to do homework, it was still primarily women's work, even when shared with other family members (see table 3). Over half of the homeworkers interviewed worked alongside female kin; nine out of ten of these homework groups included mother-daughter teams. The interview forms tell very little about the social dynamics of these family work groups, but two comments are suggestive. Byrne commented of Lucy Palumbo's husband, an irregularly employed mule spinner: "Husb[and] most annoyed at having to sit and pull lace. He could arrange things better if he were President."[31] Olive Faria's daugh-

Table 3. Composition of Homeworkers' Work Groups

	Number	Percent
Principal homeworker working alone	75	31.1
P.H. working with other woman/women only	66	27.4
P.H. working with other woman/women and man/men	58	24.1
P.H. working with man/men only	42	17.4
Kin combinations:		
Mother-daughter	111	46.1
Wife-husband	67	27.8
Mother-son	48	19.9

ter indignantly told Byrne, "Can I sit here and see my mother work hard [and] not help her? Of course they think she can do it alone, but she can't."[32] Probably not all husbands were as ill-tempered as Palumbo's, nor all daughters as solicitous as Faria's, but these comments reflect the fact that female kin ties were the backbone of industrial homework.

Female networks extended beyond the household and outside family relationships. Nina Ouellette and her mother, who lived in different flats of the same Pawtucket tenement, worked together pulling lace.[33] Angela Germani frequently went upstairs to work with her sister-in-law, Giulia Catalano.[34] Six of the nine women who pulled lace for the Bestwick Lace Works in rural Washington were kin.[35] Jeanne Marcel, in the same village, "always divides the lace she gets with a friend."[36] In all, thirty-five of the homeworkers (four-fifths of them in lace) shared their work with a female relative outside their household; forty-four (all but one in lace) shared with women to whom they were not related; and five (three in lace) mentioned that they had been initiated into homework by a female relative.

The partner system among workers for the Bancroft Lace Company provides a particularly interesting example of the ways in which women's networks could administer homework. While most pullers simply called for their lace at the factory, pullers for the Bancroft firm had to take delivery from the company truck, which charged twenty-five cents per web of lace. Although these women had signed the pledge to do the work themselves, they not only shared it within their households but also developed stable partnerships with women outside their households. The truck delivered the lace to the house of the "boss partner" and the other partner came to collect it. The partners split the delivery costs, paying the odd penny in alternate weeks. The manufacturer gave de facto recognition to the arrangement, partly because it suited his purposes: when there was a rush job, he relied on the boss partners to recruit others to help finish the lace quickly.[37] There is no suggestion whatever that the boss partners acted as contractors or exploited their partners; the system was simply a way to spread the work and lessen the burden of delivery costs—an instance of women taking the initiative in allocating a scarce means of wage earning.

The homeworkers were involved in a wide variety of reciprocal relationships with one another and with other women, exchanging money and services. Three Portuguese-born lace pullers—Isabella Alves, her mother, and her aunt—in Providence's Fox Point section pooled resources. Blair reported that Alves told her that "they all help each other out when in need if possible. Sometimes they haven't 10 cents to loan."[38] Anna Tavares, an East Providence lace puller, gave a fourth of her week's homework income to her sister, whose husband was unemployed.[39] Aileen MacDonald lived with her husband, her three young children, her sister and brother-in-law, and her niece. While the men worked outside the home, MacDonald mended worsteds and her sister handled the housework and childcare.[40] Mary Hewitt's bookkeeping for the lace she distributed to her neighbors was "complicated by the fact that the women buy things (eggs etc.) from one another and ask that she deduct the amount from one pay check and add it to the check of the woman to whom they owe the money."[41] As Blair interviewed Rosa Pereira, who pulled lace for Bancroft, Pereira was working on a rush job to help out a friend who worked for Valley Lace.[42] Homework fit nicely into the exchange networks among women: it was adaptable to family demands, it was easily integrated into the sharing of services, and it provided cash income which could circulate to those in special need.

Geographic and ethnic connections reinforced the network links among the homeworkers. Homeworkers clustered in neighborhood groups. All but five of the seventy-three West Warwick lace pullers lived within less than half a square mile around the mills which supplied them; these workers were well situated to trade information about rates and conditions at the three mills. Those who worked for American Textile lived in three clusters: five in Providence's Fox Point, seven within a few blocks just across the river in East Providence, and fourteen in a Pawtucket neighborhood bisected by Main Street. The five women who pulled for New England Lace lived in the same neighborhood, and the ten who worked for Rhode Island Lace lived within a few doors of one another along a country road in Barrington. Eight of the thirteen tag workers lived in the Central Falls neighborhood east of Broad Street, and another lived just across the river in Paw-tucket. Twenty-two of the worsted menders lived near the Wanskuck Mill in Providence's north end, and eight jewelry workers resided in a small area of Federal Hill. The artificial flower makers and the garter makers were more dispersed, although three of the former and two of the latter were close neighbors.

Ethnic connections overlapped with neighborhood ties. The ethnic differentiation among industries and firms was sharp—partly, but not solely, because of residence patterns. Over two-thirds (68.5 percent) of the West Warwick lace pullers and 60 percent of the American Textile lace pullers were either of Portuguese birth or had a Portuguese surname. In fact, only one Portuguese woman, a garter maker, did any other type of homework. All of the artificial flower makers and ten of the twelve jewelry workers were Italian by birth or by surname. All the lace pullers for Rhode Island Lace were Italian, as were about one in ten of the West Warwick pullers. Nine of ten who worked for New England Lace, Seekonk Lace, and United Net in Pawtucket-Central Falls were French or French Canadian, as opposed to only 30 percent of those who pulled lace for American Textile. Over three-quarters (76.9 percent) of the tag workers had immigrated from Poland or Lith-uania. Finally, 93 percent of the worsted menders were English/Irish/Scots by birth or descent, as were 90 percent of the pullers for Rich-mond Lace and 58.6 percent of those for Linwood Lace, both rural firms in the southwestern part of the state. Homework in Rhode Island in the mid-1930s was thus imbedded in a tangled series of gender, family, neighborhood, and ethnic links. Far from isolated and without resources, these women drew on a variety of connections, using home-work even as it used them.

A final consideration is the work patterns of homeworkers and their families and their consciousness of themselves as homeworkers. The interview schedules tell little about the work histories of these women; although the interviewers always asked about other kinds of homework done, they did not systematically gather data about paid labor outside the home. Still, they recorded some information about outside work for sixty-nine women, a third of them worsted menders. Domestic service, long the resort of the disadvantaged women worker, had played a relatively small part in their lives: only eight women—five of whom lived in the rural portion of the state—reported working as maids or laundresses. Fewer than one in seven (13.0 percent) of the lace pullers had worked or were still working in a textile mill, while well over half (55.2 percent) of the worsted menders had done the same or a similar job inside a mill. Only seven women in all—three who pulled lace for American Textile, three who made artificial flowers, and one garter maker—had done other types of homework. The vast majority had done homework only in their present industry, and a healthy proportion of those who had worked outside their homes had worked in the same industry as that for which they did homework.

The wage earning of other household members further linked homeworkers to their industries. In nearly six in ten (58.2 percent) of the lace pullers' households, at least one family member, and sometimes as many as five, worked in the textile industry. Similarly, over a third (34.5 percent) of the worsted menders lived with someone working in that industry, nine of them in the Wanskuck Mill or other worsted mills owned by the same family. Four of the ten artificial flower makers lived with kin who were employed inside the California Artificial Flower Company, and one fishing tackle worker was married to an inside worker at the company from which she secured homework.

Such figures lead to several conclusions about the place of homework in the lives and consciousness of these women. First, they further undermine the cliche of the homeworker's isolation. Through their kin and their own experience, these homeworkers were in touch with developments in the local economy, often being closely tied to a single industry. Second, their work at home was one of a variety of work patterns which they and their kin used or were forced to use by economic circumstances; the spectrum included homework, temporary employment during times of special need, employment linked to a stage of the life cycle, voluntary or involuntary sporadic employment, and steady long-term employment. In a context in which jobs of the last type were increasingly rare, homework was not anomalous but one of many tactics for attacking the job market. That many of the homeworkers were able to earn money when the family's main breadwinner, or indeed all other family members, were unemployed underlines this point. These women took part in a varied labor market in the lace, worsted, or artificial flower industries; they were linked to a broader industrial community. There was no single labor market for Rhode Island homeworkers, but rather a very complex one with wide cleavages along industrial as well as ethnic and geographic lines.

Homework was both a flexible wage-earning strategy and a vital source of family income. For example, Jane Cormack, a worsted mender, had worked inside the mill "off and on for a good many years," staying home periodically to care for her ailing mother.[43] Rosa Vieira had worked inside a lace mill before her marriage, at which point she began to do the same work at home.[44] And Ines Silva, who preferred to work outside her home, pulled lace when she was between jobs.[45] But even though homework might not be steady work, its earnings made important contributions—about a quarter of total earnings—to family income (see table 4). Those working for American Textile in Pawtucket contributed a median of 40 percent, those pulling lace for Linwood Lace 50 percent, and those making artificial flowers an impressive 57.1 percent. Even the three garter workers, who provided by far the smallest share of the family budget, contributed about one dollar out of every six. Industrial homework by no means secured a comfortable living, but its meager rewards loomed large in the individual family budget. Life without it would have been notably more difficult. Janine Boucher, whose family depended upon lace pulling for over half its income, doubtless spoke for many when she told Byrne, "I'll say if it wasn't for lace we couldn't get along."[46]

For some of these women, wage earning in the home was a longstanding pattern; for others, it was a recent expedient. The first group—those whom we might call the career homeworkers—largely consisted of women who pulled lace, nearly half (47.2 percent) of whom had done so for ten years or more. By contrast, just over one in ten (11.1 percent) of those in other industries had been doing homework that long (see table 5). The division between career homeworkers and Depression homeworkers is most marked in the lace industry: over nine tenths (92.1 percent) of the lace pullers had been at the work for

Table 4. Homework Earnings, Weekly and as Percentage of Family Income*

	Amount of homework earnings, median	Homework earnings as percentage of family income, median
Bancroft Lace	$ 8.78	27.4
Valley Lace	7.15	25.8
Riverpoint Lace	8.00	25.6
Richmond Lace	4.99	31.4
Linwood Lace	9.08	50.0
American Textile	8.64	40.0
Miscellaneous Lace	6.92	26.1
Wanskuck Mill	6.53	25.5
Tags	2.00	23.5
Jewelry	6.25	27.0
California Artificial Flower	13.50	57.1
Moore Fabrics	3.50	16.7

*This table is based on earnings in the week before the interviews. Income data were not provided for Ashaway Line and Twine workers.

Table 5. Years at Homework, by Firm

	Number of homeworkers working for each number of years						
	25 or more	20–24	15–19	10–14	5–9	1–4	less than 1
Bancroft Lace	3	4	7	10	4	5	1
Valley Lace	0	3	1	3	0	2	11
Riverpoint Lace	2	2	1	2	4	8	0
Richmond Lace	3	2	3	3	4	4	1
Linwood Lace	0	0	0	0	0	27	2
American Textile	8	5	3	4	1	7	2
Miscellaneous lace	3	6	2	2	1	7	2
All lace	15	15	14	20	10	27	15
Wanskuck Mill	0	0	1	1	5	12	9
Tags	0	0	0	3	5	3	1
Jewelry	0	0	0	2	3	4	1
California Artificial Flower	0	0	1	1	0	7	1
Moore Fabrics	0	0	0	0	1	1	1
Ashaway Line and Twine	0	0	0	0	1	2	0

over ten or less than five years. Most of the other homeworkers had begun since 1930: three-quarters of the worsted menders, four-fifths of the artificial flower makers, half of the jewelry workers, and two-thirds of the garter makers and fishing tackle workers.

The division between the groups is not a function of their age; years worked do not neatly correlate with age. Two twenty-six-year-olds had been pulling lace for twenty years; two women in their sixties had pulled lace for only a few months. One thirty-six-year-old woman had worked on lace for seventeen years, another for only three weeks. The immediate cause of this two-peaked distribution was the hardship of the Depression, but for some of the women the crisis of the early 1930s masked the early stages of an even more disturbing secular trend: that of the deindustrialization of the Northeast. Thirteen of the home-workers resorted to industrial homework because the factories in which they or their kin worked had not simply cut back temporarily but had closed for good. Anne Powell, for example, lived with a sister who had worked at a worsted mill for thirty years; the unmarried women were stunned when it closed down: "They had never expected such a thing could happen."[47]

The women's reasons for doing homework reflect these two career patterns. While none of the women working outside the lace industry indicated that their work was tied into their traditions or culture, about one in twelve (8.5 percent) of the lace pullers did. As Carolina Pinto of West Warwick put it, she "was born pulling lace."[48] Moreover, women working in other industries were over twice as likely as those in the lace industry to state that they had tried and failed to find work outside the home (22.0 percent and 9.0 percent respectively). In explaining why they were doing homework, women pulling lace tended to mention inadequate family income in a general way more often than did non–lace workers: seven in ten (70.1 percent) of the former and just half (49.2 percent) of the latter couched their concerns in this manner. These differences suggest that the lace workers and the non–lace workers saw their work differently. For the former, wage earning was more thoroughly rooted in tradition and in a home setting, and their reasons for doing homework reflected a general concern with their contribution to the family fund.

Among the homeworkers in general, however, traditional imperatives competed with newer outlooks. In explaining why they chose to work at home, well over a third of the women interviewed (36.2 percent) stated either that factory work was unsuitable for them (because, for example, of their age or infirmity) or that they preferred or needed to be at home. A few calculated the economic advantage of staying at home: two lace pullers, for example, maintained that they would not make enough extra money inside the mills to make it worth their while.[49] More often, the desire to be a good housekeeper led women into industrial homework. Nina Motta, for example, spoke censoriously of those who claimed to pull huge amounts of lace; she felt that they were either lying or slighting their housework, two equally serious sins in her mind.[50] Delphine Gaudet also put household chores first: on the day that the agent interviewed her, she had spent the morning doing her wash and was considering going to the mill for lace in the afternoon.[51] Odette Brouillard showed the other side of the coin, complaining bitterly to Blair: "Must put aside housework and do nothing but lace. Doesn't have time to cook a decent meal."[52] Deidre Horton simply rescheduled her housework, putting her laundry off until Saturday, to accommodate lace pulling when there was lace available.[53] Comments by Byrne and Blair about the homeworkers' houses underline the importance of keeping house for these women. They judged the vast majority of the homes they visited as "clean," frequently adding such adjectives as "spotless" and "immaculate." They made negative comments about the housekeeping of only fourteen women, five of whom lived in hopelessly dilapidated company housing in Washington.

A number of women revealed an interest in consumption rather than in traditional domesticity. Five homeworkers said that they were working for "extras," five more stated that their earnings went into clothing for their children, and two were working to keep their children in high school or normal school. In these cases, industrial homework undermined, rather than encouraged, child labor, allowing women to move into the emerging pattern of maternal wage earning in order to give children more education or higher standards of living. The Rhode Island homeworkers were, like many others then and now, caught between the conflicting demands of domesticity and consumption. Blair and Byrne recorded only two comments about "woman's place," but in their contradiction they point to homework's adaptability to diverse outlooks. To Virginia Hayes, homework could protect female virtue, allowing "girls to stay home pulling lace [rather] than to be walking streets."[54] For Diane Martin's mother, who pulled lace so that "she can be somewhat independent," it was a route to increased autonomy.[55]

The interview schedules unfortunately do not provide systematic information about time budgeting, but the limited evidence indicates that the rhythm and length of the work day varied widely. Marie St. Onge, who worked from 7 A.M. to 8 P.M. to buy medicine and "thank[ed] God that she [was] well enough to do lace" was balanced off by Christine LaChapelle, who pulled lace five hours a day and considered herself a full-time worker.[56] She, and the numerous others who defined a full day as eight hours or less, traded off money for time, cutting short their wage-earning hours to accommodate household tasks and exploiting the flexibility of homework to achieve a more humane work schedule than they would have in the factory. Even so, the home was insulated, but not immune, from the time discipline of the factory: more than one in six (17.8 percent) homeworkers reported that they frequently had rush jobs which required them to set aside other chores.

Lace pulling and worsted mending both had some of the attributes of skilled work, and the women in these occupations used some of male craftsmen's techniques to administer that skill.[57] They passed it along from woman to woman. Jane Cormack, who proudly told Byrne that it took four years to learn the skill of worsted mending, taught it to her daughter as a fallback occupation in case she couldn't get a job suited to her high school education.[58] Ellen Marshall had learned to mend lace, a better-paid trade than pulling, from her mother.[59] Many women learned their homework skills from their mothers: twenty-six had begun their work before the age of twenty, and another five mentioned that they had learned to work on lace as a child. Some home-workers received recognition for their skills: Teresa Ardita and Carmela Lombardo had demonstrated lace pulling at the local town hall, and Ardita had been recruited by the firm to teach newcomers to the trade.[60] Skill could make a real difference in earnings: Maria Pontes, whose speed was the envy of West Warwick lace pullers, could pull 100 bands per day, earning from $3.00 to $4.50.[61] Although limitation of output was not a realistic option for most homeworkers, the worsted menders' skill was so much in demand that they could refuse to do work they disdained. Two women who mended for the Wanskuck Mill refused to take on more fabric because too large a proportion of it was black.[62] Moreover, after World War II, when the worsted industry boomed and skilled menders were in even shorter supply, home-workers insisted on continuing to work in their homes, indicating that they still considered Wanskuck's management methods as "wicked" as Maureen Connolly and Ellen Taylor had in 1934.[63] Probably more typical, though, was Elizabeth Hollinshead's protest: annoyed with the Linwood Mill's "bad lace," she told the distributor of her grievances in no uncertain terms and switched to Bestwick Lace.[64]

Complaints about the work itself were rare, although many women objected to the rates, to conditions set by employers, or to bad work. The interviewers recorded only one outright negative opinion of the work: Janet Crompton, a mender, was trained as a bookkeeper and "very upset" at having to do homework.[65] Maureen Connolly, in the same occupation, "love[d]" the work; Marianne Tetreault, Myrtle Barnes, and Rita Morris all liked to pull lace.[66] Some women had chosen the work over other possibilities: Elizabeth Ainsworth, who had been a chambermaid, much preferred mending worsteds, but Alice Graham, who had also been a chambermaid, found it easier work than mending.[67] In general, lace pullers less often stood off from their work and assessed it than did worsted menders, possibly because of the denser network connections that tied them into their work and the limited wage-earning alternatives in the relatively isolated Pawtuxet Valley and in the rural areas of southwestern Rhode Island. Although the evidence of the homeworkers' attitudes toward their work is frag-mentary, it clearly suggests that they were far from a monolithic group and that there was no single response either to industrial homework or to any single homework occupation. Again, the adaptability and flexibility of homework modify its oppressive quality.

An understanding of industrial homework in Depression Rhode Island helps to explain the paradox the woman who wrote to the *Providence*

Journal encountered when she sought homework. Industrial homework, despite recent attempts to ease regulations, is still by and large illegal. And it still flourishes. On the one hand, the reformers of the first half of the twentieth century have carried the day: they have outlawed this most exploitative form of wage labor. On the other, neither reformers nor economists have been able to eradicate the factors which led women into this bottom-of-the-barrel wage earning. Women still feel the strongest pull of domestic and child care responsibilities; when they go to work outside the home, they often fail to earn enough to cover their personal and day care expenses. They therefore continue to rely on network connections with kin and friends to help them squeak out a living. The social welfare system remains stingy and grudging, its inadequacies forcing many into industrial homework. Factory work has become even more relentlessly rationalized and managers even more singularly dedicated to efficiency, making the comparative autonomy of work in the home an attractive alternative. As the proportion of full-time positions with decent pay and benefits shrinks, the distinction between industrial homework and the growing number of part-time jobs seems less dramatic. And, finally, deindustrialization has intensified and left many women with a desperate need for some income, any income. "Southern competition" has been replaced by "foreign competition," but both have encouraged managers to continue to seek a cut-rate labor force.

Industrial homework has persisted because it has been surprisingly adaptable to the needs of both workers and employers. If we are to deal humanely and intelligently with the abuses of wage earning in the home, we must remember that it is not simply a rotten branch that can be pruned away; it was and is imbedded in people's lives and closely linked to ties of gender, family, residence, ethnicity, and community economy. What we have learned about these Rhode Islanders should alert us to the complexity, variety, resilience, and power of women's networks to make the best of what was in the final analysis not a very good thing, to marshall resources to cope with a larger economic situation that was not of their making.

NOTES

I am grateful to Barbara Melosh, Judith Smith, and Kate Monteiro for assistance in the research for this article. A portion of the research was supported by National Institute of Mental Health grant. Many thanks to Edward Benson, Julia Kirk Blackwelder, Maurine Greenwald, Louise Lamphere, Barbara Melosh, Christina Simmons, and Judith Smith for helpful and perceptive comments on earlier drafts.

1. Among the many reports which made these arguments are Massachusetts Bureau of Statistics of Labor, *Industrial Home Work in Massachusetts,* Bulletin no. 101 (Boston, 1914); U.S. Department of Labor, Women's Bureau, *Home Work in Bridgeport, Connecticut, December, 1919,* Bulletin no. 9 (Washington, D.C.: GPO, 1920); Pennsylvania Department of Labor and Industry, *Industrial Home Work and Child Labor,* Special Bulletin no. 11 (Harrisburg, 1926); New York State Department of Labor, Bureau of Women in Industry, *Homework in the Men's Clothing Industry in New York and Rochester,* Special Bulletin no. 158 (Albany: State Department of Labor, 1929); and Emily C. Brown, *Industrial Homework,* Women's Bureau, Bulletin no. 79 (Washington, D.C.: GPO, 1930).

2. For a good digest of these arguments see "Regulations, Recommendations, and Policies," *Homework in Bridgeport, Connecticut,* pt. 3, pp. 21–26. William L. O'Neill uses the term *Social Feminism* to refer to women who campaigned for social reform rather than women's rights alone. See his *Everyone Was Brave: The Rise and Fall of Feminism in America* (Chicago: Quadrangle, 1969), x.

3. *Homework in Bridgeport, Connecticut,* pp. 22–35.

4. U.S. Department of Labor, Women's Bureau, *The Commercialization of the Home through Industrial Homework,* Bulletin no. 135 (Washington, D.C.: GPO, 1935), pp. 39–48.

5. *Annual Report of the Rhode Island Department of Labor,* 1942, p. 35.

6. Harriet A. Byrne and Bertha Blair, *Industrial Home Work in Rhode Island, with Special Reference to the Lace Industry,* Women's Bureau, Bulletin no. 131 (Washington, D.C.: GPO, 1935). The raw data for this report is available in the National Archives, Record Group 86, Boxes 297 and 298. All interviews cited below are filed in Box 297.

7. Those who pulled lace at home had only to sign an agreement framed by the American Lace Manufacturers Associations covering wages, hours, sanitary regulations, and restrictions on child labor. See Blair and Byrne, *Industrial Home Work in Rhode Island,* p. 27, for the text of the agreement.

8. See Blair and Byrne, *Industrial Homework in Rhode Island,* pp. 3, 20; [Bertha Blair], memo, April 11, 1934, Box 297.

9. Margaret Ackroyd and Anna Tucker, interviews with Nina Shapiro-Perl, and author, September 4 and 27, 1979, respectively.

10. Harriet Byrne, memo, April 11, 1934, Box 297.

11. Lace pullers, interviews with Blair and Byrne, interview 5–2–18. I have given ethnically appropriate pseudonyms to the homeworkers; I cite the interview schedules by the penciled numbers on them or, if unnumbered, by the folder in which they are found.

12. Box 297, file "R.I. Rough Material, Miscellaneous Interviews," hereafter referred to as Box 297, Miscellaneous.

13. 5–1–15.

14. 6–2–3. 6–2–30.

15. Blair and Byrne, p. 4; 3–2–22.

16. 6–2–30.

17. 6–2–2, 6–2–19, 6–2–20.
18. Box 297, Miscellaneous.
19. 2–3–3, 5–2–17.
20. Hugh Brady, interview with Blair and Byrne, April 6, 1934, Box 297.
21. 5–1–3, 5–1–4.
22. 1–1–16, 1–1–9, 1–1–20, 1–1–6
23. Ackroyd and Tucker, interviews, September 4 and 24, 1979.
24. 5–3–6.
25. Dennis O'Neil, interview with Blair and Byrne, April 23, 1934, Box 297.
26. 1–1–1.
27. 3–1–1.
28. The information on jewelry workers is particularly sketchy, giving no hint as to why they were so much younger than the other homeworkers.
29. 1–1–12
30. 5–3–10.
31. 2–1–30.
32. 2–1–7.
33. 2–1–4, 2–1–5.
34. 5–3–16, 5–3–18.
35. 3–1–1.
36. 3–2–7.
37. 5–1–5, 5–1–21, 5–1–33.
38. Box 297, Miscellaneous.
39. Box 297, Miscellaneous.
40. 6–2–22.
41. 1–1–1.
42. 5–1–16.
43. 6–2–8.
44. Box 297, Miscellaneous.
45. 5–1–10.
46. 3–2–8.
47. 3–2–12.
48. 5–1–5.
49. Box 297, Miscellaneous; 5–2–19.
50. 5–1–17.
51. 5–2–16.
52. Box 297, Miscellaneous.
53. 3–2–24.
54. 3–2–2.
55. 3–2–18.
56. 2–1–13; Box 297, Miscellaneous.
57. The Women's Bureau characterized these occupations as skilled work. See *The Commercialization of the Home through Industrial Home Work*, p. 11.
58. 6–2–8.
59. 1–1–8.

60. Box 297, Miscellaneous.

61. 5–1–3.

62. 6–2–3, 6–2–30.

63. 6–2–23, 6–2–26; on the worsted industry and homework, see *Annual Report of the Rhode Island Department of Labor,* 1947, p. 47; 1948, p. 47; 1950, p. 45.

64. 3–1–5.

65. 6–2–11.

66. 6–2–23, 2–1–10, 1–1–4, 1–1–11.

67. 6–2–28. 6–2–13.

4

Texas Homeworkers in the 1930s

JULIA KIRK BLACKWELDER

During the 1930s Texas homeworkers spent long hours bent over tedious tasks that earned them mere pennies a day. In San Antonio,
described by a local labor paper as a "pest hole of low paid labor,"
social and economic conditions interacted to encourage the growth of
industrial homework before and during the Depression. Deploring the
exploitative aspects of home labor, the paper's editor complained, "The
New Deal glorified the fact that the sweat shop of the home had been
abolished. The sweat shop in the home still continues in this city, and
if anything is on the increase." Laredo was another Texas city where
homework flourished in the 1930s. Two federal studies preserved the
stories of Texas homeworkers. In 1932 the Women's Bureau completed
survey research on the wages and working conditions of women in
Texas industries. The study included 123 personal interviews with
homeworkers in San Antonio and Laredo. In the late 1930s Selden
Menefee and Orin C. Cassmore collected data on the pecan shelling
industry in San Antonio. Their research, published by the WPA, documented the emergence of homework where factory employment had
once prevailed.[1]

Hand sewing and pecan shelling were the two major areas of industrial employment for San Antonio homeworkers, with approximately 4,000 persons deriving income in each of these areas during
the mid-1930s. In 1937 it was estimated that some 15,000 to 20,000
families in and around San Antonio existed on homework.[2] There were
fewer homeworkers in Laredo and they were principally garment workers. Although the sewing trades were exclusively female, men as well
as women worked as pecan shellers. The vast majority of industrial
homeworkers were Chicano, a situation that reflected ethnic discrimination in the labor market and the dislocation of Mexican agricultural
workers. In San Antonio the geographic segregation of Chicanos on

the city's West Side further encouraged Chicana domination of garment work.

World War I labor shortages and the overall decline of immigration to the United States encouraged mechanization in many sectors of the American economy. However, a dramatic rise in immigration from Mexico offset wartime labor shortages for farmers in the Southwest. In Texas manual labor persisted as the backbone of production. The extremity of Depression conditions in Mexico in the twenties guaranteed that Mexican immigrants would undercut Anglo or black workers in unskilled labor just as "illegal aliens" have undercut other U.S. workers in the 1980s. The eagerness of Mexicans to cross the border likewise guaranteed that Chicanos could not withhold their labor to bargain for higher wages. As the oldest and largest city in the U.S. with a distinctively Mexican heritage and identity, San Antonio acted as a magnet for those immigrants who chose not to return to Mexico after the harvests had ended. Consequently, San Antonio emerged as the national marketing point for migrant workers with labor agents from as far away as Michigan maintaining recruitment offices in the city. Many other immigrants adopted border towns like El Paso and Laredo, Texas, as their permanent homes. Chicanos in Texas were an internal colony of laborers. Driven from their homeland by the intense poverty of the 1920s, migrants from rural Mexico had become the harvesters of our nation's crops. As migrant workers, Chicanos earned lower wages than any other occupational grouping. During the late fall and early winter, little if any agricultural work could be found and Texas Chicanos returned to San Antonio and many smaller cities and towns along the Mexican border. In their winter homes, Chicanos took work when and where they could find it.[3]

The presence of thousands of low-paid, temporarily unemployed migrant families in San Antonio encouraged the expansion of non-mechanized industrial work in the city while the national economy was moving away from hand labor. Similar developments occurred on a smaller scale in Texas border towns like Laredo. The shelling of pecans was one area of winter employment. Pecans gathered in late summer could be shelled later, after migrant workers had returned from harvests elsewhere. During the Depression much of the pecan shelling activity in Texas moved from organized plants into workers' homes.[4] In greater San Antonio pecan shelling emerged as a significant occupation of Chicano men as well as women.

Texas Chicanas also presented the unique attraction that lured manufacturers to Texas in the 1920s. Taught by nuns, grandmothers, and mothers over generations, many Chicanas had practiced embroidery and fine sewing since early childhood. The artistry of these women and the cheapness of their labor encouraged the establishment of garment factories in many Texas cities. In San Antonio and in Laredo and other border towns, the infants' and children's wear industry grew especially strong. The small dresses, gowns, and other items of children's clothing had little machine sewing and featured fine embroidery. Such skills were readily available in few U.S. locations and virtually no U.S. labor market was cost-competitive with the Texas towns. While larger, machine-sewn garments were produced mostly in sweat shops or factories, infants' and children's wear was produced just as easily at home as in a plant. In San Antonio and Laredo homeworkers also hemmed handkerchiefs. The garment industry became the major employer of home workers in the 1920s. This homework persisted through the Depression.

During the 1930s industrial homework flourished in Texas despite the existence of federal policies to eliminate it. High unemployment and federal preoccupation with broad economic issues undermined policies intended to restrict home production.[5] In San Antonio and Laredo NRA regulations that controlled the wages and conditions of homework were flagrantly violated and homework conditions in the late 1930s mirrored a situation that the National Recovery Administration had tried to eradicate. The NRA homework provisions required certification that workers were free of contagious disease and that they maintained sanitary surroundings. The failure of the San Antonio health department to insure these standards among workers led to a local ban on industrial homework in 1940. The NRA codes also stipulated that "all material and findings must be supplied by the employer and delivered and returned without expense to the worker. No deductions may be made for spoiled work. The homeworker must pledge himself not to allow other persons to assist in any part of the homework. The assignment of more work than it is possible to complete in the applicable code hours is prohibited."[6] When interviewed by representatives of the Women's Bureau in 1932, San Antonio and Laredo workers consistently complained of the continuance of exploitative conditions that the NRA would outlaw. Not only were the NRA codes unenforceable because compliance was voluntary, but an authority to oversee the code for the shelling industry was never selected.

Although the abundance of cheap Chicano labor gave rise to both home shelling and home sewing, the pattern of growth for the two industries in San Antonio was somewhat different. As pecans are native to East Texas, commercial shelling had existed in the state long before the 1920s. By the early 1920s machinery to crack the nuts and separate the shells from the meats had been developed. The introduction of shelling machines led to an expansion of the pecan trade in San Antonio, where the largest plants operated. However, by 1926 the large number of Mexican immigrants in the city had depressed the wages of unskilled labor to the point that hand labor was cheaper than machine shelling, so owners of shelling plants gradually replaced the shelling machines with hand labor.[7] In St. Louis, the other major pecan-shelling location in the United States, the reconversion to hand labor did not occur. As hand shelling required a lower level of capital outlay than the mechanized plants, cheap labor attracted many marginal entrepreneurs to the industry. The adoption of the contract system of shelling, which could be initiated with even less capital than the hand-shelling plants, brought still further expansion of the industry in San Antonio and its hinterland. In the 1920s contractors frequently delivered pecans to the workers' homes and returned for the shelled nuts.

During the years of expansion in the shelling industry, piece rates of six-to-eight cents per pound prevailed. In the 1920s a single worker might average six to seven dollars per week, engaging in such labor at home or in the shelling plants, but wages fell rapidly during the Depression. By the late 1930s wages had fallen as low as four cents per pound with work available less regularly. Whole families working together could not earn enough for the barest level of subsistence. Weekly shelling incomes fell to an average of $2.50 for adult workers.

Chicanos in San Antonio initially entered into pecan shelling and provided an attractive labor supply for shellers because the work was seasonal and could be taken up after the agricultural harvest. Shelling plants were concentrated on the West Side, where Mexican-American residence centered and where high population density allowed workers to walk to the sheds. As few Anglos or blacks lived in the area, few had much knowledge of the shelling industry and fewer still sought employment in pecans. As the contract system was adopted, pecan shelling became less centralized. Individual contractors used workers in points distant from the west side, frequently outside Bexar County (San Antonio), but the pattern of Chicano dominance persisted.

During the 1920s some shelling was conducted throughout the year, but most of the shelling was done from October through May, providing opportunities for steady employment for many agricultural workers who wintered in San Antonio. With the onset of the Depression opportunities for migrant employment dwindled, enlarging the importance of income from shelling. At the same time, however, the price of pecans fell, driving some shellers out of business and compelling others to cut wages. The use of the contract system, which cut overhead by eliminating the costs of maintaining a plant, became more attractive as prices fell. An El Paso man who operated a shelling plant stated in 1932 that he had cut wages 20 percent, but that he could no longer maintain even the lower wage level because of falling prices. He told a Women's Bureau agent that he planned to close his plant and sell unshelled pecans to home shellers and buy back the meats because he saw no other way to compete with San Antonio shellers who were driving down rates and prices through this arrangement. The plant owner said he had complained of the situation to the federal government and received a reply that the prohibition of homework was a state matter.[8] In 1934 a strike against the shelling plants dramatized the plight of pecan workers. The striking workers sought the support of home shellers and endeavored to prevent contractors' distribution of pecans to homeworkers. While the 1934 strike and the more protracted and violent strike of 1938 did close down several plants, they were ineffective in curtailing home shelling.[9] The persistence of the homeworkers encouraged plant owners to adopt the contract system.

The children's wear and handkerchief industries were not as seasonal in their labor demands as was pecan shelling. Garment workers did not and generally had not followed the crops, although their male relatives may have done so. They were available for garment employment because of their permanent residence in Laredo, San Antonio, or other urban centers. Although they needed to work, a variety of factors had discouraged Chicana garment workers from other employments. Inadequate education and ethnic prejudices excluded Mexican-American women from most sales and clerical jobs, and Mexican familial values discouraged Chicanas from accepting domestic employment in Anglo homes. San Antonio and Dallas emerged as major garment centers that drew largely on underemployed Chicana labor. In Laredo, which offered even fewer employment opportunities for Chicanas than the major Texas cities, the children's wear and handkerchief industries did not have to compete with sectors of the garment industry that were mainly factory based.

The farming out of garment sewing from pieces cut in New York City, either to homeworkers or workshops, was not unique to Texas. Connecticut, New Jersey, and Pennsylvania all received such work from the New York garment district before and during the Depression. In the 1920s the passage of New York state labor laws governing hours and conditions of female and child employment—laws stricter than those in other states—had encouraged the decentralization of hand sewing. Sending the work as far as Texas clearly reflected the lower wage levels among Mexican-American workers. An Anglo handworker interviewed by the U.S. Women's Bureau in 1932 stated that the Chicanas set the pace for speed and quality of work and that it was up to the Anglos to keep up or look for other work.[10]

While the low wages in Texas made the decentralization of New York's industries feasible, the expansion of the garment industries in the 1920s also rested on the belief that Mexican-American women represented a peculiar combination of skills and attitudes. These factors were an ideal situation for investment in the 1920s, and as late as the 1960s the sociologist Robert G. Landolt reported that

> Mexican-American women were found characteristically to have the dexterity and temperament for being adept at both hand and machine needlework. Their ability to work well on highly repetitious jobs was attributed to their Indian ancestry. Their particular proficiency in the skills of garment making was attributed to the centuries-old practice of the Catholic nuns of teaching Mexican and Indian women to sew, and the emphasis on excellence in needlework was handed down from mothers to daughters.[11]

The sewing and embroidering done by Texas handworkers was extremely exacting. In addition to the fine stitching required for infants' clothing, the women often smocked, appliqued, and embroidered the garments. The Women's Bureau reported that "the articles usually were of so fine and delicate a texture that the utmost care was required in handling so as to preserve their freshness and daintiness."[12]

Employers supplied materials for workers that included patterns, cut fabric, and thread. Workers then returned the finished garments or handkerchiefs, but contractors paid only for those products that met their satisfaction. The work was then pressed at the shops and sent on to buyers or to the home offices. Although the work was precut, none of the designs or smocking patterns was stamped on the materials. The worker had to be extremely skillful to get the exact amount of tautness in smocking or drawn work that the employer desired and had to have a well-practiced knowledge of embroidery to copy the intricate designs from the patterns.

As all homeworkers, except a privileged few who sewed designers' samples, were required to call for and deliver their work, the vast majority of workers lived near the manufacturers' offices or plants. Wage levels were too low to accommodate carfare for the weekly trip which most of the women made to the plants. In San Antonio employers located plants on the West Side because they calculated their profits on employing skilled Chicanas for whom few employment alternatives existed. The Women's Bureau survey of 1932 revealed that a few Anglo women living in north San Antonio had taken up home sewing because of Depression emergencies, but the West Side location of the industry discouraged both black and Anglo women from seeking such work, even if they would accept the low pay. None of the manufacturing concerns surveyed by the Women's Bureau employed black women to do sewing.

The Women's Bureau interviewed 100 San Antonio home sewers, eighty-four of whom were Chicana, sixteen Anglo, and none black. The women ranged in age from sixteen years to sixty-five, with the majority being over the age of thirty (see table 1). That the majority of the women were currently married or had been married supports the view that homework appealed primarily to women who were homebound by child care or other household responsibilities (see table 2). That all of the single homeworkers were Chicana may reflect either the Mexican preference for keeping daughters at home whenever possible or the relative lack of alternative employment options for Mexican women. Certainly Anglo women had access to better jobs that were denied Mexican Americans, but occasionally an interviewee commented on her preference for homework over alternatives. One Chicana reported

Table 1. Age Distribution of Homeworkers in San Antonio and Laredo

Ages	San Antonio	Laredo
16–19	11	6
20–29	26	9
30–39	33	3
40–49	17	3
50 & older	13	2
	100	23

Table 2. Marital Status of Homeworkers in San Antonio and Laredo

Status	San Antonio Chicana	Anglo	Total	Laredo all Chicana
Single	28	0	28	10
Married	35	11	46	9
Separated or divorced	7	1	8	1
Widowed	14	4	18	3
	84	16	100	23

that her daughter had been working as a maid for $3 per week but that she quit that job because she could "make that much at home without killing herself." A young Mexican-American girl stated that sewing paid poorly but that housework was the only other job that she could get and that she "would not feel right staying in another house." Two of the San Antonio workers told bureau representatives that home sewing was preferable to factory work. One of these workers questioned the interviewer as to the Women's Bureau's intentions because the "foreman of [the] factory told her that the Labor Department women were going around trying to get information to be used in discontinuing homework for Mexicans." Another worker said factory wages were no better and that workers were fired for talking on the job.[13]

The conditions under which women entered and continued homework differed significantly between Anglos and Chicanas. A number of the Chicanas reported that they had learned needlework from other homeworkers in their families, but none of the Anglo women commented on acquiring their skills in this way and none of the Anglos had relatives who assisted them in fine sewing. Many of the Chicanas had done the work for several years, while the Anglos were mostly newcomers who had taken up handwork because of sudden changes in economic conditions. One Anglo told the interviewer she had previously been a seamstress and milliner but that this was the only work she could get at present. Another Anglo had taken up homework after her husband and daughter had lost their jobs. The family was able to get by temporarily by moving in with her mother and sharing expenses with a brother who also lived in the house. Unlike virtually all of the Chicana workers, the Anglos did not walk to the factory but drove or rode the bus to the plant periodically to deliver and collect their work.

The Women's Bureau interviewed twenty-three homeworkers, all Chicanas, in Laredo. Proportionally more of the Laredo workers than the San Antonio Chicana subjects were under thirty years of age and ten of the twenty-three were single (see tables 1 and 2). The significant difference between the San Antonio and Laredo respondents is the conditions under which they accepted homework. Unlike the San Antonio women, none of the Laredo workers said that she did homework because other employment options were unsuitable. Most of the women pursued homework because it was the only employment they could find. Laredo workers who were not homebound by child care or other equally confining situations often expressed a preference for other work.

Not all Chicana homeworkers came from the lowest socioeconomic brackets, but they generally did. Two young Chicanas were supported by their fathers but did sewing in order to have spending money. A single woman from an educated family engaged in homework because she wanted to be of some assistance in getting through the hard times of the Depression. The family finally made her give up the work, claiming that she was expending a greater cost in shoe leather walking back and forth to the factory than she was earning.[14]

As in the case of shellers, pay for hand sewers was extremely low. One worker reported that she was paid forty-two cents for twelve hours work on a single dress that the Women's Bureau reported could be purchased in an eastern shop for eight dollars. Fifty-three of the 123 homeworkers in Laredo and San Antonio reported hourly earnings under five cents. Outside Texas, wages reported by homeworkers were markedly higher. A 1936 Women's Bureau study documented wages in New Jersey and Pennsylvania that ranged from five cents to eleven cents per hour for inexperienced homeworkers while the most skilled needle workers averaged twenty-one cents per hour.[15]

Based on the estimated wages workers reported to the interviewers, the *average* wage per person among home sewers in San Antonio and Laredo was approximately $2.20 per week for anywhere from a few hours per day part of the week to a sixty-hour week. The highest wage reported by any of the workers was $5.53 and the lowest was $.83. In contrast the study found the *median* wage of workers in four San Antonio garment factories to be $5.70 per week. Of one worker who claimed to earn only one dollar per week as the sole supporter of children and an unemployed spouse, the interviewer noted, "Mystery to me how they live."[16] Many families like this one got by from day to day only through the charity of friends and relatives. Only two of the workers stated that they had received any relief assistance. Other families got by only through the combined efforts of two or more homeworkers. While some reported that the work was steadily available, others found sewing work only periodically.

Although some of the women were not at their sewing tasks full-time, most claimed to work in excess of eight hours per day at least six days a week. Many Laredo workers alternated homework with factory work but this rarely happened in San Antonio, where the factory work differed from homework. San Antonio garment factories produced machine-sewn women's clothing, and the garment factories offered higher wages than the hand workers could earn. For Laredo workers, factory employment was not essentially different from home sewing. The Kewpie Company Juvenile Manufacturing Company, which was the major employer in the industry and operated in Laredo and San Antonio, paid the same piece rates in both cities. There was little if any machine sewing in the manufacture of these garments. A few of the Laredo workers had their own machines and did this work at home.

While San Antonio workers were hostile to the garment companies, the Laredo workers did not feel that the firms exploited them. However, the Laredo women saw the subcontractors, who distributed and collected the work and who paid them, as being responsible for many of their employment complaints. Two of the Laredo workers believed that the subcontractor skimmed off part of the wage that the firms paid workers. One of the interviewees told the bureau representative that her supervisor was opposed to the interviews because she feared the bureau would discover that she had cheated the workers.[17]

One San Antonio homeworker complained that the manufacturers exploited the sewers, paying them almost nothing while the garments sold for high prices. Another woman stated that her employer had started as a garment cutter himself and "now they've got a big factory, own big cars, have a beautiful home, and pay the workers very little. Their factories get bigger and bigger and they pay us less and less. We make very little and work so much." One employer countered that he was not exploiting workers more than he was being exploited. A San Antonio manager, who contracted hand-embroidered garments for a New York employer, complained of the low rates after the home office had instituted a number of cuts in 1931 and 1932. He was informed by New York that San Antonio "must compete with cheap Puerto Rican labor or lose the contract." The Women's Bureau cited a 1932 report, issued by the governor of Puerto Rico, that listed handwork rates ranging from $2.67 to $2.77 per week per worker with more than twelve million women's and children's garments and one and half million handkerchiefs entering the U.S. from Puerto Rico from July of 1931 through June of 1932.[18]

Some employers of homeworkers, like the Texas Infant Dress Company and the Randolph-Kohlman Company, were locally owned concerns that operated factories to supplement the labor of homeworkers. Other companies, like the Juvenile Manufacturing Company, were branches of New York firms that sent bundles of cut work to San Antonio and Laredo for distribution to the workers. Women who worked for this category of firm frequently complained of long delays in receiving their wages as requisitions for payment came from New York after the San Antonio office had certified the amount of work completed.

However, individuals were anxious not to make themselves conspicuous to employers as complainers or troublemakers. They believed they would be fired if they complained, and many had no other work experience. In the 1930s, when the repatriation movement flourished, the fear of "voluntary" deportation was an ever-present concern to all Mexican Americans. And the experience of workers in San Antonio, even at wage levels well below subsistence, was that employers could pick and choose among workers because of the abundance of labor. Many believed, not always without knowledge of conditions in Mexican and border communities, that there were people earning even less than they.

In fact, the workers had fairly clear notions of the rates offered by various local employers. The most consistent complaint of the Laredo and San Antonio sewers was that the rates had been cut 50 percent since the onset of the Depression. A characteristic comment was that a garment maker "used to earn more and didn't work so hard."[19] But despite the cuts the sewers kept on with their jobs. The lower the rates, the harder they drove themselves. Of the 123 workers whom the Women's Bureau investigated, only two had quit work because of the wage cuts.

As San Antonio's lowest paid workers, pecan shellers and home garment workers endured some of the nation's worst living conditions. Many of the workers lived in the "corrals" of West San Antonio—one- or two- room shacks without plumbing or electricity. Housing conditions among the Laredo workers were comparable. An interviewer for the Women's Bureau, asked to describe the housing of one respondent, commented simply, "indescribable." This house was a one-room structure renting for four dollars per month. The renter had no light and cooked all of her meals outside the house. She shared central water and toilet facilities with fifteen other families. Despite these difficulties, the interviewer noted, the garment maker was "herself immaculate."[20]

Early in the Depression the low wages and poor working conditions in the San Antonio garment industry attracted the attention of national labor organizations. Labor leaders reasoned that improvements had to be achieved in San Antonio to prevent cheap labor there from driving down wages or destroying jobs in eastern garment-making centers. In 1934 the International Ladies Garment Workers began organizing in San Antonio. Emily Jordan of the United Garment Workers also began similar work in the city earlier in the same year. Unlike the UGW, the ILGWU undertook, as a considered aspect of organizational strategy, to include hand sewers and embroiderers as well as machine workers in their drive. Meyer Perlstein of the ILGWU, who was in the Alamo City after the first local had been organized, explained that "the problem of organization in [Texas] cities is very complicated because of the nationality question, and also because the Mexican border is open for immigration, and at any time that the Mexicans who reside in this country want to organize or ask for any improvement, they are let out and new Mexicans brought in to take their place."[21] The reality of the situation in San Antonio was that very few immigrants were arriving from Mexico, but the staggering unemployment among the city's Mexican Americans made the replacement of troublesome workers a simple matter. Perlstein reported that a group of Anglo women and Chicanas had formed a local affiliated with the ILGWU about a year before his visit but that manufacturers began to blacklist the women and that only the local charter remained by the end of 1934. Before Perlstein left the city, the garment workers had succeeded in resurrecting their local. In subsequent weeks the ILGWU obtained a contract with a local firm. The agreement brought some improvement to the handworkers covered, but the vast majority of homeworkers were not covered and the union's success was short lived.

In 1936 Perlstein returned to San Antonio. With Perlstein came one of the ILGWU's chief organizers, David Dubinsky, who would remain there for several months. However, most of the 1936 labor activity centered around a strike at the Dorothy Frocks factory, which was not a contractor of homework, and the ILGWU secured no subsequent contracts involving homeworkers. From 1937 to 1938 the ILGWU made the Texas Infant Dress Company, a major employer of homeworkers, its primary target. The International members struck and picketed in May of 1937 and again in March of 1938, but by this time the split between San Antonio's factory-based machine workers and home-based hand sewers was an accomplished fact. Although union organizers had wanted to unite the two groups, the pickets' demands included a minimum wage for machine operators, a forty-hour week, and the termination of homework. Thus, the cottage laborers were deprived of the one voice that had spoken for the improvement of their situation as opposed to the destruction of their jobs.

In 1938 Congress passed the Fair Labor Standards Act, which mandated a fifteen-cents-per-hour minimum wage. The Fair Labor Standards Act eventually guaranteed a living wage for shellers and garment workers, but in the process the majority of jobs in both industries disappeared in San Antonio and Laredo. The initial response of employers to the legislation was avoidance, accomplished partly through the replacement of plant labor with homework. Some pecan plant owners as well as contractors for home shelling sold the unshelled nuts to workers and bought back the meats, asserting that the shellers were independent businessmen, not employees, and that the Fair Labor

Standards Act therefore did not apply. Although the majority of plant owners did not convert to home shelling, the number of home shellers reportedly increased in 1938 and continued to increase in areas surrounding San Antonio through 1939.[22] Although the reintroduction of machine shelling was well underway before the end of 1939, home shellers were still operating in the city in 1940.

In San Antonio the Women's Bureau's 1932 investigation of conditions in pecan shelling and garment making rallied organized labor, women's groups, and a number of public officials behind a movement to eliminate homework. In September of 1936, L. P. Bishop, head of the San Antonio health department, appeared before the city council to request passage of an ordinance which would appropriate funds for the health department to enforce sanitation standards in the shelling industry. Bishop testified that the health department destroyed any pecans that it knew had been shelled in homes but that the bulk of the nuts escaped health department notice. Although the city had initiated a system of issuing health cards to food handlers and food processors in May of the same year, it was simply beyond the health department's capacities to administer physicals to San Antonio's many thousands of food workers. The physicals therefore were perfunctory and home shellers were most certainly ignored.

The release of the Women's Bureau's findings sparked an alliance of middle-class club women and working-class men who set out to reform homework in San Antonio. In December of 1936, William B. Arnold, editor of the trades council's *Weekly Dispatch,* reported that he had interviewed a number of home sewers in their homes and that he "found in one instance the worker sitting along the side of the bed where her husband was lying (he had a case of tuberculosis) sewing infants' garments and the garments were spread out on the bed. . . . In another hole in the wall two women were sewing garments and by the side of one were piled several pieces of goods and a small mangy dog was sleeping on them."[23]

The following February Bexar County representative William Carssaw introduced a bill in the Texas legislature to regulate homework in the garment industry. The initial goal of Carssaw, the *Dispatch,* and women's groups was to establish systems of health cards for workers and to require sterilization of the finished products. Clearly the predicament of thousands of exploited workers was not the central concern. In the succeeding months the *Dispatch* carried a series of articles supporting Carssaw's bill that carried scare headlines about disease-infected products.

Carssaw's bill failed to pass, but in 1940 the San Antonio city council adopted an ordinance forbidding both the home shelling of pecans and the sale of garments manufactured by homeworkers. The council had been embarassed by a 1938 *Focus* magazine article about home shelling.[24] *Focus* condemned local officials for endangering public welfare by not eradicating unhealthful conditions among the city's homeworkers. The institution of a ban rather than a set of controls on homework was enforceable, and homework declined precipitously after 1940. In addition, the Fair Labor Standards Act had begun to be enforced against shelling. Puerto Rican workers had already undercut the pitifully low wages of Texas home needleworkers and the children's and infants' wear industries declined in Laredo as well as San Antonio. By 1940, then, there was little reason for managers in either the pecan or garment industries to oppose a ban on homework.

The history of Texas home shellers and hand sewers illustrates both the grimmest consequences of the economics of discrimination and the vested interest of employers in maintaining occupational segregation. The abundance of locally noncompetitive workers in San Antonio and Laredo encouraged employment expansion in the 1920s, but the expansion was calculated on minimal capital investment or the replacement of capital with labor. As the Depression deepened, the trend toward increasing labor intensity continued. There appeared to be no wage level below which shellers and garment workers would overwhelmingly refuse employment. The Fair Labor Standards Act destroyed Texans' competitive edge over other garment and pecan producers. Consequently, sewing machine operators replaced hand sewers and cracking and sorting machines replaced hand shellers. For the garment industry the change meant that hand embroidery and other fine sewing would be given over to foreign producers. The guaranteed wage meant fewer jobs for Chicanas because it destroyed their advantage in the national market without affecting the pattern of discrimination that excluded them from other jobs. After the Depression ended, many handworkers moved into the garment factories, but these women remained disadvantaged because occupational segregation persisted and a continued influx of labor into Texas held wages down.

NOTES

1. *San Antonio Weekly Dispatch,* July 20, 1934; Mary Loretta Sullivan and Bertha Blair, *Women in Texas Industries,* Women's Bureau Bulletin no. 126 (Washington, D.C.: GPO, 1936). The interview materials in this essay come largely from the survey materials for this study. The materials are part of the

records of the Women's Bureau National Archives, Washington, D.C. Seldon Menefee and Orin C. Cassmore, *The Pecan Shellers of San Antonio,* Works Progress Administration (Washington, D.C.: GPO, 1940).

2. *San Antonio Weekly Dispatch,* January 15, 1937.

3. Neither scholar nor government statistician has attempted more than a rough estimate of Mexican immigration to the U.S. for any decade. Careful records were not kept on immigrants who returned to Mexico, and illegal immigration was heavy during the 1920s. Robert G. Landolt estimated that legal immigration from Mexico numbered 49,642 persons from 1901–10; 219,004 from 1911–20; 459,259 from 1921–30; and 22,666 from 1931–40; *The Mexican-American Workers of San Antonio, Texas, The Chicano Heritage* (New York: Arno, 1976), p. 32.

4. "Working Conditions of Pecan Shellers in San Antonio," *Monthly Labor Review* 45 (March 1939): 549–50.

5. U.S. Bureau of Labor Statistics, "Homework and Sweatshops," in *Handbook of Labor Statistics: 1936,* Bulletin no. 615 (Washington, D.C.: GPO, 1936), pp. 196–204; Bertha M. Nienberg, *A Policy Insuring Value to Women Buyers and a Livelihood to Apparel Makers,* Women's Bureau, Bulletin no. 146 (Washington, D.C.: GPO, 1936), pp. 18–21.

6. National Recovery Administration, press release no. 9861, January 28, 1935.

7. Menefee and Cassmore, *The Pecan Shellers of San Antonio,* p. 16; "Working Conditions of Pecan Shellers in San Antonio," 549–50

8. T. Azar, interview, Materials Relating to Bulletin no. 126, Records of the Women's Bureau, the National Archives, Washington, D.C.

9. Menefee and Cassmore, *The Pecan Shellers of San Antonio* pp. 23–26; "Working Conditions of Pecan Shellers in San Antonio:" 549–50.

10. San Antonio homeworker interview no. 77, Materials Relating to Bulletin no. 126, Records of the Women's Bureau.

11. Landolt, *The Mexican American Workers of San Antonio, Texas,* pp. 184–85.

12. Sullivan and Blair, *Women in Texas Industries,* p. 72.

13. San Antonio homeworkers' interviews nos. 5, 71, 34, Materials Relating to Bulletin no. 126, Records of the Women's Bureau.

14. Laredo homeworker, interview no. 16, San Antonio homeworker, interview no. 23, Materials Relating to Bulletin no. 126, Records of the Women's Bureau; Carmen Perry, interview with author, May 22, 1979.

15. Nienberg, *A Policy Insuring Value to the Women Buyer and a Livelihood to Apparel Makers,* pp. 17–18.

16. San Antonio homeworker, interview no. 36, Materials Relating to Bulletin No. 126, Records of the Women's Bureau.

17. Laredo homeworker, interviews no. 4 and 20, Materials Relating to Bulletin No. 126, Records of the Women's Bureau.

18. Typescript report on homeworkers, Materials Relating to Bulletin No. 126, Records of the Women's Bureau.

19. San Antonio homeworker, interview no. 25, Materials Relating to Bulletin No. 126, Records of the Women's Bureau.

20. San Antonio homeworker, interview no. 96, Materials Relating to Bulletin No. 126, Records of the Women's Bureau

21. Meyer Perlstein, quoted in Menefee and Cassmore, *San Antonio Weekly Dispatch,* December 21, 1934.

22. *San Antonio Weekly Dispatch,* April 26, 1940; *The Pecan Shellers of San Antonio,* pp. 21–22.

23. William B. Arnold, quoted in *San Antonio Weekly Dispatch,* December 4, 1936.

24. "Disease and Politics in Your Food: The Case of San Antonio," *Focus,* April 1938, p. 3.

SECTION TWO

Images of Homework:
A Pictorial Essay

EILEEN BORIS
and CYNTHIA R. DANIELS

The task of treating the "Tasks in the Tenements" is one that is
truly Herculean. The subject always makes me see red—not
merely because it raises memories of twenty-four hour shifts
tripping up and down the tenement stairs, six or seven flights of
them (for the good things are always at the top), loaded down
with several tons of camera equipment; . . . [i]t is because when
I stop to consider it in all of its damnable ramifications,
tenement home work seems to me one of the most iniquitous
phases of child-slavery that we have.
>   —Lewis Hine,
>   "Tasks in the Tenements."
>   *Child Labor Magazine* 3
>   (May 1914):95

Much of our historical memory of homework derives from photographs created by social reformers and government investigators who
sought to regulate or prohibit such labor. During the late nineteenth
century, fledging garment unions and the New York State Department
of Labor joined journalists like Jacob Riis to create images of how
"the other half lives" and expose the perils of tenement homework to
the consumer of cigars and clothing. In the process, they revealed the
material culture of working-class life and documented social relations
in homeworking households: who did what kinds of homework with
whom. Most notable of the social investigators of tenement homework

was Lewis Hine, who from 1908 until the late teens photographed child labor for the National Child Labor Committee (NCLC). Used by the NCLC to move middle-class onlookers to join their campaign against sweated labor and what they considered to be its destruction of the home and childlife, Hine's photographs reveal the dignity of homeworkers as well as the burdens of their labor.

During the late 1920s and 1930s, the Women's and Children's Bureaus of the U.S. Department of Labor carried on the fight against industrial homework. Investigators enhanced their social surveys of the hours, wages, work process, and family life of homeworkers with photographs that strikingly visualize this other data. Sometimes in tenements and shacks, othertimes in decent houses, homeworking women continued to draw their children into their labor as they worked with friends and kin to provide for families during the economic crisis.

Homework in the 1980s embraces even a wider range of work situations and processes than in the past. Social photographers continue to document the world of immigrant homeworkers. But homework has entered the modern age, with some workers assembling the component parts for high tech industry and others using them in their homes. While the politics of homework still generates images and old forms linger, the computer industry offers us new portraits of women working at home. Despite changes in the ethnicity of homeworkers and the expansion of clerical homework, the central figure—a woman, often a mother—persists. In this period, however, a photograph of homework is just as likely to be an advertisement for business machines as it is a social commentary.

In the late nineteenth century the United Garment Workers of America instituted the union label to distinguish factory-made from home-made garments, playing on the fear of "contamination" from garments made at home.

(Top left) Although *In Re Jacobs* (98 N.Y. 98) struck down New York's initial law of 1884 prohibiting tenement homework, the New York State Bureau of Labor Statistics continued to monitor tenement-made cigars. A decade later it reported on the persistence of homework in an industry which deployed a family labor system, with men as well as women and children engaged in rolling cigars. This photograph captures the intrusion of factory investigators into the tenement home. Source: New York State, Bureau of Labor Statistics, *Thirteenth Annual Report for the Year 1895* (Albany: Wynkeop Hallenbeck Crawford Co., 1896).

(Bottom left) Children often conveyed homework between the factory and the home. In fieldnotes accompanying this picture of a girl under a pile of garments, Lewis Hine wrote: "A Load of Kimonos just finished. Girl very reticent. Thompson St., NY." c. 1911. Source: National Archives.

(Bottom) Hine commented on this New York City scene: "Mrs. Lucy Libertine and family:—Johnnie, 4 years old, Mary 6 years, Millie 9 years, picking nuts in the basement tenement 143 Hudson St. Mary was standing on the open mouth of the bag holding the cracked nuts (to be picked), with her dirty shoes on, and using a huge dirty jacknife." Source: National Archives.

Hine created poster montages for the National Child Labor Committee to exhibit the evils of homework. This one appeared at the Women's Industrial Exhibit, the Pure Food and Domestic Science Congress, and the Child Labor Exhibit and traveled to cities from Los Angeles, California, to Duluth, Minnesota, and Frankfort, Kentucky, during 1912. Source: Library of Congress, Prints and Photographs Division.

During the Great Depression, men could be found doing "women's work" at home, as witnessed in this portrait of Mrs. Anna Price and her family in the Philadelphia area in April 1936. Note that even when not engaged in the work, children stayed close by their parents. This is a rare portrait of an African-American doing homework. Source: National Archives.

The Women's Bureau photographed Mrs. Jennie Figaro and daughter Jennie finishing men's coats in April 1936 in the Philadelphia area. Source: National Archives.

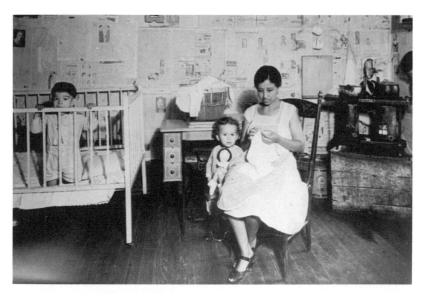

"Mexican Industrial Home Worker Making Infants' Fine Garments" read the caption to this photograph when published in Mary Loretta Sullivan and Bertha Blair, *Women in Texas Industries,* U.S. Department of Labor, Women's Bureau, Bulletin no. 126 (Washington, D.C.: GPO, 1936). The photograph was taken in San Antonio in 1932. Source: National Archives.

"Mexican Women on porch of miserable home doing homework on infants dresses" commented the Women's Bureau on this photograph taken as part of their Texas survey on October 3, 1934, in San Antonio. Source: National Archives.

Cambodian immigrant woman making bows in the Bronx, 1986. Most of these women work around nine hours a day and earn about $2.50 for a dozen simple bows. Many of the homeworkers are older women, mothers who stay at home, or widows; many are also welfare recipients. They often live in large groups, up to twelve people in an apartment. They find out about the homework through neighbors and friends and receive the work from Cambodian contractors who pick up and drop off the bows. Photograph by Leah Melnick.

Home-Based Clerical Worker, as presented in an advertisement for Lanier Voice Products Division which argues, "Some of the best people in your office could be sitting at home," especially "People who stay at home to take care of their families . . . who can't afford the high cost of commuting [, or] who are handicapped." Source: Lanier Voice Products Division, Atlanta, Georgia.

Protesting Reagan Deregulation. 1986 Source: Mike Konopacki, Press Associates Inc.

SECTION THREE

The Persistence of Homework

5

The Demand for Homework: Evidence from the U.S. Census

HILARY SILVER

Since the rediscovery of homework in the 1970s, most empirical research has investigated homeworkers themselves—their social characteristics, earnings, and personal motivations for working in their residences. As a result, we now know more about the supply of homeworkers than about the demand for them.[1]

In this chapter I consider some aspects of employers' demand for homeworkers. I will discuss the historical demand for homework, and then, building on the few studies of homeworkers' employers currently available,[2] will test several hypotheses about contemporary demand using the 1980 Census of Population: Has homework increased in recent years? Is it concentrated in particular sectors of the economy? Is it associated with fluctuations in the demand for labor?

Economic Change and the Role of Homework

The term *homework* often refers to a wide variety of work arrangements. In order to analyze the demand for homeworkers, an important distinction should be made between wage laborers, who sell their productive capacities to a single employer in competition with other workers, and independent producers, who sell their final goods or services in commodity, rather than labor, markets. Consequently, at any given time, the number of homeworkers must be viewed as a composite of the demand for wage labor and the number of independent producers sustained by demand in various commodity markets. These two groups have different life chances, work conditions, and historical antecedents.

Historical Demand

Most historical attention has been given to the demand for home-workers who compete with other wage laborers, referred to here as "waged" homeworkers.[3] Many labor markets arose with the putting-out system, in which households producing for their own use or the local community were organized by petty merchant capitalists who sold them raw materials and purchased their final product, intervening between them and the market. Workers became dependent on employers who engaged them to perform part-processes of production, rather than make a final product, in return for payment by results on a piece-rate basis.

This industrial homework arrangement differed from the employment conditions of factory laborers, who earned wages by the hour regardless of output and were directly supervised and told how to produce during formally set work hours. In contrast, industrial home-workers retained somewhat more autonomy and control. Nevertheless, from the perspective of employers seeking to minimize wages and organized workers trying to raise them, homework directly competed with factory labor.

The total demand for homeworkers rose during the industrial revolution, but the introduction and persistence of homework varied by industry.[4] In America, the earliest homework was found in textiles. As spinning machines increased production, work was subdivided between factories and homeworkers, each producing part of a finished product. The length of time that factories and homeworkers co-existed in such interdependence was also uneven across industries. In cotton textiles, all partial processes moved into factories in the 1840s, with the development of the power loom. In wool, silk, linen, and lace, with limited consumer demand, homework persisted much longer. At the same time, homework developed in new industries, some of which were originally artisan crafts that had moved into manufactories, such as boot, shoe, and cigar making.

In the garment industry, homework both complemented factory work, as each specialized in different tasks, and competed with it in terms of labor and overhead costs for the same tasks. Hand sewing of clothing in the home was the rule until the invention of the sewing machine in 1846. However, this new technology did not replace homework because machines required little investment capital and foot power could compete with steam or electric energy. Thus, homework increased after the Civil War, reaching its peak in the late nineteenth century, when the minutely divided Boston system of clothing production and the passage of antisweating laws appeared to reduce the number of sweatshops. However, garment-finishing tasks continued to be performed in the home during the 1890s. The flow of East European and Italian immigrants provided cheap labor, and employers could avoid the additional cost of the space the two to four homeworkers needed to finish the work of one factory employee.[5]

Indeed, in the early twentieth century, homework demand remained strong in a diverse group of industries, despite new factory-based technologies, labor organization, raising wages, and attempts to regulate or abolish it.[6] During the 1930s, the federal NRA codes temporarily banned homework in many industries until declared unconstitutional. Indeed, industries with employer associations, composed of large, better-capitalized, mechanized, and unionized firms, often supported the elimination of homework on the grounds of unfair competition. Nevertheless, in response to the Depression, other employers and industries introduced homework to cut costs.[7]

In sum, there appears to be a historical pattern, varying by industry, in which industrial homework increased alongside factory production for a time. Some industries set up factories early but shifted work out after union agitation, economic crisis, or technological innovation. Other industries evolved directly from household production through a stage in which homeworkers and factories coexisted until all work was finally consolidated on site.

Many believe that after World War II labor laws and sustained economic growth diminished the demand for waged homework until the recent period of economic restructuring.[8] We need more research to sustain this assertion. For example, a postwar decline in homework in the regulated manufacturing industries may not have been matched in the booming service and white-collar sectors.

If industrial homework, like waged factory labor, has roots in the putting-out system, independent homeworking producers originated in artisanal handicraft production. Several characteristics of commodity production by independent producers set it apart from wage labor. The workers themselves produce an entire commodity, which they market directly. This requires control over some capital or physical means of production as well as control over skills. Professions and some crafts have been able to monopolize certain complex, specialized skills and thereby regulate who and how many may attain them. Abstract knowledge permits independent producers to readily adapt products to changing market conditions. Similarly, traditional skills handed down through personal apprenticeships allow the perpetuation of quality standards. Some entrepreneurs deliberately limit the size of their enterprises in order to retain personal oversight of production. Specialization, personal tailoring of a good or service, and an emphasis on quality create market niches that permit independent producers to survive with a limited clientele. Where markets are sufficiently small and demand is segmented, specialized, or fluctuates by fashion or season, the economies of scale achieved by capital-intensive mass-production factories are largely irrelevant.[9]

These work conditions indicate that homeworkers belong to more than one social class. The number of homework jobs is therefore not simply a function of segmented labor market demand but of demand in segmented commodity markets as well. Independent or artisanal homeworkers themselves face different market situations.[10] *Traditional* artisans carry on pre-industrial production techniques under conditions of free competition. Other artisans are *dependent* upon the decentralization of production from large enterprises to cheaper or more specialized subcontractors who hire nominally self-employed workers who closely resemble waged homeworkers. *Innovative* artisans decentralize production on their own. Through collegial or professional collaboration with competitors, these skilled and entrepreneurial artisans in effect protect their own markets and create new ones with flexible techniques, product innovation, and political cooperation.

Many have predicted that independent artisanal producers would disappear in competition with large organizations. Indeed, over the twentieth century, self-employment in the U.S. did decline. Nevertheless, large numbers of artisans persisted in Italy, France, and other countries, while even in the U.S., independent professionals continued to hang out shingles, artists to work in their studios, and shopkeepers to live over the store.[11] Considerable media attention has been given to the new "workshop economy" in which market demand for high quality or unique commodities, produced with special skills and increasingly cheap technology and subsidized in the start-up phase by the income of second earners, has promoted growth of home-based "worksteaders."[12]

Although few doubt that self-employment is currently enjoying a resurgence in America, ending its long-term decline, it remains unclear whether this is a structural or only a cyclical trend.[13] Since the 1970s, unemployment rates have been very high and increasing numbers of working women have heightened competition in the labor market. It is not inconceivable that small business start ups reflect a lack of alternative or desirable employment, particularly in areas hard hit by farm failures and factory closings.[14] Whether the upward trend in home-based businesses is sustainable, therefore, requires closer examination of the success and failure rates of these small businesses.

Historically, the number of small shopkeepers and service workers tended to rise and fall with the business cycle.[15] Most small businesses were precarious enterprises that failed within a couple of years. Although offering upward mobility to a few, most were established by manual workers who neither intended to, nor in fact did, earn more than modest livings for long hours of work and who, in time, skidded back into employee status.[16] More recent evidence also indicates the self-employed work longer hours and earn less than other workers.[17]

Another reason why the current rise in self-employment may be cyclically induced is suggested by the recent increase in marginal proprietorship. The vast majority of self-employed workers are sole proprietors of unincorporated businesses; side businesses have grown fastest in recent years. Similarly, between 1975 and 1985, the number of self-employed women rose over six times faster than self-employed men (75 percent versus 12 percent).[18] However, most women's businesses have no employees, are financed from the owners' personal savings, have annual receipts of under $ 5000, and almost half—327,112 of them—are operated from the home.[19] But even more than other female entrepreneurs, home-based businesswomen are more likely to start their own businesses without partners, use smaller start-up capital, have lower expenses, employ fewer people, and earn lower profits.[20] Moreover, some female entrepreneurs explicitly start businesses because of inadequate opportunities in the labor market, especially to work flexible hours. Others choose small business as an escape route from arbitrary employers, discrimination, or unsatisfactory jobs.[21] At the same time, self-employment reaffirms the values of independence, autonomy, competition, rewards for individual effort, and the "right to work"—precisely the classical liberal values to which contemporary defenders of homework appeal.[22]

The precarious nature of many small businesses not only suggests that the contemporary surge in entrepreneurial homework is cyclical but also makes ambiguous the employment status of many who regard themselves as independent producers or contractors. The answer hinges on whether the trend reflects dependent or independent decentralization. Many home-based businesses rely primarily upon orders from larger firms. Subcontracting chains can create a "diffused factory" tying the self-employed by "invisible threads." The mythical nature of labor-only independent contracting has long been recognized. In 1939, for example, the courts required garment manufacturers to pay restitution to ten thousand homeworkers for evading wage, hours, workers compensation, and social security laws through a purchase and sales agreement under which homeworkers bought raw materials from and sold their finished products to the same employer.[23] Similar disputes have resurfaced in recent years over the application of Fair Labor Standards Act (FLSA) standards to electronic clerical homeworkers. Independent contractors are deemed to be employees if they cannot hire others, set their own hours and deadlines, profit or lose money, risk some investment, take intiative, or turn to different clients or customers.[24] Thus, the main issues are the degree of control over the labor process and the extent of dependence on one employer who contracts only for labor, rather than on numerous clients or customers in commodity markets.

Even if people's self-identification does not accord with their legal employment status, which may be ambiguous, distinguishing this group from wage earners remains theoretically significant. Not only do the two groups of homeworkers have different historical antecedents, but they continue to work under different conditions. In sum, the total number of homeworking jobs in America is composed not only of employer demand for wage labor but also of the extent of self-employment, which itself may indirectly reflect labor market conditions.

Trends in the Demand for Homework

There is some indication that the number of homeworkers grows during periods of economic distress, rising poverty, and unemployment.[25] This suggests that the demand for homework has been increasing in recent years.

Until 1960 reliable national data on trends in the demand for homework is unavailable. In the early twentieth century and during the 1930s a number of estimates, based on licensing records and investigations, were made for various states and the nation. However, wide evasions of regulations made the data unreliable. Because the movement of production into factories was very uneven, data is available only for varying sets of regulated industries that are not comparable over time. Similarly, there is little systematic evidence for the 1940s and 1950s. After the FLSA ban on homework in seven industries, little research was done to guarantee its enforcement.[26]

In 1960, however, a more reliable source of counting American homeworkers became available. The decennial censuses asked about means of transportation to work, with "work at home" as an alternative response. These data are not ideal, because homeworkers who answered this question referred only to their principal place of work in their primary job during the week surveyed. The answers exclude moonlighters—who have grown from 4.0 million in 1970 to 5.7 million in 1985—and those who occasionally bring work home from the office.[27] In addition, the census did not count those who work less than fifteen hours a week.

My preliminary work with the nationally representative 1977 *Quality of Employment Survey* indicates that 36 percent of the labor force worked at home some time during the year, but a mere 3 percent worked only at home. A survey by the Bureau of Labor Statistics in May 1985 also included occasional homeworkers.[28] Respondents were asked whether, as part of their regularly scheduled work for their principal employer, they did any work at home and, if so, the number of hours they did so. Of more than eighteen million who worked at home some time during the month, half did so for less than eight hours a week and only five percent did so full time. At-home moonlighters, however, were not identified in either survey.

These government sources indicate that, contrary to expectation, homeworking is declining over time, both absolutely and relatively. The data from the 1960, 1970, and 1980 censuses indicate that the number of those who worked primarily at home fell from 4.7 million to 2.2 million over the two decades. If farmers are excluded, the total fell from 2.3 million in 1960 to 1.5 million twenty years later (see table 1).[29]

The BLS survey is not directly comparable to the census, since the data were obtained by means of a different question. Indeed, the report explicitly cautioned that "because this was the first time this survey has been conducted, it is not possible to determine if this number of homeworkers has been increasing or decreasing."[30] Nevertheless, if we assume that only those who worked exclusively at home responded affirmatively to the census question on means of transportation, a comparable estimate can be made for 1985 from the BLS Current Population Survey. It shows that during the reference week, only 2.2 million worked exclusively at home, of whom less than 1.9 million were nonfarm homeworkers. The last figure is comprised for a mere 953,000 full-time homeworkers, leaving a million nonfarm part-timers who work only at home.

Published census data on homeworkers is not broken down by employment status, so separate trends in self-employment cannot be discerned without special tabulations. My own analysis of the 1980 Census Public Use Sample indicated there were approximately 910,000 nonfarm homeworkers who identified themselves as self-employed. Most were sole proprietors, not employees of their own companies.

Table 1. Trends in Homeworking

	1960	1970	1980	May 1985*
Total who work at home	4,662,750	2,685,144	2,179,863	2,243,000
Percent of all U.S. workers	7.2	3.5	2.3	2.1
Urban homeworkers	1,357,400	1,081,570	1,026,604	1,853,000
Rural nonfarm homeworkers	991,701	483,058	501,151	
Rural farm homeworkers	2,313,649	1,120,516	652,108	390,000
Spanish heritage origin		53,287	57,525	
Nonfarm, full-time, self-employed homeworkers			536,900	694,980

Source: U.S. Bureau of the Census, *Censuses of Population 1960, 1970, and 1980*; Current Population Survey (May 1985) reported in *Monthly Labor Review* 109 (November 1986): 34–35.

*1985 figures refer to those who worked exclusively at home.

Of these 910,000, full-timers numbered 536,900. Assuming home-workers who work thirty-five hours a week or more at home do so as a primary job, the comparable BLS figure for the nonfarm self-employed in 1985 was 694,980. Thus, the recent rise in self-employment appears to account for any increase in homework in the early 1980s.

In sum, the evidence indicates that the total number of American homeworkers has basically held steady during the 1980s, that nonfarm homework has increased slightly, and that, as a share of the total labor force, homework continued to decline. Greater competition, changing markets, economic restructuring, new technologies, and a weakened labor movement may have increased the demand for nonfarm home-workers in the past few years, as was hypothesized, but the official statistics as a whole provide only limited support for this assertion. First, economic distress and immigration increased during the 1970s, but during that decade the number of homeworkers declined. Second, the aggregate figures include not only employees but also the rising number of self-employed. Finally, any increase during the 1980s was modest, particularly in comparison with growth in the labor force working outside the home. Of course, turnover among a larger number of temporary homeworkers may explain the absence of a net gain, but only longitudinal data can confirm this.

Can the official statistics be trusted? After all, they are difficult to compare over time, omit homework done as a second job, and, most importantly, may have missed undocumented immigrants. Field workers and anthropologists as well as local governments have discovered large numbers of illegal aliens working at home.

For example, the California state labor department, investigating violations of its homework laws, estimated 40,000 illegal homeworkers in Los Angeles alone.[31] Similarly, the New York state labor department reported that in 1980 there were 50,000 illegal homeworkers in New York City.[32] During the 1970s, approximately a hundred thousand people were found to be working illegally in the Midwest.[33] Theoretically, one would expect this growth in illegal homework to be connected to the formal economy through subcontracting chains. For example, thousands of Hispanic and Asian homeworkers stuff circuit boards in Silicon Valley and are paid off the books.[34] Subcontractors in San Francisco's Chinatown have set up hundreds of garment industry sweatshops from which, it has been estimated, almost half the employees take work home to evade union rules.[35] Homework in the garment industry was also pervasive in Miami during the early 1980s.[36] For these reasons, we must ask whether the census counted those employed in the underground economy.

It is very difficult to estimate the size of the underground labor force. Some suggest it has increased; others maintain it is stable. Estimates of illegal aliens since 1970 have ranged from two to ten million, but there is some evidence that 88 percent of them work on the books.[37]

The census itself estimates its undercount of the number of illegal aliens in the United States through the "error of closure" statistic. This represents the difference between the actual 1980 count and the estimate for 1980 based on the 1970 count and intercensal population changes from birth, death, and net immigration figures. In 1980 the census reported an overcount of 5.5 million persons, of which two million were estimated to be illegal aliens. Indeed, every million undocumented persons add only 0.4–0.5 percent to the undercount.[38] Moreover, although the coverage of the decennial census improved between 1970 and 1980, the number of homeworkers still declined. Finally, the census reported a rise in the number of Hispanic homeworkers between 1970 and 1980, when homeworkers as a whole were declining, which suggests that many new immigrants were in fact enumerated (see table 1). Thus, there is little reason to suspect that a lack of data on undocumented immigrants has produced a bias in the data on homeworkers.

When compared to other estimates of American homeworkers, the census data appear conservative. For example, the Internal Revenue Service enumerated 5.1 million nonfarm proprietorships located in the home in 1980. However, the discrepancy with the census figures can be attributed to the inclusion of special groups: homeworkers with more than one business; moonlighters who report only their primary job; and those who devote less than fifteen hours a week to a business or hobby and are therefore not counted by the census. These groups are large. For example, one survey found that only 56 percent of self-employed homeworkers operate home businesses and over 10 percent of the latter are operated by moonlighters.[39] The casual nature of these types of homework suggests cyclical factors are indeed operating.

Other higher estimates, particularly those made by high-technology-related businesses, are less reliable. For example, estimates by AT&T (23 million), Electronic Services Unlimited (13–14 million in 1985 and 52 million by 1990), and LINK Resources (23 million in 1987) hinge on an expanded definition of homework to include any work performed at home, even that occasionally taken home from the office.[40] Without a consistent notion of homework, these figures are difficult to compare or reconcile. In sum, despite changes in the economy, growth in immigrant labor, and new technologies, homework is not significantly on the rise in the United States.

Contemporary Demand

Although the number of homeworkers has not increased significantly the nature of homework may have changed. During the past decade, increasing international competition has pressured firms in virtually all industries to cut costs or raise productivity through so-called "flexible" production. In the labor market, it results in segmented demand for different types of workers. In commodity markets, it increases demand for specialized goods and services provided by small firms and entrepreneurs who seek market niches or vigorously compete among themselves for business.

Larger firms have sufficient capital to automate production and eliminate peripheral in-house functions. In this way, they shed some workers and still maintain a well-paid, secure "core" labor force. They also have the economic power to transfer the risks of new investment and the pressure of rising competition to smaller firms (or low-wage areas) by decentralizing production through a subcontracting hierarchy. The subcontracting chain can be local, regional, national, or even international.[41] Multisourcing from a number of subcontractors also subverts strikes and union demands. As in the sweating system, smaller firms are forced to compete for corporate contracts, cutting production costs themselves by employing or contracting with "contingent" workers: freelancers, temporaries, and homeworkers.

The employment of homeworkers depends on a number of factors:[42] *The cost of technology relative to labor.* If technology is relatively cheap, barriers to entry by new employers of homeworkers are lower. This enhances competition and forces down wages. It also makes possible the decentralization of production, even to the extent of homeworkers themselves being able to purchase or rent their own equipment. But if technology is expensive, and especially if demand is unstable, firms that might otherwise adopt it may decide to contract out at least the unstable segment of the market, transferring investment costs to subcontractors or, more likely, encouraging them to produce in less efficient, labor-intensive ways—i.e., with homeworkers.

Seasonality, fluctuations, or uncertainty of demand. While large firms tend to produce for mass standardized markets, surges in demand and small-scale or temporary bottlenecks often require additional capacity and capital investment to address in-house. Rather than purchase machines and space that would be unused during downturns or hire more in-house workers who would be more difficult and costly to fire, large firms contract out rush orders to small, marginally profitable, dependent firms in the "peripheral" economy. Local homeworkers are especially desirable when short lead times and proximity to markets are essential.

Consumer preferences. As the market becomes global in scope, it becomes possible to efficiently produce large enough quantities of very specialized products to sustain independent firms. Highly differentiated or segmented markets may rely on demand for quality goods, innovatively designed products, or personally tailored services. Small firms remain viable if they can adjust to often fickle shifts in consumer preferences, new technologies, or special practices adopted by business clients.[43] Independent producers may enter these risky markets and, to keep costs down, often establish businesses in their homes.

A labor process that can be fragmented and decentralized. In cases where production does not require collective use of large-scale machinery and where immediate supervision or interaction among workers is unnecessary, the labor process can be subdivided into smaller routine and unskilled tasks assigned to homeworkers. Payment by result both intensifies labor and ensures discipline.

The size of the available labor pool. Although unemployment has been high since the 1970s, shortages of both unskilled and skilled labor are projected for the next decade.[44] Industrial homeworkers have traditionally been unskilled, drawn from the most insecure segments of the labor market, particularly rural dwellers, immigrants, and women, and often serve as a reserve army under the most competitive of conditions. In this way, homework serves to reinforce existing divisions between workers, keep wages low in the secondary labor market, and forestall unionization. Additionally, many employers face shortages of skilled workers, especially those familiar with new techniques needed for restructuring. Subcontracting with home-based professionals or women employees who would otherwise withdraw from the labor force are ways to acquire or retain access to skills in great demand. It also avoids permanent hiring or training of expensive skilled labor not needed on a long-term basis.

Unionization. Concentrating workers in a large factory facilitates organization, which may lead to increases in direct and indirect labor costs as well as disruptions of production and inflexible work rules. There are many instances of employers transferring work to homeworkers in the wake of unionization drives. Homeworkers, in contrast, are difficult to organize. Their social isolation simplifies labor discipline. Interaction moves up the hierarchy of control instead of laterally.[45]

Labor legislation and taxes. Where government regulations require minimum wages, worker compensation, old age insurance, health and safety standards, and other benefits that increase the costs of hiring additional employees, employers have an incentive to move underground, hire illegal or part-time homeworkers who do not qualify for benefits, or set up homeworkers as independent contractors. Hours, child labor, and safety standards are also easier to evade in the privacy of people's homes.[46]

The cost of overhead. Where the relative costs of rent, energy, equipment, transportation, and wastage are high, employers can transfer them to homeworkers as conditions of employment.

The dividing line between formal, core sector firms and peripheral, dependent ones is somewhat ambiguous but is clearly related to size and market concentration. As the global restructuring of production proceeds, it appears to have reinforced the segmentation of labor demand. At the same time, many current labor market conditions resemble those that in the past encouraged a rise in demand for waged homeworkers. Increasing economic competition together with high unemployment, a growing supply of female and immigrant labor, and political setbacks to unions provide the incentives and opportunities for employers to cut costs by hiring homeworkers.

Moreover, in many cases, shrinking profits discourage investment in new technology and favor a reorganization of production with low-wage labor at its base. Even when computer technology has been adopted, it has often not significantly reduced wage bills or increased productivity.[47]

/ None of this is to say that firms employing homeworkers are less profitable than conventional establishments. Studies have found that they invest and grow more than firms in the same industry that do not employ homeworkers and that telecommuters are more productive than identical workers who commute to work.[48] Indeed, this provides some of the motivation of employers to use them. Nevertheless, in part because managers resist the erosion of corporate culture and supervising those they cannot see, large firms tend not to employ homeworkers themselves but subcontract with those who do. Thus, homework is in demand largely among smaller firms or is pursued by the self-employed. Indeed, the coming labor shortages will be particularly acute for skilled workers, who may find demand for their services sufficient to set up their own home businesses, accentuating the decentralization trend.

Homework in a Dual Economy

The criteria used to empirically distinguish core sector industries from those in the periphery of the economy make it likely that core sector firms will contract out for specialized and auxiliary goods and services, transferring market uncertainties, investment risks, and competition to smaller enterprises in the peripheral sector.[49] In some cases, entrepreneurs may set up businesses in their homes to reduce costs below their competitors'. In other instances, existing labor-intensive, but less profitable, firms may turn to homeworkers to meet market pressures, exploiting existing labor market segmentation to lower wages.[50]

All this suggests that homeworkers are more likely to be found in industries of the peripheral sector of the economy than the labor force at large. With the census of population, it is possible to test this hypothesis (see table 2). First, three-fourths of all homeworkers were found in peripheral industries of the economy in 1979. Second, this share far exceeds the proportion of all American workers in the periphery, which Tolbert, Horan, and Beck reported as 55 percent in 1976. Third, the annual earnings of core-sector homeworkers are $6,000 more than those in the periphery. Finally, homeworking women, who

Table 2. Sectoral Distribution of Homeworkers by Selected Characteristics

	Periphery	Core	Total
Total homeworkers	75.4	24.6	100.0
Percent female	57.5	41.5	53.6
Percent employee	35.8	38.9	36.5
Percent self-employed/unpaid family worker	60.7	53.1	58.8
Percent government worker	3.6	8.1	4.7
Percent part-time	39.7	37.5	39.1
Mean weeks unemployed	1.0	1.4	1.2
Mean annual income	$10,005	$16,856	$11,720

All Chi-square and F-statistics significant at .05 level.

earn less and have traditionally been segregated in the secondary labor market, disproportionately comprise the peripheral homework sector. Male homeworkers are a majority among core sector homeworkers. These findings are all in line with theoretical expectations.

However, economic segmentation may occur among firms within the same industry as well as between industries. In the event of surges in demand for a particular commodity which large firms do not have the capacity or willingness to supply, smaller firms within the same commodity market may try to fill the gap. The fact that they face greater instability in demand may encourage them to seek out flexible labor, including homeworkers. Thus, there may also be homeworkers in the more insecure secondary labor market employed within core sector industries that the above analysis could not distinguish. Indeed, even full-time, year-round homeworkers earn only 76 percent of what comparable in-house workers make.[51] But without firm level data, this issue must be left for future research.

The Demand for Homeworkers by Industry and Occupation

Studies from the early twentieth century noted the great diversity of industries engaging homeworkers. Although, as discussed later, waged and self-employed homeworkers are found in different sets of industries, the industrial distribution of all homeworkers indicates that demand was still broadly based in 1979 (see table 3).

Homework appears to be in greater demand, or is performed by more independent producers, in a number of traditional pre-industrial pursuits which have been declining over time: agriculture, forestry and fisheries, private household services, personal services, and religious

Table 3. Industrial Distribution of Homeworkers and Total U.S. Labor
Force by Employment Status* (1979)

	Labor Force Total	Homeworkers		
		Nonfarm	Employed	Self-employed
Agriculture, forestry, fisheries	3%	9.6%	5.6%	12.5%
Mining	1	.2	.4	.2
Construction	6	5.6	5.2	6.0
Nondurable manufacturing	9	4.2	6.6	3.1
Durable manufacturing	14	4.1	5.7	3.5
Transportation	4	1.9	2.2	1.7
Communications	1	.2	.4	.1
Utilities	1	.4	.5	.2
Wholesale trade	4	3.5	3.8	3.5
Retail trade	17	11.2	10.6	12.4
Finance	3	1.0	1.4	.8
Insurance	2	1.4	2.1	1.2
Real estate	1	4.8	8.2	3.1
Business and repair services	4	9.6	5.1	12.8
Computer data processing	.4	.4	.4	.4
Private households	1	4.2	11.4	.2
Personal services	2	13.6	7.9	18.0
Entertainment/recreation	1	1.3	1.2	1.4
Health services	7	1.6	1.4	1.8
Professional (exc. health)	12	14.7	11.7	13.6
Child day care services	0	1.9	1.0	2.3
Religious organizations	1	3.2	7.1	1.2
Public administration	5	1.4	0	0

*Government workers not shown—one-third are found in public administration, another
half in professional services.

organizations. Yet, homework is found in some of the leading growth
industries of the economy as well: real estate, business and repair
services, child care, and nonmedical professional services. This diversity makes it difficult to generalize about the nature of the demand
for homework, except to note that firms and workplaces in these industries tend to be small and nonbureaucratic, attributes typical of the
peripheral sector. The greatest concentrations of homeworkers are in
professional and personal services; the proportion of homeworkers in
these industries is twice that of the labor force as a whole.

The occupational distribution of homeworkers is in line with the
findings about industries (see table 4). In comparison with the entire
American labor force, homeworkers are more likely to be core sector

executives, administrators, or managers, and peripheral sector sales-persons and especially service workers. Although slightly underrepresented in most professions, homeworkers are disproportionately artists and writers, occupations traditionally pursued in home studios.

The census data includes all home-based workers and does not permit distinguishing between those who remain *at* home all day and those who use home as a base *from* which to work. However, the industrial distribution does suggest that many have jobs that take them to a variety of workplaces, leaving administrative activities to be performed in the home. For example, real estate agents or repairpersons may travel to other people's homes to perform some tasks while still spending considerable time at home organizing their work. Moreover, home-based workers in household services or religious organizations may actually be described more precisely as living *at* work than working at home.

Turning to industries in which homeworkers are underrepresented reveals some unexpected findings. First, the data do not support optimistic claims that the development and deployment of new, cheaper, "flexible" technologies has led to a massive increase in homework or

Table 4. Occupational Distribution of Homeworkers and U.S. Labor Force*

	Labor Force	Homeworkers			
	Total	Nonfarm	Employed	Self-employed	Core
Executive, administrative managerial workers	10%	13.7%	13.8%	13.7%	16.2%
Professional, exc. writers	12	10.2	9.8	9.4	11.4
Writers and artists	1	6.9	2.8	9.7	4.3
Technicians	3	1.2	1.3	.9	1.8
Sales	10	11.7	11.5	12.6	11.2
Administrative support	17	12.5	17.7	8.5	23.9
Service occupations	13	19.9	24.3	16.8	3.1
Farming and forestry	1	8.9	5.2	11.6	.3
Precision production and craft	13	8.8	5.2	11.5	15.9
Operators, fabricators, and laborers	20	6.4	8.3	5.3	11.9

*Government employed, not shown, are evenly divided among professional, administrative support, and service occupations.

"telework."[52] Despite the publicity given these work arrangements, less than 1 percent of homeworkers are found in computer and data processing services, a proportion similar to that found for the labor force as a whole. Of course, computers may be used in other industries, but most studies find only a small minority of homeworkers have need of new technologies.[53] Home computer sales have been lower than expected, and few of these are used for paid work.[54] Moreover, corporations have been slow to adapt to the innovative potential of information technology, as organizational culture places constraints on the acceptance of "telecommuting."[55] At best, technology is facilitative, not determinate of, the social organization of work.

At the same time, manufacturing homework, which is of greatest concern to organized labor, is performed by only 6 percent of American homeworkers. Of course, this is in line with the overall restructuring of the economy toward service industries, but even in 1979, 23 percent of the labor force as a whole worked in manufacturing. In line with theoretical expectations, the gap between homeworkers and the entire labor force is greater in durable manufacturing, where the technological constraints of large-scale capital-intensive production make it more difficult to decentralize tasks to workers' homes. Nevertheless, about equal proportions of homeworkers are in durable and nondurable manufacturing.

The occupational data further support these findings. Homeworkers are underrepresented among operatives, technicians, and craft workers, who constitute the bulk of the blue-collar manufacturing labor force, as well as among administrative support workers, the white-collar occupations unions and others have equated with industrial ones in terms of pay and work conditions. However, of the operatives, technicians, and administrative support workers who do work at home, most are employees in core sector industries, suggesting that even larger, more powerful firms—or their competitors—turn to homeworkers for flexible labor. Craftspersons are also disproportionately in the core, although they tend to be self-employed. Their scarce skills may be in sufficient demand to permit them to remain independent and contract directly with core sector firms.

Although industrial homework pales beside the numbers of homeworkers in services, this does not mean that it no longer should be regulated. Indeed, regulation may be responsible for the low figures. Rather, the finding points to the need to consider whether homework in the growing service sector, particularly that performed by clerical workers, should receive similar protective legislation.

Employment Stability

Homeworkers provide employers with flexibility in hiring in response to fluctuating market demand. Thus, it might be expected that the number of weeks worked by homeworkers during the year is lower than for the labor force as a whole. Similarly, the hours worked each week by homeworkers is hypothesized to be lower than the hours of the average American worker. However, homeworkers taken as a whole, and especially those in the core industries, work more weeks a year than most Americans (see table 5). The difference is due largely to the self-employed homeworkers, who, responsible for their own often marginal businesses, are less likely to take vacations. Employed homeworkers tend to work the same number of weeks as the national labor force. They do not appear to suffer from greater employment instability by virtue of their place of employment.

Homeworkers are more likely to work both shorter and much longer hours than most Americans (see table 5). While only 21 percent of the labor force are part-time workers, this is true of 41 percent of homeworkers, whether they are self-employed or in the core sector. These part-time self-employed may actually be wage workers disguised as independent contractors. Yet, there is also a relatively larger proportion of homeworkers who put in a longer-than-average work week. In particular, 31 percent of self-employed homeworkers devoted over forty

Table 5. Employment Stability of Homeworkers and U.S. Labor Force

	Labor Force Total	Homeworkers		
		Nonfarm	Self-Employed	Core
Weeks worked in 1979:				
50–52	.60	.62	.64	.67
48–49	.04	.05	.05	.04
40–47	.09	.10	.10	.09
27–39	.08	.08	.08	.07
14–26	.09	.09	.08	.07
1–13	.09	.06	.05	.06
Hours worked in survey week:				
1–14	.05	.15	.13	.15
15–34	.15	.26	.28	.26
35–40	.52	.30	.28	.35
41 or more	.25	.28	.31	.24

hours to their businesses, compared to 25 percent of the labor force as a whole. This is in line with findings about the hours of owners of newly formed businesses more generally, 53 percent of whom spend more than 60 hours a week at work.[56]

In sum, if employers seek to adapt flexibly to seasonal demand by hiring homeworkers, it is not reflected in the number of weeks home-workers are employed during the year. Wage-earning homeworkers had no greater employment instability during 1979 than most Americans. Of course, it is always possible that homeworkers quickly switch among a number of employers over the year, as work for one dries up and is quickly replaced by work for another. Employed homeworkers did experience more weeks of unemployment than self-employed home-workers (on the average, half a week more). In addition, the use of homeworkers as a flexible, contingent labor force is apparent in the number of hours of work available. Employed homeworkers are more likely to find or choose part-time work than the average worker. This is also true of a larger than average segment of self-employed home-workers, who may be fictitious independent contractors.

However, about a third of home-based businesspersons work very long hours, as do entrepreneurs in general. They are not only more likely to work between fifty and fifty two weeks a year but are much more prone to working longer than eight-hour days in comparison to other homeworkers and most Americans. The marginal nature of their businesses may explain why they appear to be "workaholics."

Self-Employed Homeworkers

These findings suggest the need to refine theories of homework to take account of true employment status. The census data on employment status is based only on the subjective reports of workers themselves, not on objective criteria of dependence or control. Although this makes it impossible to distinguish independent contractors from true entre-preneurs, a closer look at the industries in which self-proclaimed self-employed homeworkers participate provides further insight into home-based businesses.

In 1979, 59 percent of all homeworkers were self-employed by their own account. However, most have unincorporated businesses and no employees. As a result, it is up to them how much they work, earn, and risk their investments. Compared to employed homeworkers, at-home entrepreneurs are more likely to be in the peripheral sector, in industries composed of a large number of small, highly competitive firms. Dependence on larger firms for contracts and general market insecurity may add to the pressure felt by some self-employed home-workers to devote long hours every week of the year to insure that their businesses succeed.

These businesses are more likely to be in agriculture, forestry and fisheries, real estate, day care services, nonmedical professional services, and especially business and repair and personal services in comparison to the industrial distribution of the labor force as a whole. Indeed, self-employed homeworkers are five times more likely to work in the last two industries than in the national labor force. These industries offer opportunities to devise highly innovative, specialized services catering to other businesses as well as to final consumers on a fee or commission basis. Thus, it is possible that these self-employed homeworkers are skilled "artisans" who, following the model of independent decentralization, provide dynamism to the economy, despite their peripheral sector status.

The occupational distribution of self-employed homeworkers tends to support this. Ten percent of the self-employed working at home are writers and artists, compared to only one percent of the entire labor force. They are also more likely to have executive, administrative, and managerial positions, sales jobs, and service occupations than the average American worker. They are underrepresented among manual occupations, except in farming and forestry. Thus, with the exception of the nonartistic professions, home-based businesspersons are more likely to work in occupations that offer scope for initiative, creativity, and personally tailored service. Yet, they are also labor-intensive, which would account for the extraordinary work effort detected among some of the self-employed.

Conclusions

I have tried to test several hypotheses about the demand for homework with data from the U.S. census. First, I considered whether demand for homework has been increasing in recent years, in line with theoretical expectations that international competition and a weakened labor movement, together with economic restructuring and new technologies, create pressures to cut labor costs. I found, however, a downward trend in the number and percentage of homeworkers between 1960 and 1980. Even the rise in undocumented immigrants, many of whom may work underground, appears to have been included in these figures. I found some evidence of a modest increase in nonfarm labor working exclusively at home between 1980 and 1985, but these findings must remain tentative until the 1990 census.

Second, the hypothesis that homeworkers are in demand dispro-portionately by the peripheral sector of the economy was confirmed. Three of every four homeworkers were in the periphery, where greater competition, more labor-intensive production, and lower wages and benefits are the rule. Thus, it appears that international competition resulting in market segmentation and the decentralization of produc-tion encourages the demand for homeworkers by the more insecure firms of the periphery sector.

Third, I found that homework is performed in diverse industries, rather than concentrated in manufacturing as existing legislation and union policy positions would imply. As the social division of labor has increased, activities have been shifted to specialized service firms that increasingly demand homeworkers. However, there is little evi-dence of an explosion in demand for computer homeworkers, despite the development of new technology making telecommuting possible.

Fourth, homeworkers in general do not experience relatively greater employment instability due to seasonality and fluctuations in demand throughout the year, contrary to expectation. This may be due to the increasing insecurity of employment more generally. However, em-ployed homeworkers were more likely to work part-time, suggesting that they serve as a flexible labor force on a daily basis.

Finally, I argued both theoretically and empirically that self-em-ployed homeworkers, whose style of work resembles that of pre-in-dustrial artisans, independent producers, and the petit bourgeoisie, should be distinguished from wage-earning homeworkers. A significant minority of the self-employed work longer hours and for more weeks of the year than most Americans. These entrepreneurial homeworkers engage in labor-intensive specialized services, where their skills and devotion may earn them particular niches in the market. During down-turns in the economy, self-employment may provide more satisfying, if more strenuous, work than that available in the wage labor market. However, because many rely on contracts from large firms in the core economy, their businesses can be very precarious.

Self-employed homeworkers, as distinct from employees, raise ques-tions for future research. To the extent that the significant minority with businesses in specialized services are innovative entrepreneurs, the alleged contribution to economic growth of starting businesses in the home can be assessed. Do these enterprises succeed in the long run? Do they tend to employ other homeworkers? Do they eventually outgrow their base in the home? How dependent are these independent producers on larger firms? Whatever the answer to these questions, it is clear that self-employed homeworkers experience their work differently than those who work in the home for a wage or piece rate. As the demand for wage-earning homeworkers shifts toward new industries, particularly for clerical tasks, this study suggests some attention might be paid to the fewer hours of employment available to these workers and the legal protection and benefits that part-time status confers. As in the putting-out system and industrial homework, wage-earning clerical workers are also paid by the piece for routine subdivided tasks. The similar motivations behind demand for such workers, their similar role in the labor process, and their lack of independence in commodity markets suggests a need for similar protection from abuses that historically characterized industrial homework.

NOTES

1. Robert E. Kraut and Patricia Grambsch, "Home-Based White-Collar Employment: Lessons from the 1980 Census," *Social Forces* 66, no. 2 (December 1987): 410–26.

2. Margrethe Olson, "An Investigation of the Impacts of Remote Work Environments and Supporting Technology," Working Paper of the Center for Research on Information Systems, no. 161, New York University, August, 1987; Margrethe Olson, "Overview of Work-At-Home Trends in the United States," Working Paper of the Center for Research on Information Systems no. 57, New York University, August, 1983; National Research Council, *Office Workstations in the Home* (Washington, D.C.: National Academy Press, 1985); Joanne H. Pratt, "Home Teleworking: A Study of Its Pioneers," *Technological Forecasting and Social Change* 25 (1984): 1–14; Catherine Hakim, "Employers' Use of Homework, Outwork, and Freelances," *Employment Gazette* (April 1984): 144–50; Lourdes Benería and Martha Roldán, *The Crossroads of Class and Gender: Industrial Homework, Subcontracting, and Household Dynamics in Mexico City* (Chicago: University of Chicago Press, 1987); Sheila Allen and Carol Wolkowitz, *Homeworking: Myths and Realities* (London: Macmillan, 1987).

3. Early studies include Edith Abbott, "Employment of Women in Industries: Cigar-Making," *Journal of Political Economy* 15 (January 1907): 1–25; U.S. Department of Labor, Women's Bureau, *The Commercialization of the Home through Industrial Home Work,* Bulletin No. 135 (Washington, D.C.: 1935); Frieda S. Miller, "Industrial Home Work in the United States," *International Labour Review* 43 (January-June 1941): 1–50; Lazare Teper and Nathan Weinberg, *Aspects of Industrial Homework in Apparel Trades* (New York: International Ladies' Garment Workers' Union, Research Department, July 1941). Secondary sources include Sandra Albrecht, "Industrial Homework in the United States: Historical Dimensions and Contemporary Perspective," *Economic and Industrial Democracy* 3 (November 1982): 413–30; Laura and

Robert Johnson, *The Seam Allowance: Industrial Home Sewing in Canada* (Toronto: Women's Educational Press, 1982); Susan Porter Benson, "Women, Work, and the Family Economy: Industrial Homework in Rhode Island, 1934," in this volume, pp. 53–74. For a discussion of the class position of industrial homeworkers, see Benería and Roldán, *The Crossroads of Class and Gender;* and Allen and Wolkowitz, *Homeworking.*

4. See, for example, Duncan Bythell, *The Sweated Trades: Outwork in the Nineteenth Century* (New York: St. Martin's Press, 1978).

5. Miller, "Industrial Home Work in the United States," p. 20.

6. One factory-investigating commission found homeworkers employed in the production of sixty-two articles in addition to the forty-one regulated by law. New York State, *Second Report of the Factory Investigating Commission* (Albany, New York State, 1913), 1: 92–93.

7. Miller, "Industrial Home Work in the United States," pp. 27–36; Women's Bureau, *The Commercialization of the Home through Industrial Home Work.* See also Eileen Boris, "Regulating Industrial Homework: The Triumph of 'Sacred Motherhood,' " *Journal of American History* 71 (March 1985): 745–63.

8. Eileen Boris, "Homework and Women's Rights: The Case of the Vermont Knitters, 1980–1985," in this volume, pp. 233–57.

9. Michael Piore and Charles Sabel, *The Second Industrial Divide* (New York: Basic, 1984), pp. 28–35, 258–77.

10. This typology is based on Sebastian Brusco and Charles Sabel, "Artisan Production and Economic Growth," in *The Dynamics of Labour Market Segmentation,* ed. Frank Wilkinson (New York: Academic, 1981), pp. 99–114.

11. Suzanne Berger and Michael J. Piore, *Dualism and Discontinuity in Industrial Societies* (Cambridge: Cambridge University Press, 1980).

12. Stephen Kindel, "The Workshop Economy," *Forbes,* April 30, 1984, pp. 62–84; Lynn Langway, "Worksteaders Clean Up: As the Network of Entrepreneurs Running Successful Home Businesses Grows, So Do Labor-Union Concerns," *Newsweek,* January 9, 1984, pp. 86–87.

13. Eugene H. Becker, "Self-Employed Workers: An Update to 1983," *Monthly Labor Review* 107 (July 1984): 14–18.

14. Steven P. Galante, "Cottage Businesses Help Ease Farm-Belt Economy Burdens," *Wall Street Journal,* June 2, 1986; "Iowa Sheep Farm's Cottage Industry," *New York Times,* June 11, 1986; Chris Gerry, "The Working Class and Small Enterprises in the UK Recession," in *Beyond Employment: Household, Gender and Subsistence,* ed. Nanneke Redclift and Enzo Mingione (London: Basil Blackwell, 1985), pp. 288–316.

15. A. J. Mayer, "The Lower Middle Classes as an Historical Problem," *Journal of Modern History* 47 (September 1975): 409–36.

16. Kurt Mayer and Sidney Goldstein, "Manual Workers as Small Businessmen," in *Blue Collar World,* ed. A. Shostak and W. Gomberg (Englewood Cliffs: Prentice-Hall, 1964), pp. 537–50.

17. Becker, "Self-Employed Workers."

18. Sheldon Haber, Enrique Lamas, and Jules Lichtenstein, "On Their Own: The Self-Employed and Others in Private Business," *Monthly Labor Review* 110 (May 1987): 17–23; Bureau of Labor Statistics data cited in Eric Schmitt, "The U.S. Woman as her Own Boss," *Herald Tribune* August 22, 1986, p. 11. See also U.S. Small Business Administration, *The State of Small Business: A Report of the President* (Washington, D.C.: 1983), p. 315; Interagency Task Force on Women Business Owners, *The Bottom Line: Unequal Enterprise in America* (Washington, D.C.: GPO, 1978), and *Annual Report to the President* (Washington, D.C.: Government Printing Office, 1980).

19. Joann Lublin, "Running a Firm from Home Gives Women More Flexibility," *Wall Street Journal*, December 31, 1984.

20. Amy Lyman, *The HUB Program for Women's Enterprise: A Survey of Philadelphia Women Business Owners* (Philadelphia: Wharton Center for Applied Research, University of Pennsylvania, 1987), p. 6.

21. Robert Goffee and Richard Scase, *Women in Charge: The Experiences of Female Entrepreneurs* (London: Allen and Unwin, 1985), pp. 40–44.

22. F. Bechhofer, B. Elliott, M. Rushforth, and R. Bland, "The Petits Bourgeois in the Class Structure: The Case of the Small Shopkeepers," in *The Social Analysis of Class Structure*, ed. Frank Parkin (London: Tavistock, 1974), and "Small Shopkeepers: Matters of Money and Meaning," *Sociological Review* 22 (November 1974): 465–82.

23. Teper and Weinberg, *Aspects of Industrial Homework in Apparel Trades*, pp. 36–37.

24. Donald Elisburg, "Legalities," in *Office Workstations in the Home*, pp. 60–61. For a discussion of the employment status of British independent contractors, see Catherine Hakim, *Home-based Work in Britain*, Research Paper no. 60 (London: Department of Employment, May, 1987), pp. 209–24.

25. Johnson and Johnson, *The Seam Allowance*, p. 50.

26. One exception was a North Carolina report that indicated that as minimum wages rose the number of homeworkers declined through the mid-1950s. Cited in Ibid., p. 54.

27. Philip Mattera, *Off the Books: The Rise of the Underground Economy* (New York: St. Martin's, 1985), p. 132; John F. Stinson, "Moonlighting by Women Jumped to Record Highs," *Monthly Labor Review* 109 (November 1986): 22–25.

28. Francis W. Horvath, "Work At Home: New Findings from the Current Population Survey," *Monthly Labor Review* 109 (November 1986): 31–35.

29. There are a number of ways to define the nonfarm labor force. In tables 2 through 5 farmers were excluded on the basis of place of residence (rural, nonfarm), thereby leaving a considerable number of those in agricultural, fishing, or forestry pursuits but excluding nonagricultural workers who reside on farms. The same procedure is used in the published census data. The CPS excluded agricultural workers by industry. If this procedure is followed, there is little difference in the substantive findings presented.

30. Horvath, "Work at Home," p. 35.

31. Jonathan Rauch, "Anatomy of a Proposition for Regulation: The Battle of Industrial Homework," *National Journal* 6 (June 1981): 1015.

32. Marilyn Webb, "Sweatshops for One: The Rise of Industrial Homework," *Village Voice,* February 10–16, 1982.

33. Johnson and Johnson, *The Seam Allowance,* p. 54.

34. Naomi Katz and David Kamnitzer, "Fast Forward: The Internationalization of Silicon Valley," in *Men, Women, and the International Division of Labor,* ed. June Nash and Maria Patricia Fernández-Kelley (Albany: SUNY Press, 1983), pp. 332–45; Rebecca Morales, "Cold Solder on a Hot Stove," in *The Technological Woman: Interfacing with Tomorrow,* ed. Jan Zimmerman (New York: Praeger, 1983).

35. Stanley Lim, "Analysis of Chinatown Garment Workers Survey Questionnaire," *Report to the Employment Committee of the Human Rights Commission* (San Francisco, October 23, 1969); Morrison G. Wong, "Chinese Sweatshops in the United States: A Look at the Garment Industry," in *Research in Sociology of Work,* vol. 2, ed. Richard and Ida Stimpson (Greenwich, Conn.: JAI Press, 1983), pp. 357–79.

36. Alejandro Portes and Saskia Sassen-Koob, "Making It Underground: Comparative Material on the Informal Sector in Western Market Economies," *American Journal of Sociology* 93 (July, 1987): 46.

37. Mattera, *Off the Books,* Appendix.

38. U.S. Bureau of the Census, "Coverage of the National Population in the 1980 Census, by Age, Sex, and Race: Preliminary Estimates by Demographic Analysis," *Current Population Reports,* P-23, No. 115 (Washington: GPO, 1982); Jeffrey S. Passel and J. Gregory Robinson, *Revised Demographic Estimates of the Coverage of the Population by Age, Sex, and Race in the 1980 Census,* Bureau of the Census, memorandum (Washington, D.C., April 8, 1985).

39. Gil Gordon, "Analysis of Data from National Survey Shows Surprising Trends, Raises Interesting Questions about Home Work," *Telecommuting Review* 5, no. 2 (February 1, 1988): 12–17.

40. Joanne H. Pratt and John A. Davis, *Measurement and Evaluation of the Populations of Family-Owned and Home-Based Businesses,* Report to the Office of Advocacy, Small Business Administration (Washington, D.C.: GPO, 1986); Electronic Services Unlimited, *Telecommuting: The State of the Art and Market Trends* (New York: ESU, 1984), p. 2; Jonathan Friendly, "The Electronic Change: House Becomes Office," *New York Times,* May 15, 1986, C-1; Robert Kraut, "Predicting the Use of Technology: The Case of Telework," in *Technology and the Transformation in White-Collar Work* (Hillsdale, N.J.: Lawrence Erlbaum, 1983); AT&T Consumer Products, news release no. 111083; Residence Market Research Group, AT&T, proprietary report, 1982; Gil Gordon, "Analysis of Data from National Survey," pp. 12–17. The LINK study did break out the number of full-time homeworkers who are not just working after hours. In 1987 the total amounted to 3.4 million Americans, including farm families, which suggests a continuing upward trend in homework.

41. Saskia Sassen-Koob, "The New Labor Demand in Global Cities," in *Cities in Transformation,* ed. Michael Peter Smith (Beverly Hills: Sage, 1984),

pp. 139–72; Benería and Roldán, *The Crossroads of Class and Gender,* pp. 31–74; José Alonso, "The Domestic Clothing Workers in the Mexican Metropolis and Their Relations to Dependent Capitalism," in *Men, Women, and the International Division of Labor,* ed. Nash and Fernández-Kelly, pp. 161–72; Allen and Wolkowitz, *Homeworking,* pp. 87–93.

42. Jill Rubery and Frank Wilkinson, "Outwork and Segmented Labour Markets," in *The Dynamics of Labour Market Segmentation,* ed. Wilkinson, pp. 115–32; John Holmes, "The Organization and Locational Structure of Production Subcontracting," in *Production, Work, Territory,* ed. Allen J. Scott and Michael Storper (Boston: Allen and Unwin, 1986), pp. 107–24; Carla Lipsig-Mumme, "La Rennaisance du Travail a Domicile dans les Economies Developpées," *Sociologie du Travail* 3 (1983): 313–35.

43. Piore and Sabel, *The Second Industrial Divide,* pp. 28–35, 258–77.

44. "Help Wanted: America Faces an Era of Worker Scarcity That May Last to the Year 2000," *Business Week,* August 10, 1987, pp. 48–53.

45. Examples include New York cigar making in 1877, clothing workers in the Philippines in the 1970s, and Wisconsin insurance claims processors in the 1980s. See Miller, "Industrial Homework in the United States"; Mattera, *Off the Books,* p. 104; Cynthia Costello, "The Office Homework Program at the Wisconsin Physicians Service Company," in this volume, pp. 198–214. Although homeworkers have organized locally in exceptional cases, they have rarely been successful in winning their demands.

46. Naomi Katz and David Kemnitzer, "Women and Work in Silicon Valley: Options and Futures," in *My Troubles Are Going to Have Trouble with Me: Everyday Trials and Triumphs of Women Workers,* ed. Karen Brodkin Sacks and Dorothy Remy (New Brunswick: Rutgers University Press, 1984), p. 214.

47. Keith Schneider, "Services Hurt by Technology: Productivity Is Declining," *New York Times,* June 29, 1987, D-1; Olson, "An Investigation of the Impacts of Remote Work Environments and Supporting Technology."

48. Charles McClintock, "Expanding the Boundaries of Work: Research on Telecommuting" (Paper presented at the American Association for the Advancement of Science, New York, May 29, 1984); Margrethe Olson, "Organizational Barriers to Professional Telework," in this volume, pp. 000–00.

49. Core-sector firms have a greater capacity for oligopoly, as indicated by market concentration and greater economic scale in assets, receipts, and employees. They exhibit oligopolistic behavior through greater advertising, political contributions, and profit rates. They also have bureaucratically organized work forces as well as higher unionization, wage levels, fringe benefits, and job stability. These criteria were used to operationalize core and periphery. Two-digit census industries were recoded into sectors based on the classification devised by Charles Tolbert, Patrick M. Horan, and E. M. Beck, "The Structure of Economic Segmentation," *American Journal of Sociology* 85 (March 1980): 1095–116.

50. Rubery and Wilkinson, "Outwork and Segmented Labour Markets"; Holmes, "The Organizational and Locational Structure of Production Subcontracting."

51. Heidi Hartmann, Robert Kraut, and Louise Tilly, *Computer Chips and Paper Clips: Technology and Women's Employment,* 2 vols. (Washington, D.C., National Academy Press, 1986), 1:146–47.

52. Robert Johnson, "Rush to Cottage Computer Work Falters Despite Advent of Inexpensive Technology," *Wall Street Journal,* June 1983; Judith Gregory, "Clerical Homeworkers and the New Office Technology," in *Office Workstations in the Home,* pp. 115–16; Jane Kingston, "Telecommuting: Its Impact on the Home," in *The World of Work,* ed. Howard Brasbury (Bethesda, Md.: World Future Society, 1983), pp. 287–99.

53. Hirshey, "How Women Feel about Working at Home," p. 70; Gordon, "Analysis of Data from National Survey," p. 15.

54. David Sanger, "The Expected Boom in Home Computers Fails to Materialize," *New York Times,* June 4, 1984, A-1. A survey by C&SN/SRI Research into reasons people wanted personal computers at home indicated that only 19 percent intended to use them to run a home business and another 9 percent to work at home.

55. Olson, "An Investigation of the Impacts of Remote Work Environments and Supporting Technology."

56. "Like 60-Hour Weeks? Try Your Own Business," *Business Week,* August 10, 1987, p. 75.

6

The Family Context of Home Shoe Work

BETTY A. BEACH

In parts of rural Maine, home shoe workers continue to participate in a putting-out system similar to that which characterized their industry in the nineteenth century. In common with those earlier women, whose family duties impelled their entry into shoe work, today's shoe workers choose the home as their workplace because it allows them to fulfill dual work and family responsibilities. For them, homework represents what one woman shoe worker called a "terrific option" which permitted her to work for income and to parent her children simultaneously. Although the continued existence of outwork fulfills the particular needs of employers, it also fits into the ways that such women view the world. In this chapter I will explore the meaning of family for contemporary home shoe workers by recreating the systems of understanding, the phenomenology, of a group of ordinary women who have striven under adverse economic circumstances to merge their family and work responsibilities into an integrated whole.

Outwork in the Shoe Industry

As shoe making evolved from an individual craft to mass market production in the late eighteenth and early nineteenth centuries, individual male boot makers were gradually transformed from independent artisans who created a custom product to outworking contractors. Merchant capitalists financed an expansion of production to meet increased demands for shoes in the domestic market by providing raw materials and therefore controlling profits; boot makers responded by increasing production as competitively as possible, drawing their wives and daughters into a previously exclusive male process. Between 1780 and 1810 women started working as shoe binders for male household heads, adding the sewing of uppers (considered a "natural" skill of women) to their other household duties. Generally, shoe binders worked within their kitchens or other domestic spaces while men reserved a separate workspace, often in an attached shed. Household duties were carried on simultaneously or interspersed with shoe-binding demands, a gender division of labor described in historical studies of the early Lynn, Massachusetts shoe industry.[1]

As Mary Blewett has so capably demonstrated, women's homework remained a part of the family economy with labor and wages controlled by men. Channeling women into shoe binding devalued that part of the labor process, while men reserved the more skilled artisan processes for themselves, effectively barring women from the shoemaking craft: "The recruitment of women in shoemaking families was instead a carefully controlled assignment of work designed to fit the role of women and to maintain gender relationships in the family, while preserving the artisan training system in its social as well as its craft aspect. Women were recruited to only a small part of the work, the sewing of the upper part of the shoe, and not to the craft itself. They were barred from apprenticeships and group work and isolated from the center of artisan life: the shoe shop."[2]

Blewett and other historians of the early shoe industry have traced the special role of married women, a role in which they remained firmly tied to their family identity, accepting the lesser wages and status consistent with a subordinate, wifely role. Predictably, married women's labor continued to fuel homework production even after men entered the shoe factory, followed soon by single women. In 1910 Edith Abbott noted this enduring cultural preference for homework among married women and widows who "preferred work which could be done in their own homes and could be neglected when household cares were pressing. Other women who could not 'be spared' at home or those who still cherished a social prejudice against 'factory hands' also preferred homework to mill work."[3]

Throughout the first half of the nineteenth century, outwork in the shoe industry increased, employing more Massachusetts women than textile factories did. Shoes were shipped for work not only to area coastal towns and to Massachusetts and New Hampshire farms but also to numerous rural Maine towns. Such extensive outwork established a precedent in the shoe industry, a precedent which obviously meshed with manufacturer's needs for a cheaper, elastic, and more tractable labor force capable of responding to the shoe industry's seasonal and market fluctuations. In return, homeworkers in rural areas augmented their farming production with wages from shoe work, particularly important in "declining agricultural regions" of Maine and New Hampshire, where "the putting out system blended nicely with traditional employment . . . (permitting) the outworker and his family to remain on the land and supplement their income from farming with wages from shoemaking."[4]

Indigenous shoe industries springing up in rural Maine continued the outwork tradition. G. H. Bass, a central Maine shoe firm that employed homeworkers until quite recently, noted its own early involvement with outwork in a company history: "Stitching was now [in 1887 after a decade of expansion] mechanized, as well as pegging, edge trimming and bottom finishing. But in spite of this indication of mechanized progress, examples of informal and individualized production still lingered on. Several farmers in the area supplemented their income by having shoe parts brought to their homes for hand sewing by members of their families, and many concessions could still be made to the idiosyncrasies of independent minded workers."[5]

Whether native or imported, small Maine shoe shop operations proliferated abundantly during the latter half of the nineteenth century. Integral to this proliferation was the putting out of shoe uppers to be sewn at home. Home labor thus accompanied the development of a major industry in an agricultural state, providing a distinctive cultural context for homework.

This heritage of outwork in the shoe industry directly affects contemporary homeworkers who labor at procedures commonly located in the shoe shop itself. Never banned by reform legislation of the 1930s, which effectively eliminated homework in many traditional women's industries, homework in the shoe industry retained its links with the past. Throughout the twentieth century, married women with young children worked at home, sewing uppers just like their historical predecessors, performing work remarkably similar in form and content. They assemble the pieces of leather on the upper part of the shoe, operating industrial weight machines (resembling large sewing machines) supplied by the factory. They also may perform "lacing," the sewing of prepunched holes with needle and waxed thread by hand. A second group of homeworkers consists of "hand sewers"—the highest skill level, most akin to craftsperson status. Once a male preserve in a trade that early divided along gender lines (with men bottoming or attaching the sole to the shoe while women sewed uppers), hand sewers now include women. They employ the traditional tools of the old time cordwainer or boot maker: awl, needle, thread, lasts, clamps, and cobbler's bench.

Although cash wages are now paid directly to the laborer, ties with the family role persist, setting forth a family context which infuses the work experience. This family context remains a powerful motivator and support for women, functioning in both ideological and pragmatic ways. As we shall see, family needs motivated women to undertake homework, family support sustained the work style, and families shared in the benefits of such work.

Present-day homework occurs, it must be emphasized, in a once prominent but now declining shoe industry. Long a principal in the Maine economy, shoe manufacture is diminishing as foreign imports increase. In 1986 slightly over ten thousand workers produced shoes in Maine, 62 percent of them women. The average shoe worker earned $5.88 an hour.[6] Wages in the shoe industry reflect the low income status of rural Maine. Census data published in 1983 (the time of this study) indicated that the state of Maine ranked forty-sixth in median household income, with the two counties contributing participants to this study ranked below the state median with incomes of $11,830 and $13,500.[7] While the decline in shoe manufacture squeezes a traditional source of employment for unskilled and semiskilled workers, opportunities for homework still exist. Some manufacturers continue to use homework as an integral part of the labor process, while others use it to meet fluctuation in contracts. Additionally, a current resurgence in hand-sewn shoe production may increase homework opportunities.

Methods and Mechanics

In 1983 I interviewed seven past and present at-home shoe workers, using a semistructured questionnaire developed for the purpose. Interviews occurred in their homes, lasting about one-and-a-half hours per subject. I took extensive notes and transcribed them immediately to improve reliability. I located participants with the snowball method; I asked each to suggest names of other home workers. In addition, I interviewed four supervisors of at-home workers in an effort to "triangulate," or cross-verify, data obtained.[8] Supervisors agreed that homeworkers generally exceeded in-shop production, that family members frequently assisted in the work, and that they were a highly motivated group which worked well without direct supervision. These supervisors also recollected that most homeworkers were mothers who preferred to be home with their children, a motivation also expressed by the homeworkers themselves. Of course, despite supervisors' and participants' observations that home shoe workers were predominantly mothers of young children motivated by family needs, it is possible that other categories of workers exist who might display different motivations and perceptions. This study does not attempt to generalize to a random sample but instead chooses to focus on the family linkages considered significant by women who were interviewed. All excerpted quotes derive from these interviews.

Homeworking participants in this study worked for four different companies, several stitchers working simultaneously or sequentially for more than one company. Variations existed among companies, one of which has since shut down due to the competing flood of shoe imports. One company put out all its handsewing to about 120 hand-sewers, treating them essentially as independent contractors. The other companies put out machine sewing or lacing, generally treating their homeworkers like factory workers, providing identical wages and benefits. The only exception was lay-off: in the predictable seasonal and market fluctuations of the shoe industry, homeworkers were laid off first. All workers reported they made equal or superior wages to factory employment, working on a piece-rate basis (although one company experimented with hourly wages on an honor system).

For stitchers, factories supplied and repaired machines, and paid a portion of the electric bill. Factories also provided all materials, delivering and picking up once or twice weekly at the stitchers' homes. Hand sewers, though, brought in and picked up their own shoes, often pooling cooperatively to take turns delivering. All workers designated their own amounts of work, above a minimum, and often varied their work load depending on other demands for their time.

Most women hired as homeworkers had worked previously in a shoe shop, establishing a prior record as a capable employee. All could still work in the shop but voluntarily chose to work at home instead. No one was unconnected to the shoe industry; all women were either former employees or wives or daughters of present shoe workers. Floor bosses approached some women or their husbands, asking if they'd like to work at home, while other women heard about the opportunity and sought it out. Employer motivations for initiating homework varied, although it clearly meshed with needs of their own. One supervisor cited a lack of experienced factory stitchers and insufficient factory space at a time of increased production demands, seeing homework as an ideal solution. Another mentioned the recurrent problem of seasonal fluctuation in shoe production in which homeworkers represented an elastic labor force. The first workers laid off in hard times, homeworkers were also given opportunities at factory openings, an option declined by most women. Finally, one supervisor recognized the potential labor pool of mothers. To capture the labor of women with school-aged children, her factory, long a family-owned firm, of-fered "mothers' hours" work shifts and summers off; homework was a natural extension of this effort.

I analyzed the interview data from homeworkers and supervisors thematically, following the method of Glaser and Strauss.[9] Family emerged repeatedly as the dominant theme running throughout these interviews. It was intimately intertwined with work experience, as might be expected given our knowledge of previous generations of home shoe-working women.

Results: The Family Context of Home Shoework

The overwhelmingly compelling reason to work at home is family: "Once you have children, they should come first. This option offered time for your kids and the chance to work—it was terrific"; "I didn't have my kids to have somebody else bring them up. . . . Someone else would get the benefit of seeing my kids' cute things—first steps, words . . ."; "Kids need a parent. . . . I don't think kids should be left on their own. Babysitters can give care, but mother's touches are missing."

All respondents cited the importance of being a parent as their prime motivation for choosing homework, perceiving the opportunity to earn wages while caring for one's own children to be an ideal combination. Some expressed negative views of day care but most described a pos-itive sense of mothering their own children, whether their children were of tender age or teenaged (when they needed even more super-vision, according to the two mothers of teenagers). All workers inter-viewed had previous out-of-the-home experience, primarily in shoe shops but also in other service jobs, and thus had a concrete under-standing of the alternatives. Their family motivations, though perhaps culturally rooted, were not merely abstract expectations of proper roles but had been tested against the "real" work world.

All participants recalled that homework had been especially ap-pealing to women with young children, a perception borne out by supervisors who confirmed that homeworkers were parents of young or school-aged children. Besides child care duties, all women acknowl-edged being principally responsible for housework—responsibilities to which they added wage labor. Most women worked six to ten hours of piece work daily, five to seven days a week in the busy season (weekend work was not popular but was usually accepted and com-pleted by Monday morning during rush times). During slow times, they worked fewer hours, chose not to work, or accepted lay off for several weeks.

Not only did these women invest tremendous energy in maintaining their family and wage earner roles, but they contributed further to the family economy in other ways: four held *additional* part-time jobs (store cashier, day care provider, cafeteria worker, foster parent) and the remaining three contributed substantially to the family economy through farm labor, raising and preserving the bulk of the family's food supply, and/or sewing their family's clothes. These were heavy work loads of wage/household labor/child care/additional wage or labor contributions to the family economy. Women handled the demands by interspersing duties. The schedule of one admittedly busy and hard-working woman who also provided day care for five children reveals how shoe work fit into household and family activities:

5:00 A.M.	Get up, get some housework done
6:00	Babysitting children start arriving, get them settled, get own family up and ready for school and work, clean up dishes
8:30 to 11:00	Sew shoes while also diapering, feeding, attending to children (Mrs. E worked in her living room and set up playpens for the children to spend the morning in)
11:00 to 12:00 P.M.	Prepare lunch (husband home), feed and diaper children. Prepare them for nap, do dishes
12:00 to 2:30	Work on shoes uninterruptedly. (She described this as her "own time")
3:00	Greet her own children returning from school, prepare day care children for going home, prepare supper
Evenings	"The evenings looked good by comparison; I could just sew on shoes all evening."

Beyond this basic schedule, Mrs. E also worked on weekends when there was work available: "I was working all the time. I was sewing all the time. There are times when I felt I was born with a needle in my hand." It was her practice to accept whatever work was offered to earn extra money ("If work was there, I took it"). At her busiest, she laced twenty-four cases of shoes per day (roughly eleven hours of work daily), extending into nights and weekends.

Another homeworker's more typical schedule reflected this interposing of work and household duties: She began lacing around 1:00 P.M. Although she would have preferred to work straight through to finish the job, she found that there were "too many interruptions." Chores were interspersed with her lacing work: trying to get housework done (e.g., throwing in a load of laundry) and meeting the demands of child and husband ("It seemed like I was always doing something either for one or the other of them.") As a result, it felt like "I was always doing (lacing) constantly," that the work was never done. Generally, she stopped around 4:00 to do afternoon chores, prepare supper, wash the dishes, and get her daughter to bed; she resumed lacing around 8:00 and worked until midnight or so, depending on what she had laced earlier. She found the constancy of the work wearying; sometimes she would call the company and refuse the next day's work if she was a case or two behind. She said the company was "very good" about this.

Despite such heavy workloads, both stitchers and supervisors recollected that no one quit homework. The opportunity to fulfill parental and household responsibilities while also earning income appealed powerfully to women with young children—a motivation which helped them to interpret homework positively. Guided by a family ideology which valued mothering, homework was part of a logical package allowing women simultaneously to nurture and contribute wages to the family economy.

However, further probing indicated that "family" emerged in a context other than simply the ideological. A component of very pragmatic family support underlay the conditions of the job, a practical and significant contribution to sustaining homework. Although women were originally motivated by family ideology, ongoing involvement by children, spouses, and kin clearly buttressed the homework system. The family worked together, interacted over homework, assisted with shoe work tasks, and redistributed household duties. Thus, "family" functioned both abstractly as a guiding ideology and concretely as a pragmatic support. Such a linkage between the ideological and the practical assisted women in interpreting homework favorably.

Husbands played a subtle yet crucial role in sustaining the homework process. Five of the seven husbands were shoe workers themselves, lending a commonality to their wives' work. Husbands so employed were directly and explicitly involved in their wives' work in both logistical and productive ways: Mrs. Q's husband worked for Shiretown Shoe Company. He would take time from work to pick up, lug, and then return her own work. He was also frequently contacted to bring special instructions for new designs or work loads to her and also represented her to the shop when she had special equipment needs or repair parts to obtain for her machine. Further, he also helped her with lacing at night when she needed assistance.

Another woman whose husband was also employed at a shoeshop. He picked up, delivered, and returned all cases for her, usually at the noon hour, as well as handling details at the shop. On the infrequent occasions when she fell behind or was overwhelmed, he helped her lace shoes at night. When they worked together like this, they would "fool around" about her work: she would "sputter" about the difficulty of the particular model or the price paid, and he would discuss how fast the girls in the shop could get that model done. Sometimes she and her husband would compete and race to see who could finish lacing first. Her husband had never been a piece worker, and she felt this gave him a biased view of the work. She described this friendly rivalry as a way of "letting off steam" at home that couldn't be done in the shop, that home "had a more relaxed atmosphere" for complaints than the shop did.

One of the women interviewed clearly worked as a partner with her husband, a skilled hand sewer who sews for a large moccasin company. Though she was trained as a hand sewer at another company seventeen years ago, she spent only one year in the factory. She considered her husband to be the more skilled hand sewer, but they worked together, sharing the same labor process. Both also held additional outside jobs: Mrs. D's work schedule was dependent on the school year. Employed as a school cafeteria aide from 7:00 A.M. until 1:00 P.M. she then came home to sew for a few hours before supper. Her husband did the bulk of the sewing, coming home from his garbage route at 2:00 and sitting down to sew five or six pairs before supper. After eating, he then sewed for the rest of the evening while watching television. On Mondays (non–garbage route days), he sewed throughout the day. Mrs. D said that her husband "loves hand sewing," that it was "very relaxing" to him. The work was not explicitly divided up, as both husband and wife shared all aspects of the labor. However, after completing his own evening's work, her husband usually set up work for her for the next morning.

This couple functioned more as an explicit production team than as a husband helping with his wife's work. Their model recalls the historical image of the shoe maker's family except that there is no gender division of labor. This resemblance extended to their workspace: they maintained a small separate room within their house to work in. In this room sat the prototypical cobbler's bench, leather-working tools, pails for soaking uppers, piles of lasted moccasins and cases of completed shoes—all undoubtedly familiar to an eighteenth-century boot maker, with the exception of the television set in the corner. Also like the prefactory shoe workers, all work and pay was in the husband's name. He was the hand sewer employed by Graff's—the one person who went to the factory to demonstrate his hand-sewing skills in order to be hired (his only visit to the factory or contact with its management). Thus, through Mr. D's efforts his wife became involved in the homework arrangement, though officially all work was done in her husband's name and with his quality control. Graff's tacitly recognized this participation by asking that a minimum of eight cases per week be completed *per household.*

This pair of handsewers, however, was the exception, possibly due to the skilled nature of their work. Most husbands functioned primarily in the support role as factory liaisons. Their importance in that role is ironically underscored by the one stitcher who frequently disliked homework and gratefully accepted lay-off when it came; her husband refused her any assistance, failing to offer any of the pragmatic help contributed by other husbands. Mrs. N described herself as being responsible for all the housework and child care. Even though her husband was unemployed when she started working, "he never helped me do a single shoe," nor would he help with any housework or child care. She characterized his attitude about shoes as "poor," seeing that her work took time away from him. Later her husband obtained employment at one of the shoe shops, and when he came home from work, he refused to help her with lacing because he felt he had already spent the day working on shoes.

Beyond assisting directly with work or acting as liaisons, husbands contributed to the family context of shoe work in other important ways. Although blue-collar families are stereotypically described as maintaining rigid sex role divisions, six of the women reported that their husbands assumed housework and child care responsibilities. Mrs. Q and her husband agreed that in addition to his nightly assistance with the shoework, he also did housework and dishes—the evening chores that needed doing while she was downstairs stitching. He readily admitted that she was "all tied up" all night and couldn't go out or get anything else done.

Another wife acknowledged that beyond lugging all the cases back and forth and actually helping her with her work when she fell behind, her husband helped in the house as well. She described him as accommodating: "He put up with a lot." That is, he put up with the inconveniences of her work at home and her sometimes self-described grumpy temperament. Though she retained overall household responsibility, he helped start meals, clear the table, start baths, and other such tasks. She mentioned that at one point he had looked seriously into getting her a dishwasher. She felt that "he always tried to meet me halfway . . ." Husbands also provided a link to the larger social world of the factory. They brought home gossip and stories, discussed new models or work loads, examined personnel crises, and brought their wives in to make social visits at the shop. One husband, employed as a shoe model patterner, made frequent trips to factories in nearby towns, and his wife would "get out for a ride" with shoes and day care kids in tow, working on shoes enroute in the car.

Husbands were not the only family members involved in shoe work. Children participated as well, though in ways which were often subtler and required patient questioning to discover. *All* women reported working in the presence of their children, with abundant opportunity for children to observe and ask questions about their work. One woman described a typical setting with her two-year-old child at her side: she worked in the living room, in a chair with the shoes piled at her side. Prior to starting, she set Karen up with toys at her side as well. Her daughter did not nap in the afternoon but played by her mother's side as she laced.

Other mothers reported work spaces in the midst of their households, usually in the kitchen or living room. For example, another woman performed most of her work in the kitchen. When her twin boys were small, she moved into the bedroom because that was the only room with a door that could be closed, thus enabling her to keep an eye on her sons while she worked. Essentially, the kitchen was her work place, and cases were stacked adjacent to her machine. Occasionally in the evening she worked in the living room, doing nonmachine tasks: cutting strings, packing, etc.

By contrast, Mrs. E's work space was in her living room, where she could also watch over children in playpens. She set up her own assembly line for efficiency, calling it her "production assembly," on her living-room sofa. She held the actual shoe she was working on in her lap, placed the shears on the sofa arm, a block of beeswax on sofa arm or side table, and the case of shoes, bag of elastics, and refuse bags at her feet; thus, "I could grab what was needed without looking." She worked steadily and always tried to complete a case rather than stopping part way through. Completed cases were stacked in the living room or, if they were to be picked up for return right away, in the kitchen.

Thus for most preschool and school-aged children, their mother's work was a constant and familiar presence. Although cognitive-developmental theory suggests that such concrete intimacy with work equipment would engender more work-related knowledge in children, mothers initially were unable to recall specific instances of their children's interest in work; apparently the blending of work and family life, space and time made such distinctions difficult. Ultimately, they recalled incidents which suggested that children were actively aware of the work and intermittently joined in labor. Mrs. J's children knew the names of some of the procedures she performed. Specifically, she mentioned "paper dolls" in which pieces are linked together by thread which needs to be cut between each individual piece. At times the kids would cut the threads between the paper dolls for her and in rush times she paid them ten cents a case to do so. Mrs. E's children not only saw her working but also displayed interest in what she did. Her older daughter often asked to help, so "we'd let her fool around with it to get the feel of what it is like." With both daughters, she looked at and talked about the individual patterns of different shoes, pieced them together like puzzles, examined the hole punches, and generally discussed procedures. Further, both daughters were casually asked to help: "Gee, Kate, hand mama something from that case box," or "Would you get me that piece that fell under the sofa?" and other requests for simple tasks. Both girls also learned not to stand too near while Mom was lacing with the needle, and they learned through observation why some shoe patterns were difficult to do. Occasionally, her kids complained about shoes, but on the whole they were good about it; they knew the extra income helped out the family and they also learned to ignore Mom's "grouchiness and tiredness" because they saw how hard she worked.

A third woman recalled that her children helped her cut strings; they wanted to help even before they were big enough to use conventional scissors, so she went out and bought them blunt-ended scissors to do the job. They also helped her with lugging, unloading, and loading (one son present during part of the interview said, "I could take *two* cases!"). Not only were her children present during her work, but she also recalled casually including them in various ways, reciting a memory of teaching her youngest daughter to count using a number of pieces of a particular shoe.

While younger children observed tools and procedures of their mothers' work, occasionally undertaking simple chores, older children expressed explicit interest in working and undertook regular tasks. Mrs. D's son helped lug the heavy cases and also expressed interest in sewing. At one point he wanted to learn, so they let him start out with prepunched shoes (not wanting to send any amateur handsewn efforts out under their own names) and he tried but subsequently lost interest. Their daughter threaded needles for them in the evening—a time-consuming task helpful to have done. Both children, of course, were regularly around when sewing occurred, particularly when Mr. D sewed in the evening while the family watched TV and talked. One other stitcher got her married daughter interested in home work. Their two machines were set up side by side in the mother's home, and each received her separate work assignments from the delivery truck. Each evening, the daughter left her small child in her husband's care to join her mother in stitching.

Beyond direct involvement in shoe work, children, like husbands, undertook more household responsibilities. Older children cared for younger ones, cleared tables, did dishes, and assisted with chores needing completion. Although all women accepted overall responsibility for household functioning, they readily listed tasks performed by husbands and children, underscoring that it was a family undertaking. One woman emphasized that this was a "family unit," (another described her work as a "family project") and there was no room for traditional "girls' tasks" and "boys' tasks"—"everyone had to pitch in."

One family involved their teenaged children in yet another way: participation in family financial planning. Women unanimously reported their work income as being for "extras" to benefit the family. (One woman translated "extras" to mean that her children could have Nikes and Levis rather than discount store clothes). Children were often the beneficiaries of these extras and were involved in decisions on family purchases. Mrs. D described her children's involvement in such a way: "They see the income and where the bills are." Her son had "pestered" them for a trail bike until he sat down with them and saw that it was financially impossible. Such involvement—no one reported spending money just on herself—further reveals homework as a crucial component of the family economy.

Family context played one other critical role in supporting the success of the homework effort. All women reported frequent interaction with kin in the area, describing themselves as coming from close families. Daily visits, phone chats, and drop-ins by family members and close friends may have provided the socialization outlet commonly ascribed to the work place. Several homeworkers described hooking telephones over their shoulders for lengthy chats "without breaking the rhythm of your work." Trips and visits with parents and siblings also occurred: "In the summer I could take work out in the yard, or visit a friend, or go to mother's and bring my boxes with me." Another woman reserved Friday mornings for shopping trips with her mother and delayed the start of work until late afternoon. Mothers and sisters particularly helped with child care when work demands increased. Two women solicited family members to undertake home stitching, and they often got together to work. One woman recalled that she and her sister did all the French cord work for one particular factory while working at home.

Drop-in visits by family and friends were frequent (several occurred while I was interviewing). One woman reported that family members often pitched in to help when she was "buried" with shoes. Most found it possible to socialize and work at the same time; friends coming to visit accepted that sewing was going on; "It doesn't bother them." A hand-sewing husband was a selectman and thus frequently people dropped by to discuss problems or politics while he was sewing. One stitcher expressed resentment that stitching sometimes got in the way of preferred family activities, but most stitchers maintained that family needs came first and that work could be put aside to meet those needs. Frequently, they cited instances of turning down or rescheduling work in order to participate in events impossible for conventionally employed parents to join in: help out in a classroom project, attend a school pageant, enjoy an unscheduled family outing on a beautiful day.

Despite objective indicators of often heavy workloads, all women emphasized their perceived autonomy—freedom to be available to their children and larger families, to arrange their work schedules, to work "without having a boss hanging over your shoulder," to put work aside and go for a walk whenever you feel "flustrated [sic]." All reported refusing to work as well, calling the factory to turn down the next day's work for reasons of their own—reasons they said were readily accepted by the company. Two women said they turned down all summer work in order to go to camp with their families, both regularly resuming work in the fall.

Though family needs or responsibilities typically prompted work refusals, women phrased this as an exercise in autonomy. They perceived themselves as having power to organize their lives in ways important to them rather than allowing work demands to structure, routinize, and overwhelm their lives. This perception of autonomy derived from two sources: positively, from the experience of responding to demonstrated family needs and, negatively, from comparison with prior factory experiences. "I was free to do as I wanted." Being one's own boss, setting one's own schedule, and being free from the heat and discomfort of the shop all represented advantages of homework. As one woman put it, compared with factory work, "home work I prefer 100 percent." When employed in the factory doing hand sewing on a piece-work basis, Mrs. D typically drove herself to produce more, making herself constantly "tense" from the pace of factory demands and the push to do "more, more, more." At home, she felt far more relaxed without the factory pressure: "I like to work at my own pace,

I don't feel any pressure." She also remembers how physically uncomfortable the shop was, and hot in the summer. Overall, she felt her production was higher now because she's "happier with her work" and doesn't "resent having to get up at 5:30 and go to work."

This perception of autonomy was echoed by one of the supervisors, who theorized that homeworkers were a "different" lot who preferred not having to work with others. Many of them, she remembered, had frequent conflicts with fellow factory workers when they worked there: they were adamant about where they'd sit, who could use their machines, and their general likes and dislikes. All of them worked successfully at home without any real supervision, displaying high degrees of independence in doing so. Objectively, these women lacked the autonomy enjoyed by a wealthy individual or by the owner of a shoe factory. Their perceived autonomy was clearly relative to their alternatives: segregating rather than integrating work and family, putting children in day care to work in an often uncomfortable and (to their minds) uncongenial setting, working with a boss hanging over your shoulder, feeling tension to keep up the pace. Studies of work satisfaction consistently pinpoint autonomy as a key variable affecting workers' job gratification, whether autonomy translates to control over corporate policy or the simple control over schedule represented by flextime. Homeworkers, while not objectively autonomous, expressed aspects of that sense of autonomy in their self-perceptions, especially when comparing homework to previous factory experiences.

Phenomenologically, these women perceived shoe homework in a favorable light. They were realistic, mentioning disadvantages such as the often unpleasant stink of leather pervading the home and the sometimes wearying work. Nor did they disregard the larger economic reality of limited work opportunities for rural women in low income areas. As the husband of a home knitter stated in another set of interviews:

> It's [having a career] very attractive if you are well educated, a professional woman who can go and take an office job where they start at $20,000 and the only way is up, you know, where within 5 years they own their own business—it sounds very good in *Cosmopolitan* magazine, but for the average housewife in a rural area in the state of Maine, you're talking ludicrous. You're talking, what would you rather do, cook and wash and look after the kids at home or would you like to go in the shoeshop? You have the choice.[10]

Although mindful of economic realities, homeworkers judged advantages to outweigh drawbacks. Part of this phenomenology emanated from ideology about family roles and part from pragmatic sources of support. They perceived the opportunity to integrate rather than segregate work and family life of overriding importance, a logical blending rather than the forced choice of work or family which confronts most women. Expressive as they were about the primacy of family in motivating home work, many supporting factors contributed to sustaining this work style: preferences for work autonomy, support from husbands and children, interaction with kin networks, and a historical tradition supporting homework in the shoe industry. For most women workers, a gulf separates work life from family life. For these women, integration of work and family life occurred in tangible ways. They saw the interspersing child care/household labor/wage labor throughout the day as a natural daily routine enabling them to allocate time and energy where they most felt the need. Valuing family life quite expressly (and disdaining factory employment options which clearly were available), these women saw homework as a desirable choice, one consonant with their perceptions and supported in pragmatic ways by their families. As such, their choices illustrate what anthropologist Micaela di Leonardo described as the "shifting but always symbiotic nature of women's household and workplace labor."[11]

NOTES

1. Mary Blewett, "Work, Gender and the Artisan Tradition in New England Shoemaking, 1789–1860," *Journal of Social History* 17 (Winter 1983): 221–48; Alan Dawley, *Class and Community: The Industrial Revolution in Lynn* (Cambridge: Harvard University Press, 1976); Paul Faler, *Mechanics and Manufacturers in the Early Industrial Revolution: Lynn, Massachusetts, 1780–1860.* (Albany: State University of New York Press, 1981).

2. Blewett, "Work, Gender and the Artisan Tradition," p. 224.

3. Edith Abbott, *Women in Industry* (New York: D. Appleton, 1910), p. 160.

4. Faler, *Mechanics and Manufacturers,* p. 223.

5. Streeter Bass, *G. H. Bass Company, 1876–1976* (Wilton, Maine: n. p. 1976).

6. Maine Department of Labor, Division of Economic Analysis and Research, verbal communication to author, February 17, 1987.

7. U.S. Bureau of the Census, *1980 Census of Population,* vol. 1, *Characteristics of the Population,* Chapter C, "General Social and Economic Characteristics, Part 21, Maine," (Washington, D.C.: GPO, 1983).

8. Egon Guba, "Criteria for Assessing the Trustworthiness of Naturalistic Inquiries," *Educational Communication and Technology Journal* 29 (1981): 75–91.

9. Barney Glaser and Anselm Strauss, *The Discovery of Grounded Theory* (New York: Aldine, 1967).

10. Betty Beach, "Working At Home: Family Life/Work Life," *Dissertation Abstracts International* (Ann Arbor: University Microfilms #8520649, 1985), pp. 81–82.

11. Micaela di Leonardo, "Women's Work, Work Culture, and Consciousness (An Introduction)," *Feminist Studies* 11 Fall 1985: 491–95.

7

Electronics Subassemblers in Central New York: Nontraditional Homeworkers in a Nontraditional Homework Industry

JAMIE FARICELLIA DANGLER

Lynn Brown found herself at odds with the state of New York in an effort to save her home-based job.[1] As the result of a state crackdown on industrial homeworking that began in 1981, she and hundreds of other homeworkers in central New York began to lose their jobs. Since then, the legal battle between the state labor department and homework distributors has raged on. Should an existing law, written in the 1940s primarily for the garment industry, be applied to Mrs. Brown's work building transformers for electronics firms?

The controversy in central New York exemplifies the issues being raised on a national scale in debates over modern-day homeworking. Is homeworking in "new" industries like electronics different from the exploitative homeworking of old? Does the employment of working and middle-class women, who have greater alternatives and more varied workplace experience than urban immigrants had, ensure against exploitation? What is at the root of the increase in women who claim that they "choose" or "prefer" to do homeworking as opposed to outside work? In an attempt to make sense of these questions, I have tried to analyze the different experiences of "traditional" and "non-traditional" homeworkers.

Recent trends indicate a steady increase in the diversity of industries that have begun to convert factory- and office-based work into home-based work. The deregulation of traditional homework activities has set the stage for the continued expansion of home-based work in a range of occupations. Accordingly, we must move beyond the narrow perception of homeworking as an exceptional phenomenon characteristic of needlework industries in order to see how it has become a viable and attractive production option for many capitalist enterprises and how the ongoing decentralization of production over the past few decades has provided a new impetus for the expansion of such work. By identifying these trends and understanding the increasing attractiveness of homeworking to employers seeking to lower wage and benefit levels, reduce overhead costs, and decrease worker bargaining power, we can more fully comprehend the motivations behind and implications of the Reagan administration's effort to lift existing homework bans. Furthermore, to understand the scope of the impact this deregulation will have on women workers, we must acknowledge the broad base of people who are prime targets for recruitment into such work. Thus, in addition to documenting the diversity of industries expanding their use of home-based workers, I will challenge the typical characterization of homework as an urban phenomenon which relies mainly on the use of immigrant labor. Instead, I will demonstrate the extent to which the labor of rural or suburban, nonimmigrant, working- and middle-class workers is coming to fuel the expansion of homework in the modern economy. Particular consideration will be given to electronics industry homeworkers in central New York. The experiences of these workers (i.e., wages, working conditions, labor market position, etc.) will be compared to those of more traditional homeworkers (i.e., urban immigrants).

This essay will incorporate data from personal interviews I conducted between October, 1983, and August, 1986. I completed in-depth interviews with thirty-nine homeworkers (thirty-six women and three men), five homework distributors, three managers from firms employing homeworkers, and a number of labor department officials and lawyers representing homeworkers in pending court cases. In addition to the thirty-nine completed interviews with homeworkers, I conducted short telephone interviews with another twenty-five homeworkers. All respondents, most of whom live within a hundred-mile radius of Syracuse, New York, were involved with homeworking in the electronics industry, though some had homework experiences in other industries as well.

Homework in the Modern U.S. Economy

The written history of homeworking in the U.S. has focused mainly on its use in needleworking industries from the turn of the century until the 1940s, when homework regulation was first adopted on a national scale under the Fair Labor Standards Act. It is a history of urban immigrants, both women and children, working in squalid conditions for long hours and at low wages. The apparent resurgence of interest in homeworking in the 1980s was sparked not only by the disclosure of its persistence in traditional industries such as garment making, but also by a series of reports issued in the early 1980s, which estimated that thousands of illegal homeworkers are employed in the garment industry in Los Angeles and New York City. In addition, labor departments in states such as New Jersey and Illinois report the existence of homework production.[2] Studies in the late eighties also showed an increase in homework in the information-processing and electronics industries. The growth of telecommuting (the movement of professional and clerical computer-based work into the home) and the discovery of extensive electronics homework operations by immigrant women in Silicon Valley, California, the region of high technology concentration in the South Bay area, have stimulated a reconsideration of traditional conceptions of home-based work.[3] No longer can homeworking be seen simply as a past chapter in the history of American workers' fight for decent employment—a chapter thought to be revisited only in isolated and unusual circumstances. Instead, it must be recognized as a viable and expanding production option for modern capitalist enterprise.

While information regarding the use of homeworkers has been limited for the most part to garment making, telecommuting, and electronics production in Silicon Valley, newly emerging studies indicate that these industries are not merely exceptional cases. Instead, home-based work is surfacing in a range of diverse industries. One way to begin uncovering the extent of homeworking in the U.S. is to examine records of legal homework permits in states that have adopted some form of homework regulation.[4] Some states, such as New Jersey and Illinois, prohibit homework in certain industries.[5] Employers in industries not singled out by these laws may hire homeworkers after obtaining special homework permits. In New York state, on the other hand, while industrial homework is prohibited in all industries, workers who are elderly, disabled, or obliged to care for invalids are exempt from this ban as long as they obtain special permits. Accordingly, legal homework operations can be maintained by following the particular permit procedures valid in each state with homework regulations. Available information about the distribution of homework permits in New York, Pennsylvania, and Illinois shows the use of homeworkers for the production of items such as toys, gloves, rugs, jewelry boxes, hand-decorated novelties, pens and pencils, book bindings, leather goods, wigs, suspenders, and luggage tags. Homework permits have also been issued for electronics assembly and the packaging of a wide range of products. In Fulton County, New York, an entire glove industry has been sustained since the 1950s with the use of homeworkers who have been issued permits because of age or disability.

Given the diversity of industries that have gone through legal channels to secure the right to hire homeworkers, it seems plausible to conclude that many other firms may simply avoid state regulation of their activities by hiring homeworkers illegally. At the very least, however, examination of these legal homework operations demonstrates the viability of this type of work for a diversity of operations. Thus, while needleworking industries may be unique in their use of homeworking as a relatively permanent production arrangement, the fact that this type of work has been used for varying amounts of time in numerous industries (perhaps seasonally, cyclically, or during the early stages of a product's life cycle) lends support to the conclusion that it has been a relatively permanent feature of the capitalist production process.

More convincing evidence to substantiate the viability and recent growth of homework is the recent discovery of illegal homework activities in an even broader array of industries. Much of the evidence has been sketchy and incomplete—derived largely from anecdotal accounts of new home-based businesses in articles lauding the new economic opportunities such work can bring to housewives. A recent article applauding the spread of home-based work in rural America explains that homework industries "run the gamut, from gourmet fudge to computer services, to arts and crafts." The author highlights the success of a rural "cottage business" in which 150 home-based workers sew appliqued designs on jogging suits for a company that expected its sales to reach $3.5 million by the end of 1986.[6] Like this article, most accounts of home-based work found in popular journals and magazines seem to focus on the use of homeworkers by small regional or national firms, many of which have been started by women who build their businesses with homework labor from the start. As such, homeworking has been portrayed as the new innovation for would-be women entrepreneurs—a unique way to break into the business world. But the spread of homeworking is by no means confined to women in the small business sector. Not only regional and national, but multinational firms have expanded their use of homeworkers in recent years.

Interviews I conducted with homeworkers in central New York revealed the home-based assembly and finishing of products for multinational firms such as IBM, Ford, Magnavox, Kodak, and Squibb. In the case of IBM and Ford, a small local firm served as subcontractor to the corporation and organized the homework activities. Magnavox recruited a local distributor (either a company employee or a person from the local community) to serve as middleman between the firm and its homeworkers.[7] Among the items produced by homeworkers in New York State were subcomponents for electrical devices (transformers, coils, circuit boards), electrical distribution units, automobile dashboard plates, dental floss, and fishing line. In addition, some homeworkers did painting and decal work on products such as air conditioners, clocks, tennis rackets, and various electronic devices, while others tested the performance of electrical instruments. Finally, some central New York homeworkers had experience in home-based craft work (one woman assembled dolls for a Florida firm), drafting, and touching up photos. While the information obtained through these personal interviews cannot reveal the true magnitude of homework in central New York (e.g., the actual numbers of homeworkers employed), it helps us to draw a preliminary picture of the scope of homework activities. In addition to the information I obtained, a Syracuse lawyer representing a homework distributor whose operations were closed down by the state labor department reported discovering, in the area between Rochester and Utica, sixty-seven firms that employed homeworkers.[8]

Various companies offer homework opportunities through the mail.[9] One electronics firm located in Florida offers workers the opportunity to assemble circuit boards in their homes. A brief assembly course and all component parts are mailed to the worker, who receives payment for each assembled circuit board mailed back. I found information about homework for this firm in a special catalog of home income opportunities produced by an agency called American Lifestyle, Inc. After warning those reading the catalog that "any person using the information in the following pages does so at her/his own risk," the brochure provides information on a variety of homework opportunities, including electronics assembly, screen printing, rubber stamp making, woodworking, photo retouching, flower making, handpainting novelty items, typing, and a variety of jobs in sales and marketing. As incomplete as it may be, such evidence clearly indicates that homeworking constitutes a viable option for labor-intensive production in a range of businesses in the modern economy.

To understand the significance of the spread of homeworking over the past few decades, we must realize that it is by no means a development unique to the United States. The increasing tendency for capitalist enterprises to expand their use of homeworkers around the world has been documented by research in both First and Third World countries. A series of studies done in Britain in the mid-1970s played a large role in drawing attention to the fact that what was typically seen as an anachronism in the modern economy has come to play a more systematic and widespread role in production. Investigations conducted by Britain's Department of Employment, trade unions, and public interest groups such as the Leicester Outwork Campaign, Low Pay Unit, and London Homeworking Group have uncovered the use of homeworkers in both blue- and white-collar occupations. Among the jobs performed by homeworkers in Britain are machine and hand sewing, knitting, toy making, box making, the manufacture of car components and transmission belts, packing and packaging, clerical work, typing, sales promotion, punch-card operating, market research, and systems analysis.[10] In other developed countries, such as Italy, France, Japan, and Australia, homeworking has been discovered in industries that range from clothing and textiles to mechanical goods and electronics.[11] In Third World countries such as India and the Philippines, homeworking in export-oriented industries has forged a link between local cottage industry establishments and multinational firms selling homeworkers' products on the world market.[12]

The expansion of industrial homework in the modern world economy can be best understood as part of the broader process of decentralization of capitalist production. Increases in various forms of subcontracting, which allow employers to increase their flexibility and lower wage, benefit, and overhead costs, has enabled corporations to dissociate themselves from a host of intermediate production processes essential to their overall operations. On a global scale, MNC's have found it more profitable to subcontract to local firms, who subcontract to middlemen, who further subcontract to petty-commodity producers or homeworkers. In this way, homeworkers can be seen as the final link in an expanding chain of subcontracting relationships.[13] Accordingly, homeworking in the U.S. must be viewed as part of these global trends in the reorganization of capitalist production, and the political movement to lift restrictions on such work in this country must be examined in this context.

Homeworkers in Central New York

While research on homeworking in Silicon Valley dispelled the myth that homework is a unique problem of the needlework industries and thus an antiquarian survival of a pervious era, it has done little to move beyond the exclusive association of this form of production with immigrant labor. Accordingly, while homeworking may no longer be seen as an exceptional phenomenon by virtue of its relegation to a specific sector of the economy, it continues to be viewed as somewhat of an aberration identified solely with the exploitation of immigrant women. In order to broaden our understanding of the viability of homeworking as a production option used under a range of nontraditional conditions in the modern economy, we must consider the new circumstances underlying its use for both clerical labor and industrial assembly operations. With regard to the latter, the situation of electronics homeworkers in central New York is instructive.

Homeworking has been used in the central New York electronics industry for at least eighteen years. Between 1969 and 1981 hundreds of rural, nonethnic, nonimmigrant, working-and middle-class women assembled basic components such as transformers, coils, and circuit boards in their homes for both national and multinational electronics firms. The only way to estimate the number of homeworkers that may have been employed in any given year is to rely on distributors' reports, which are quite imprecise. One distributor reported that she trained and employed about 300 people during her three years of organizing homework operations. Another distributor, who was in business for twelve years, claimed to have had between 150 and 200 people working for her at any one time. A third made a similar claim, while a fourth had forty-two homeworkers working for her when her operations were closed down in 1981. One of the distributors estimated that the electronics industry in central New York employed about 800 homeworkers at a time during the 1970s and into the 1980s. All of the distributors except one were former homeworkers who became middlemen between the firms and workers in order to earn more money. All of the distributors lived in the communities where they distributed homework and were often well known to homeworkers or their friends and relatives. Since the distributors handled all work and payment of wages, homeworkers had no contact with the firms. The relationship between homeworkers and their distributors was generally very congenial and most workers felt that their distributors were fair and honest. The homeworkers ranged in age from twenty-one to sixty-one. Most had two, three, or four children, one woman had eight children, two had none, and four had children who were grown and living away from home.

While many homeworkers continue to be employed in this capacity, their numbers have decreased substantially as a result of the 1981 crackdown by the New York State Department of Labor. Since that time, the labor department and homework distributors have engaged in an ongoing battle over the legality of electronics home assembly. While the state's Industrial Board of Appeals has ruled in favor of the homeworkers in cases brought against specific distributors, the labor department continues to appeal these decisions to higher levels of the judicial system. Since the controversy began, firms wary of the negative publicity and ongoing disruption of their operations have transferred most of the assembly formerly performed by New York state homeworkers to Third World countries such as India, Sri Lanka, and Haiti.[14] Thus, the future of electronics industry homeworkers in New York state remains uncertain. While the labor department continues to fight against a rising tide of national support for home-based work, the homeworkers continue to hope that the situation will be resolved in their favor so they might return to the pre-1981 security of the almost unlimited availability of homework jobs.

While there are qualitative differences between the experiences of women from central New York and immigrant and urban-based homeworkers, the conditions under which they work are very similar. The situation faced by the homeworkers I studied by no means reflects the autonomy, economic prosperity, and contentment that proponents of homeworking associate with modern-day cottage industry. Instead, the homeworking jobs found in central New York are typically a cut below the standard minimum wage jobs available for women in the larger labor market, and while homeworkers support efforts to allow them to continue their work, they do so more out of absolute necessity (i.e., a lack of alternative employment that fits their specific needs) than out of a genuine desire to do homework.

The main job of central New York homeworkers in the electronics industry is to build transformers, a basic component used in a range of electronic devices. Homeworkers are employed to wind fine, coated wires around small magnetic cores. The piece rate paid for each completed transformer varies from two cents to fifteen cents, depending on the size of the transformer and the number of times the wire has to be wound around the hole in the core. Most homeworkers earned between two cents and five cents a piece for work on cores.

As with garment industry homeworkers in cities like New York and Los Angeles and electronics industry homeworkers in Silicon Valley, the ability of a central New York homeworker to make minimum wage or above depended on how fast she was able to work. Of those interviewed, roughly half claimed that it was very difficult, if not impossible, for them to make minimum wage, while the other half seemed to have developed sufficient skill to increase their speed in order to earn more.

The lowest average wage reported by a homeworker was $1.20 an hour while the highest was $8.35 an hour. Many homeworkers expressed the belief that it took a "special kind of person," someone who could adapt well to "boring and tedious work," to be able to earn good wages doing homework. They spoke of the need to develop a rhythm in order to keep up the pace required to wind enough cores in one hour to earn minimum wage. "If you were very fast, you could almost make minimum wage, but mostly you would come up short of the minimum," explained an eleven-year veteran of electronics homework. It seems clear that in the case of central New York homeworkers, as with their urban counterparts, pressure to increase the pace and intensity of work is a normal part of trying to earn decent wages under the piece-work system.

While studies of urban homeworkers in garment making and electronics have found child labor to be an important factor in workers' ability to increase their earnings, only eight of those interviewed in central New York reported having family members help with their work. One explained that her children sometimes helped her sort wires according to size and color, while the other seven reported that their husbands helped occasionally (usually to count and trim wires). For the most part, child labor did not appear to be a significant part of these homework operations.[15]

In addition to the relative lack of child labor, the experiences of central New York homeworkers seemed to be qualitatively better than that of their urban, immigrant counterparts in a number of other ways. For example, the payment of kickbacks to homework employers for the "privilege" of receiving a homework job and the vulnerability to abuses such as sexual harassment, nonpayment of wages, and payment of phony "taxes" to employers do not appear to be a part of the experiences of these white, nonimmigrant, working-class women.[16] Furthermore, the electronics homework in central New York did not involve the use of toxic chemicals, as is frequently the case in Silicon Valley, nor were women forced to complete quotas dictated by their employers.[17]

While the working conditions in central New York homework operations appear to be better than those faced by immigrant homeworkers in urban areas, important similarities can be found when comparing the income needs, labor market position, and domestic responsibilities facing both groups. Most accounts of urban homeworkers have stressed the fact that homeworking and poverty seem to go hand in hand. For most traditional homeworkers the income earned from their activities is a primary source of financial support. Despite the characterization of new forms of home-based work as either marginal to family income (pin money) or as supplemental income provided by middle-class wives to help raise their families' discretionary spending, the situation of central New York homeworkers demonstrates the extent to which such work can be an essential component of family income that keeps many working-class families above the poverty level. Of the thirty-nine homeworkers interviewed, only six reported family incomes above $20,000 a year. The rest ranged between $10,000 and $20,000.[18] While the majority reported homework as one of two essential incomes, many emphasized that the periodic unemployment of their husbands due to lay-offs in blue-collar jobs often made their income from homeworking their only support. Only four reported that their income from homeworking was extra money used for personal luxuries. One woman summarized the economic situation facing homeworkers in her area in the following way: "Most people I know are not living the good life. They're just managing, just getting by. They don't even have enough money to take their kids to the movies. They have no savings, nothing to fall back on in an emergency. We're all just living from week to week." To illustrate the desperation of many of the homeworkers she employed, one distributor explained that she had people driving from as far as an hour and a half away every two weeks to pick up materials for work.

Many respondents related stories of how difficult it was for those who lost the opportunity to do homework to maintain decent living standards after the labor department crackdown in 1981. They explained that while some were able to get minimum-wage jobs to replace homeworking others were forced to apply for welfare or simply "make due," "get by," and "settle for much less." "I'm really not sure what they [unemployed homeworkers] are doing now," explained one woman, speaking of a friend who had such a difficult time adjusting after losing her income from homeworking that "she may have lost a baby over it." The importance of the income from this work to the maintenance of adequate living standards for central New York homeworkers clearly demonstrates the extent to which current depictions of "cottage industry" as a new source of "pin money" for well-off women seeking constructive uses for their time is mistaken. As one homeworker put it, "It's not a fun job. People who do it do it because they need the money."

The importance of homework as a source of income for central New York women living in rural areas can only be understood in the context of two related factors: the subordinate position they occupy in the local labor market (i.e., their lack of other employment options or relegation to low-wage jobs) and the subordinate position they occupy in the household economy (i.e. the fact that they bear primary responsibility for household maintenance and child care). When asked why they decided to do homework instead of outside work, all of the female respondents indicated that they needed to remain at home with their children, were unable to "afford" an outside job, or both.[19] In fact, a combination of factors relating to their labor market options, their position in the sexual division of labor in the household, and the particular conditions of rural living that placed constraints on their mobility made homeworking an attractive and practical work alternative. Simply put, given the fact that for most of these women minimum-wage jobs were the only outside jobs available (amply demonstrated by their employment histories), the cost of traveling to work from their remote residences and the cost of child care meant that working outside the home "didn't pay."[20] According to one homeworker, "It doesn't pay to work outside because of travel and overwork and the cost of child care. People making minimum wage in outside jobs are taken advantage of. When you work at home, you don't need to make minimum wage because you don't have expenses for travel, clothes, and babysitters." Most of those interviewed believed that even at wages below the minimum homeworking yielded more spendable income than minimum-wage jobs outside the home.[21]

In addition to travel and child-care problems, many of these homeworkers faced particular constraints imposed by rural life that increased the attractiveness of homeworking. Some had small farms, large garden plots, or a few farm animals which provided a major source of support and needed considerable care—care that could be provided between hours spent on homeworking. Others heated their homes in winter with wood stoves that needed constant tending.

Aside from the economic considerations that made homework a more practical alternative than outside minimum-wage jobs, some women expressed their preference for homeworking in terms of its potential to provide them with a more satisfying and dignified work experience than they could hope to get in outside jobs available to them. They spoke of the unpleasantness of working on assembly lines—of tedium, boredom, overwork, and sexual harassment. As one woman put it, "People get more abuse in the shop than they do at home." In the words of another, although electronics homework is just as tedious and boring as assembly-line work, "At least at home you can break up the boredom by doing other things in between." Once again, in the context of other available job opportunities, homeworking provided these women with comparable pay plus the added benefits of convenience, flexibility, and a sense of greater control over their work experiences.

While homeworkers in central New York expressed appreciation of the slight advantages of homework compared to their outside work options, they also had ambiguous feelings about the quality of their work lives. Most homeworkers recognized the pressure placed on them by the piece-rate system. The need to increase income caused many workers to push themselves as much as possible to increase productivity, which often caused family tensions. The following comments are indicative.

> It takes a lot of hours and time when you're doing homework. You can neglect your kids. If you work outside and your kids are in school, when you come home you can be with them. When you get behind in your homework, this takes away from your kids. At times you get angry at them when they interfere with your work.

> My husband complained if I was behind and had to do the wires at night and couldn't spend time with him.

> Doing homework was easy when my daughter was young and napping all the time. When she got older and started demanding more of my time, things were a lot harder.

Others complained of the constant isolation of working at home. "Once in a while you feel you want to get away from the kids and the house." Still, when weighing these disadvantages against the disadvantages of working in minimum-wage factory or service jobs, most women revealed their qualified preference for remaining at home. "This kind of work at home is too monotonous to do as a full-time job," explained a woman who gave up her homework job to work in hospice care for five dollars an hour. "But if I had to go back 'on the line' I might choose homework as an alternative."

Their ambiguity regarding the benefits of homeworking was also evident in workers' varying points of view concerning the role government might play in regulating this type of work. A few women expressed the belief that the state had no business at all interfering with people's right to work at home. For example, some stated their feeling that homeworkers were not taken advantage of—that even if they failed to make minimum wage and received no benefits, it was their choice to work at home. In the words of one woman, "The state shouldn't regulate what you do in your home. You know what the homework job is before you take it." In the words of another, "If homework was regulated, it wouldn't be as flexible. If we had rules like minimum wage, we might have to work a certain amount of time, or do a certain amount of work. Now we're not penalized if we can't work for a week—like if our kids get sick. With regulation there would be more pressure. Now we do what we want."

The comments of most other homeworkers, however, reflected the paradoxical nature of their relationship to the state under given circumstances. Many who said they did not want the state to get involved qualified their objections by admitting that, while their situation seemed free from abuses such as nonpayment of wages and forced quotas, the conditions faced by other homeworkers in their area might not be as good. "I don't want the state involved, but [my distributor] is fair and responsible. Maybe other distributors aren't as responsible," one woman commented. "Some distributors aren't paying good. The labor department should help there. But [my distributor] should have been left alone," said another.

While some electronics workers recognized the problems historically associated with homework in the U.S., they felt that their type of work was somehow exceptional.

> The state doesn't need to get involved out here, with the type of work we're doing. But it's probably important for them to be involved in cities because you don't know what kinds of things can go on there.

> We need some control over homeworking, but not too much. Maybe it shouldn't be allowed in the garment industry.

In general, while most of those interviewed admitted that the state might have a legitimate role in trying to curb homework abuses, their main concern was that government regulation not result in the prohibition of their work. The following comments illustrate this view.

> I wouldn't mind if the state regulated homework—for example, by making sure everyone paid their taxes. But they shouldn't stop it.

> I would like to see homeworkers get benefits, but the state shouldn't take the work away. They should leave it up to the homeworkers if they want to work this way.

> I can understand the state's concern, but I don't know why they pushed it so hard and ruined it. They could just promote it better and set up standards. They should have talked to the people involved before taking action. Keeping homework jobs here would have helped the state and the economy.

The sentiments expressed in these comments were common among respondents and reflected their anger at the fact that most of the jobs they lost after the 1981 crackdown were transferred directly overseas (a fact acknowledged by company officials). They saw the banning of homework as a step which intensified the movement of U.S. jobs to Third World countries and exacerbated an already severe unemployment problem in their communities. Accordingly, while homeworkers recognized the many disadvantages of this form of work, homework provided a vital source of income for people with few other alternatives. Economic necessity was the bottom line to most homeworkers in central New York.

Conclusion

The emergence of industrial homework in the central New York electronics industry demonstrates the viability of this type of production for modern capitalist enterprise. The conditions leading up to its use illustrate how the interaction of specific supply and demand factors (factors that could be present for a range of industries in a variety of geographic locations) can foster its adoption in the modern economy. In particular, industrial homework can become a practical production option in any industry characterized by two specific, co-existing conditions: a reliance on labor-intensive production that can be decentralized plus the availability of a ready supply of homework labor. In other words, when an industry engages in labor-intensive operations that can be easily decentralized and physically dispersed, industrial homework becomes one of many production options. In the absence of legal restrictions on homeworking (or when legal restrictions are loosely enforced), whether or not that option is chosen depends on the circumstances specific to an area or company. While in some New York State firms employers actively sought potential homeworkers, in others workers themselves began requesting to do work in their homes. What is clear, however, is that once homeworking took root in one firm, word quickly spread through the informal networks of workers and managers in the area, ultimately resulting in the adoption of homeworking in other area firms. This, in turn, caused its spread from neighborhood to neighborhood through networks of friends and relatives.

Accordingly, in addition to recognizing the significance of homework as an effective means for employers to reduce production costs and stave off worker organization, we must consider the extent to which the current spread of homeworking in places like central New York can be seen, in part, as the result of workers' response to the growing insecurity of outside employment, a desire to break away from the monotony and confinement of factory and service work, and the need to forge new work alternatives given the fact that factory and office work is organized without the needs of women in mind.

The attractiveness of homeworking to women seeking more creative solutions to the problem of their "double burden" cannot be over-emphasized. In the case of central New York workers, homeworking must be viewed simply as the best of a bad lot. While exploitative conditions remain an inevitable feature of all forms of homeworking (from rural electronics work to urban garment making, to suburban telecommuting) the apparent support for homeworking voiced by many women workers can only be understood with an eye toward the broader context of economic, social, and political powerlessness from which women make the choice to become homeworkers. In the absence of structural changes that would allow women to participate in more full and meaningful work experiences (changes such as alterations in the sexual division of labor in the household, an end to discrimination against women in the labor market, establishment of flexible work time for all workers, and provision of high-quality, low-cost child care), the resurgence of homework in the modern economy promises to con-tribute to the continued subordination of women in economic, polit-ical, and social aspects of life. As it stands now, most women home-workers lack a vision of better and realistic alternatives around which to organize their lives, and as a nation we have failed to provide the structural basis for such a new vision. If this void persists, home-workers will continue to press for the right to choose homework from among a group of equally dismal employment alternatives.

NOTES

Research for the essay was funded by a grant from the Business and Profes-sional Women's Foundation.

1. Any homeworkers mentioned in this paper have been given fictitious names because, in view of their involvement in on-going court cases, the author agreed to protect their anonymity.

2. For estimates of homeworking in the garment industry in New York City see New York State Department of Labor, Division of Labor Standards, "Study of State-Federal Employment Standards in New York City," (February 1982). For estimates of garment industry homeworking in New Jersey, see Lisa Schlein, "Los Angeles' Garment District Sews a Cloak of Shame," *Los Angeles Times,* March 5, 1978, V-3. Further documentation of the existence of homework in the garment industry in New York, New Jersey, and Illinois can be found in International Ladies Garment Workers Union, "Statement of ILGWU in Op-position to the Removal of Restrictions on Industrial Homework," (July 1,

1981); Franz Leichter, "The Return of the Sweatshop: A Call for State Action," New York State Senate (October, 1979); Franz Leichter, "The Return of the Sweatshop: Part II," New York State Senate (February 26, 1981); Franz Leichter, "Sweatshops to Shakedowns: Organized Crime in New York's Garment Industry," New York State Senate (March, 1982); New York State Department of Labor, "Public Hearing on Industrial Homework," transcript of proceedings (April 2, 1981); New York State Department of Labor, "Report to the Governor and Legislature on the Garment Manufacturing Industry and Industrial Homework," Lillian Roberts, commissioner (February, 1982); New Jersey Department of Labor, "Study on Industrial Homework," Division of Workplace Standards (1982); and Illinois Department of Labor, Annual Reports (1974–80).

3. For information on telecommuting see "A Company That Works at Home," *Business Week,* January 26, 1979, p. 98; "The Potential for Telecommuting," *Business Week,* January 26, 1981, pp. 94–98; Robert Grieves, "Telecommuting from a Flexiplace," *Time Magazine,* January 30, 1984, p. 63; Philip Mattera, "Home Computer Sweatshops," *The Nation,* 236, no. 13, (April 2, 1983): 390–92; Reagan Mays Ramsower, *Telecommuting: The Organizational and Behavioral Effects of Working at Home,* (Ann Arbor: UMI Research Press, 1985). For information on electronics homework in Silicon Valley see Pete Carey and Michael Malone, "Black Market in Silicon Valley," *San Jose Mercury News,* August 31, 1980, A-1; Rebecca Morales, "Cold Solder on a Hot Stove," in *The Technological Woman,* ed. Jan Zimmerman (New York: Praeger, 1983).

4. Eighteen states adopted some form of homework regulation in the 1940s. For more information see Milton Derber, "Industrial Homework, Part I: An Old Problem Lingers On," *Industrial Bulletin* (New York State Department of Labor, March, 1959), pp. 8–11.

5. New Jersey labor law prohibits homework for the following: (1) articles of food or drink; (2) articles for use in connection with the serving of food or drink; (3) toys and dolls; (4) tobacco; (5) drugs and poisons; (6) bandages and other sanitary goods; (7) explosives, fireworks, and articles of like character; (8) articles of infants' and children's wearing apparel; (9) articles, the processing of which requires exposure to substances determined by the commissioner to be hazardous to the health or safety of persons so exposed; (10) the manufacture or distribution of dolls' clothing in any tenement house. (New Jersey Department of Labor, Division of Workplace Standards, "Industrial Home Work Laws and Regulations," compiled September 1982). The kinds of homework prohibited under Illinois labor law are the processing or preparation of (1) articles of food or drink; (2) drugs or poisons; (3) medical and surgical bandages and dressings, sanitary napkins, and cotton batting; (4) fireworks, explosives, and articles of similar character; (5) toys and dolls; (6) tobacco; (7) metal springs; (8) any other article the department of labor determines to be injurious to the health of the homeworker or the public. (State of Illinois, Department of Labor, "Industrial Homework Law").

6. Laurent Bolsie, "Home-Based Industries Take Root in Rural America," *Christian Science Monitor,* August 25, 1986, 3.

7. I have not fully explored the process of distributing homework used by Kodak and Squibb.

8. The details of this research were not revealed to the author. The interview with this respondent was conducted in November 1983.

9. I obtained this information through correspondence with the companies mentioned.

10. Cf. Catherine Hakim and Roger Dennis, *Homeworking in Wages Council Industries: A Study Based on Wages Inspectorate Records of Pay and Earnings,* Research Paper no. 37, (London: Department of Employment, 1982); P. Edwards and P. Flounders, "The Lace Outworkers of Nottingham," in *Are Low Wages Inevitable?* ed. F. Field (London: Spokesman Books, 1976), pp. 47–53; Arnold Cragg and Tim Dawson, *Qualitative Research among Homeworkers,* Research Paper no. 21, (London: Department of Employment, 1981); National Board for Prices and Income, *Pay and Conditions in the Clothing Manufacturing Industries,* Report no. 110 (London: HMSO, 1969); Commission on Industrial Relations, Clothing Wages Council, Report no. 77, (London: HMSO, 1974); Commission on Industrial Relations, Pin, Hook and Eye, and Snap Fasterner Wages Council, Report no. 49 (London: HMSO, 1973); Advisory Conciliation and Arbitration Service, Toy Manufacturing Wages Council, Report no. 13, (London: ACAS, 1978); Advisory, Conciliation and Arbitration Service, Report on Button Manufacturing Wages Council, Report no. 11, (London: ACAS, 1978).

11. Cf. Australia Asia Worker Links, "Outwork: Undermining Union Gains or an Alternative Way of Working?" Case Study no. 6, (December 1982); Philip Mattera, "Small Is Not Beautiful: Decentralized Production and the Underground Economy in Italy," *Radical America* 14, no. 5 (September–October 1980): 68; Geoffrey Murray, "Japan's Cottage Workers—Vital Cogs in Big Machine," *Christian Science Monitor,* June 23, 1981, 2.

12. Cf. R. Pineda-Ofreneo, "Philippine Domestic Outwork: Subcontracting for Export-Oriented Industries," *Journal of Contemporary Asia,* 12, no. 3 (1982): 281–93; Rukmini Rao and Sabka Husain, "Women Workers in the Delhi Garment Export Industry," *Newsletter of International Labor Studies* 21 (1984): 22–25.

13. For a more detailed discussion of global trends in the decentralization of production and expansion of industrial homework, see Jamie Faricellia Dangler, "Industrial Homework in the Modern World Economy," *Contemporary Crisis* 10, no. 3 (1987): 257–79.

14. This information was obtained in interviews with managers from firms employing homeworkers in central New York.

15. Since most homeworkers were aware that child labor was an important concern for the state, they might not have admitted that their children helped them occasionally. In fact, one woman claimed to have known many people in her area who made "a lot of money doing homework" but who had family members, especialy children, helping them.

16. The existence of such abusive practices has been documented by Carey and Malone, "Black Market in Silicon Valley," and Morales, "Cold Solder on a Hot Stove."

17. Once again, homework distributors in central New York were generally viewed as trusted members of the community and usually allowed considerable flexibility in their dealings with homeworkers. For example, the homeworkers typically decided how much work they wanted to do in a given week (thus there were no forced quotas). In addition, workers reported that during slack periods distributors would often go out of their way to distribute the available work evenly so no one would be without employment.

18. Most of the homeworkers' husbands were blue-collar workers. Many worked in various area factories. Some of the other jobs held included that of custodian, gas mechanic, bus driver, carpenter, trucker, sheriff's officer, and salesman. A few were full- or part-time farmers.

19. Two of the men who did homework did it "on the side," to supplement the income from their regular jobs. One man, along with his wife, did homework full-time as his only occupation.

20. The typical jobs held by homeworkers in the past were assembly line worker, cleaner, waitress, cashier, secretary/typist, and telephone operator. Most of the women had more than one previous job before doing homework. In fact, most had moved from job to job, spending only a few years at each.

21. In this case the fact that people could earn more in take-home pay doing homework than if they worked outside at minimum wage was not due to the fact that they failed to pay taxes on their homeworking income, as many might assume. Of those interviewed, only four reported that they neglected to file for income tax on their earnings. Seven, however, reported that they neglected to pay social security taxes. Nevertheless, in claiming that homeworking yielded more spendable income, those interviewed did not consider the cost of overhead expenses they may have incurred, such as heating and lighting.

8

Hispanic Women and Homework: Women in the Informal Economy of Miami and Los Angeles

M. PATRICIA FERNÁNDEZ-KELLY and ANNA M. GARCÍA

In the latter part of the twentieth century, underground economies are expanding in industrial regions like the United States and western Europe. The proliferation of sweat shops, unlicensed industrial operations, and homework seems incongruous in information-based societies in which multinational corporations rely upon advanced technology. Nevertheless, a growing body of quantitative and qualitative evidence points to economic informalization as a distinctive and ongoing process in advanced industrial nations.[1] Low-tech industries like apparel and high-tech industries like electronics share this feature.

A considerable degree of internal variation characterizes informal economies. An understanding of this differentiation should entail the study of labor market conditions and of the household structures to which informal workers and employers belong. It is within the household that the constraints of class and gender mesh, resulting in various modes of adaptation to the surrounding economic system and in differing patterns of employment. A comparison between Miami and Los Angeles provides an invaluable opportunity to illustrate this point. Homework involving Hispanic women, particularly immigrants and refugees, is widespread in the two locations, especially in the garment industry. On the surface, the two cases seem to be similar outcomes resulting from identical economic processes. However, as we will see, in Miami the existence of an ethnic enclave formed by Cuban entrepreneurs, most of them political exiles, enabled women from the same families and community to transform homework into a strategy for maximizing earnings and for reconciling cultural and economic demands. Theirs is a position of qualified vulnerability when judged against the totality of economic and political interactions. By contrast, in Los Angeles the high degree of proletarianization of Mexican women (partly resulting from their working-class background, undocumented immigrant status, and particular household characteristics) has accentuated their vulnerability in the labor market. For many of these women, industrial homework and even the purchase of small assembly shops are measures of last resort; they are strategies to stay a step above poverty.

The comparison proposed in this chapter not only illuminates diversity within the informal economy but also suggests that the meaning of homework varies with the economic, political, and social context of women's lives. This is true even among Hispanic women, who are usually regarded as an undifferentiated whole. Class, ethnicity, and household composition intersect with regional economic structures to define the function of homework. Thus, home assembly cannot be fully understood without regard for the economic significance to the household; the articulation between domestic labor and wage employment shapes and is shaped by the informal economy.

Two hypotheses guide this comparative analysis. (1) Proletarianization—that is, dependence on the larger mechanisms of the wage labor market—reduces the possibility of upholding patriarchal norms of reciprocity between men and women. This, in turn, translates into high levels of economic and political vulnerability. (2) Conversely, the existence of an ethnic entrepreneurial class predicated upon patriarchal notions of reciprocity can improve the bargaining ability of women in the labor market and raise the political strength of the group as a whole. The first proposition applies to Mexican women employed in garment and electronics manufacture in southern California. The second refers to Cuban garment workers in southern Florida.

A Social Portrait of Hispanic Women in Wage Labor

Although Hispanics are often portrayed as a uniform population, their employment and social profiles show differences as well as similarities when national backgrounds, educational levels, citizen status, and length of residence in the U.S. are considered. For example, Mexicans comprised more than half of all Hispanics between eighteen and sixty-four years of age living in the U.S. in 1976. Of these, approximately 70 percent had been born in this country. Average levels of education were low; less than 50 percent graduated from high school. About 60 percent of working-age Mexicans were under thirty-five years of age compared with less than 50 percent of working-age, non-Hispanic white workers. Cubans, on the other hand, represented less than 7 percent of the Hispanic population. They were mostly foreign born and had a mean age of thirty-nine years. They also had a higher level of education than Mexicans. Fifty-eight percent of Cubans had twelve or more years of formal schooling in 1976.[2]

On the other hand, Cubans and Mexicans share similar marital profiles and household compositions. Intact marriages as well as a relatively low percentage of households headed by women are distinguishing features in both groups. Seventeen percent of Cuban and 16 percent of Mexican households are headed by females, compared to about 8 percent of white domestic units in the same situation. Sixty-seven percent of Mexican and 64 percent of Cuban women were married and living with their spouses in 1976. Sixty-five percent of Mexican men and 70 percent of Cuban males lived in stable marital unions. Finally, about 74 percent of Mexican women had children living with them. The equivalent figure for Cubans was 62 percent.[3]

Both Cuban and Mexican women have had a prominent representation as remunerated workers in the United States. Their labor force participation rates dispel the widespread notion that work outside the home is a rare experience among Hispanic women. For instance, 50 percent of native-born and 45 percent of foreign-born Mexican women were employed outside the home in 1976. The equivalent figure for foreign-born Cubans was 65 percent (despite the fact that their labor participation rate prior to their arrival in the United States was about 30 percent). Thus, current levels of employment among Mexican and Cuban women in the U.S. approximate or surpass the labor force participation of non-Hispanic white women, of whom 57 percent work outside the home. Moreover, while other ethnic groups in the United States have diminished their participation in blue-collar employment, Hispanic women have increased their relative share in it, particularly in the production of nondurable goods.[4]

The importance of minority women's employment in assembly is readily apparent in southern California, where 67 percent of working women classified as "operators, fabricators, and laborers" belong to ethnic minority groups. Fifty-one percent of those are Hispanic. These findings contradict the assumption that Hispanic women's participation in the labor force is confined to the service sector. Census figures for Los Angeles County further confirm the significance of Hispanic women's employment in manufacturing: 73.7 percent of all female "operators, fabricators, and laborers" (136,937 persons) are members of ethnic minorities. Almost 60 percent of that subgroup (105,621 individuals) are Hispanic. Even more revealing is the composition of workers classified as "textile, apparel, and furnishings machine operators." Approximately 46,219 women are employed in that occupation in Los Angeles. Almost 91 percent of those are minorities; 71.76 percent, Hispanic. Equivalent data for New York and Miami (the two other areas with the fastest growing Hispanic populations) indicate that we are looking at a substantial percentage of the manufacturing labor force.[5] However, census material may underestimate the actual involvement of Hispanic women in wage labor: many are part of the underground economy; they are found in small unregulated assembly shops or doing piece work and industrial homework.

The preceding summary is useful for comparative purposes. However, some features vary when observations are limited to certain industries, their correspondent labor market incorporation patterns, and household characteristics prevalent among their workers. For example, in both southern California and southern Florida most direct production workers in the garment industry are Hispanic. In Los Angeles and Miami apparel firms approximately 75 percent of the operatives are Mexican; 85 percent, Cuban. In contrast to the characteristics of the population at large, among Los Angeles garment workers approximately 29 percent are female-headed households, a figure much larger than that for Mexicans living in the United States in general (16 percent). By contrast, there is little variation when comparing the number of female-headed households in the Florida needle trade industry with the population as a whole. About 17 percent of Cuban households are headed by females; the equivalent figure for the Florida garment industry is 19 percent.[6]

The large number of female-headed households in the Los Angeles garment industry calls for an explanation. Because Cubans and Mexicans share many cultural characteristics, that explanation cannot rely exclusively on differences regarding values and attitudes about family life or sex roles. Instead, it must take into consideration the differential modes of incorporation of the two ethnic groups into their receiving economic milieu. Before addressing this question, we provide a description of apparel manufacturing in the two locations under study.

Structures of the Garment Industry
in California and Florida

For many generations, garment production has provided a locus in which immigrant women, including Hispanics of various national backgrounds, have found entry-level jobs. But the development and nature of the industry has varied over time and by region, affecting the incorporation of immigrant labor and the use of homeworkers. To understand the current position of Mexican and Cuban homeworkers, we must first compare garment manufacture in Los Angeles and Miami. The two sites differ in the timing of the industry, its evolution, maturity, and restructuring. In Los Angeles, garment production is not only older, developing first in the late nineteenth century with the gold rush and waves of Chinese immigrants. It is also rooted in specific events such as the Great Depression, changing conditions of assembly and unionization in New York, emphasis on new definitions of casual wear, and, finally, continued reorganization during the seventies and eighties as a response to the impact of foreign imports. Restructuring in the Los Angeles garment industry has led to a decreasing number of large firms and a proliferation of small, subcontracted shops, many of which fall partly or totally outside government supervision. Sixty-two percent of the 2,717 apparel and textile manufacturers in Los Angeles County in 1984 employed between one and nineteen workers.

Several studies show that the predominance of small, productive establishments in a given industry raises the probability of informal activities such as tax and licensing evasions and violations of the labor code. The prevalence of small shops accounts, to a large extent, for the survival of the garment industry in Los Angeles. Thus, contrary to a widespread impression, garment production in the area is actually growing quickly, due to the expansion of the informal sector. Between 30 and 50 percent of the $3.5 billion in 1983 Los Angeles garment industry sales may have originated in home production or unregulated shops, the majority of which are small.[7]

Apparel production in Miami has had a shorter history and a less diversified experience. In the early sixties Miami's industry was highly seasonal, employed fewer than 7,000 workers, and depended on New York entrepreneurs feeding U.S. and European luxury markets in belts, gloves, and purses. As retired manufacturers from New York living in Miami saw the advantages of opening new businesses and hiring large numbers of freshly arrived Cubans, Miami expanded by 1973 to employ more than 24,000 people, the vast majority of whom were Cuban women. This same process led to the predominance of Cuban males among contractors. From its inception, then, apparel manufacturing in Miami illustrated gender and ethnic stratification: 70 percent of the manufacturers were Jewish; 90 percent of the contractors, Cuban men; and 95 percent of the work force, Cuban females. As in Los Angeles in the early eighties, many of the 716 firms in Miami employed fewer than thirty workers, and a substantial proportion of the industry (at least one third) originated in unregulated shops and homes.

However, unlike Los Angeles, since the late seventies Florida has suffered labor shortages caused by the relatively advanced age (over forty) of the work force and the absence of a new labor supply. The decreasing availability of Cuban women's labor has contributed, as we shall see, to the expansion of homework in Miami.[8]

The two locations also differ in the availability of a favored labor supply. The growth of the Los Angeles clothing industry resulted from capitalists' ability to rely on steady waves of Mexican immigrants, many of whom were undocumented. Over the last century this continuous migration has ensured a permanent supply of workers. From the twenties, Mexican women dominated the work force; the majority were below the age of thirty, two-thirds were born in the United States, and nine-tenths were unmarried. By 1944, when the number of garment manufacturers had grown to 900, 75 percent of their 28,000 employees were Mexican women and girls.[9] By contrast, garment production in Miami expanded because of an unprecedented influx of exiles ejected by a unique political event. Cubans working in the Florida apparel industry arrived in the United States as refugees, protected and relatively privileged. Their exile was filled with uncertainty and the possibility of dislocation but not, as in the case of undocumented Mexican aliens, with the probability of harassment, detention, and deportation.

Implicit in the previous point is a differentiation in social class between the two groups of newcomers. For more than a century, the majority of Mexican immigrants have had a markedly proletarian background. Until the seventies, the majority had rural roots; in more recent times the number of urban immigrants has grown.[10] In sharp contrast, Cuban waves of migration have included a larger proportion of professionals, mid-level service providers, and various types of entrepreneurs ranging from those with previous experience in large companies to those able to start small family enterprises. Research has shown that entrepreneurial experience among Cubans and reliance on their own ethnic network accounts, to a large extent, for their success in business formation and appropriation in Miami.[11] Thus, while Mexican migration has been characterized by a relative homogeneity regarding class background, Cuban exile resulted in the transposition of an almost intact class structure containing investors and professionals as well as unskilled, semiskilled and skilled workers.

In addition to disparate class compositions, the two groups differ in the degree of their homogeneity by place of birth. Besides the sizable undocumented contingent, the Los Angeles garment industry also employs U.S.-born citizens of Mexican heritage. Although no systematic studies have been done on the subject, first-hand reports and anecdotal evidence indicate a fragmentation between "Chicanas" and "Mexicans," with the latter occupying the lower rungs in the labor hierarchy. Differences in citizenship status, length of residence in the United States, and skill often result in open or latent conflict among the two groups. Recently arrived Mexican immigrants point to discrimination and prejudice from workers with whom they share a common ethnic background. Cubans, on the other hand, were a highly cohesive population until recently, when the arrival of the Port of Mariel refugees resulted in a potentially damaging fragmentation of the community.

Perhaps the most important difference between Mexicans in Los Angeles and Cubans in Florida is related to their distinctive patterns of labor market insertion. Historically, Mexicans have arrived in the U.S. labor market in a highly individuated and dispersed manner. As a result, they have been extremely dependent on labor supply and demand—forces beyond their control. Their working-class background and the stigma attached to their frequent undocumented status has accentuated even further their vulnerability vis-à-vis employers. By contrast, Cubans have been able to consolidate an economic enclave containing immigrant businesses which hire workers of a common culture and national background.[12]

This economic enclave operates as a buffer zone, separating and often shielding members of the same ethnic group from the market forces at work in the larger society. The existence of an economic enclave does not preclude exploitation on the basis of class; indeed, it is predicated upon the existence of a highly diversified immigrant class structure. However, the quantitative and qualitative evidence suggests that commonalities of culture, national background, and language between immigrant employers and workers can become a mechanism for collective improvement of income levels and standards of living. As a result, differences in labor market insertion patterns among Mexicans and Cubans have led to varying social profiles and a dissimilar potential for socioeconomic attainment.

Household Organization and the Politics of Home and Work

Neither proletarian atomization among Mexicans nor participation in an economic enclave among Cubans can be explained without consideration of the role played by households and families in the allocation of workers to different segments of the labor market.[13] Both Mexican and Cuban women have sought homework as one way to reconcile the responsibilities of family and domestic care with the need to earn a wage. Employers, in turn, have found in homework a vehicle to lower the wage bill, evade government regulations, and maintain competitiveness in the market. While these two aspects have remained constant, the circumstances surrounding homework in southern California and southern Florida highlight the varying impact that class has on household composition and that class-defined households have on various types of labor force participation. Differences in class background and household composition have led to the contrasting experiences of Mexican and Cuban homeworkers.

Both Cubans and Mexicans prize the idealized family—long-term, stable unions in which men act as main providers and women as principal caretakers of children. However, the possibility of forming such family units over extended periods of time vary in consonance with several factors including class background. Stable nuclear families and clearly defined sex roles are often found among the middle and upper classes; the poor must often live in highly flexible households in which resources and services flow constantly but adherence to the norms of the patriarchal family are unattainable. As we will illustrate below, the large number of female-headed households in the Los Angeles garment industry can be partly explained as an outcome of proletarianization and the absence of an ethnic enclave in which the injuries of class are mitigated.

The experience of Petra R., a thirty-two-year-old native from Torreón, Coahuila (Mexico), exemplifies the conditions surrounding many recently arrived Mexican immigrants:[14] "I've worked in several garment shops since I came to California five years ago. At first I lived with my aunt and uncle and another Mexican family with whom we shared an apartment. None of us had papers, but that didn't matter so much. The problem was the language—how to make yourself understood when looking for a job. So I ended up sewing . . . then I got pregnant. I didn't want to live with relatives then, so I had to work at home. Fortunately, the old man [her employer] gives me enough so that I don't have to go to the shop."

The employment history of Amelia Ruiz, a U.S.-born woman of Mexican ancestry, more fully illustrates the ways that economic uncertainty, cultural expectations, and household stability lead women to homework. She was born into a family of six children in El Cerrito, Los Angeles County. Her mother, a descendant of Native American Indians, married at a young age the son of Mexican immigrants. Among Amelia's memories are the fragmentary stories of her paternal grandparents working in fields and, occasionally, in canneries. On the other hand, her father was not a stoop laborer but a trained upholsterer. Her mother was always a homemaker. Amelia grew up with a distinct sense of the contradictions that plague the relationships between men and women: "All the while I was a child, I had this feeling that my parents weren't happy. My mother was smart but she could never make much of herself. Her parents taught her that the fate of woman is to be a wife and mother; they advised her to find a good man and marry him. And that she did. My father was dependable, and I think he was faithful, but he was also distant; he lived in his own world. He would come home and expect to be served hand on foot. My mother would wait on him, but she was always angry about it."

After getting her high school diploma, Amelia took up odd jobs in all the predictable places: as a counter clerk in a dress shop, as a cashier in a fast food establishment, and as a waitress in two restaurants. When she was twenty, she met Miguel. He was a consummate survivor, having worked in the construction field, as a truck driver, and even as an ESL (English as a Second Language) instructor. At the age of twenty-one and despite her misgivings, Amelia was married: "For a while I kept my job, but when I became pregnant, Miguel didn't want me to work anymore. Two more children followed and then, little by little, Miguel became abusive. He wanted to have total authority over me and the children. He said a man should know how to take care of a family and get respect, but it was hard to take him seriously when he kept changing jobs and when the money he brought home was barely enough to keep ends together." After the birth of her second child, Amelia started work at Shirley's, a women's wear factory in the area. Miguel was opposed to the idea. For Amelia, work outside the home was an evident need prompted by financial stress. At first, it was also a means to escape growing disillusion: "I saw myself turning into my mother, and I started thinking that to be free of men was best for women. Maybe if Miguel had had a better job, maybe if he had kept the one he had, things would have been different. . . . We started drifting apart."

She had worked at Shirley's for almost a year when one late afternoon, after collecting the three children from her parents' house, she returned to an empty home. She knew, as soon as she stepped inside, that something was amiss. In muted shock she confirmed the obvious: Miguel had left, taking with him all personal possessions; even the wedding picture in the living room had been removed. No explanations had been left behind. Amelia was then twenty-eight years of age, alone, and the mother of three small children.

Under the circumstances, employment became even more desirable, but the difficulty of reconciling home responsibilities with wage work persisted. Amelia was well regarded at Shirley's and her condition struck a cord of sympathy among other factory women. In a casual conversation, her supervisor described how other women were leasing industrial sewing machines from the local Singer distributor and doing piece work at home. By combining factory work and home assembly, she could earn more money without further neglecting her children. Mr. Driscoll, Shirley's owner and general manager, made regular use of homeworkers, most of whom were former employees. That had allowed him to retain a stable core of about twenty employees and to depend on approximately ten homeworkers during peak seasons.

Between 1979, the year of her desertion, and 1985 when we met her, Amelia had struggled hard, working most of the time and making some progress. Her combined earnings before taxes fluctuated between $950 and $1,150. In 1985 almost half of her income went to rent for the two-bedroom apartment which she shared with the children. She was in debt and used to working at least twelve hours a day. On the other hand, she had bought a double-needle sewing machine and was thinking of leasing another one to enable a neighbor to help with additional sewing. She had high hopes: "Maybe some day I'll have my own business; I'll be a liberated women. . . . I won't have to take orders from a man. Maybe Miguel did me a favor when he left after all."

Although there are individual variations, Amelia's life history is shared by many garment workers in southern California. Two aspects are worth noting in this experience. First, marriage and a stable family life are seen as desirable objectives which are, nonetheless, fraught with ambivalent feelings and responsibilities. Second, tensions surrounding home life express a contradiction between the intent to fulfill sexual roles defined according to a shared culture and the absence of the economic base necessary for their implementation. Male unemployment and women's need to become breadwinners militate against the maintenance of patriarchal standards. Male desertion adds to the vulnerability of women. Mexican garment workers, especially those who are heads of households, face great disadvantages in the labor market. They are targeted as a preferred labor force for jobs which offer the lowest wages paid to industrial workers in the United States; they also have among the lowest unionization rates in the country. Ironically, household atomization, partly caused by proletarianization and the ensuing breakdown of patriarchal norms, has not been followed by the elimination of similar patriarchal standards in the labor market.

Although our focus is on women employed in the garment industry, it is worth noting some commonalities in electronics production. Mexican women working in southern California's booming electronics industry reflect similar reasons for homework; like their counterparts in garments, they provide a large labor pool attractive to entrepreneurs who find in them the flexibility needed in highly competitive sectors of the economy. When activity peaks, some employees take batches of components to their own homes, where they assemble them at piece rates (as low as seven cents per unit), often aided by friends and family members.[15] Several aspects are striking in this case. The public image of high-tech industries appears antithetical to practices such as the putting out of assembly work among Hispanic and Indo-Chinese workers in southern California. However, for a large number of electronics firms, this is a customary practice. In Kearny Mesa, an area in San Diego County where there is a large concentration of electronics producers, 75 percent of firms make regular use of homeworkers. Maribel Guzmán, who has worked at one electronics firm for two years, thinks homework is a good idea: "I'm always looking for ways to earn a little more. . . . I have worked in all sorts of jobs. But with a family to look after, and the cost of child care what it is, I can use the extra money. Sometimes, my neighbor helps and I give her part of what I get. She can't leave home because she has a baby and doesn't speak a word of English, but she too needs the money."

Tales like the ones related above can be found among Cuban and Central American women in Miami. However, a larger proportion have had a different trajectory than Mexicans in Los Angeles. Among the first waves of refugees were many who worked hard to bring the standards of living of their families to the same level or higher than those they had been familiar with in their countries of origin. The consolidation of an ethnic enclave allowed many Cuban men to become successful entrepreneurs. While their wives toiled in garment factories, they entered the world of business. Eventually, they purchased homes, put their children through school, and achieved comfortable styles of life. At that point, many Cuban men pressed their wives to stop working outside the home. They had only allowed them to work in the first place out of economic necessity. In the words of a prominent manufacturer in the area:

> You have to understand that Cuban workers were willing to do anything to survive. When they became prosperous, the women saw the advantage of staying at home and still earning additional income. Because they had the skill, owners couldn't take them for granted. Eventually, owners couldn't get operators anymore. The most skilled would tell a manager,

"My husband doesn't let me work out of the home." This was a worker's initiative based on the values of the culture. I would put ads in the paper and forty people would call and everyone would say, "I only do homework." That's how we got this problem of labor shortages.

This testimony partly shows that decisions made at the level of the household can remove workers highly desired by employers from the marketplace, thus endangering certain types of production. In those cases, loyalty to familial values can act against the interests of capitalist firms. Interviews with Cuban women involved in homework confirm this general interpretation. By capitalizing on their skill and experience, many of these women became subcontractors, employing their own neighbors and transforming so-called "Florida rooms" (the covered porches in their houses) into sewing shops.

In one of those improvised sewing shops we interviewed Elvira Gómez. She was thirty-four when she arrived in Miami with her four children, ages three to twelve, in 1961.

Leaving Havana was the most painful thing that ever happened to us. We loved our country, we would have never left willingly. Cuba was not like Mexico: we didn't have immigrants in large numbers. But Castro betrayed us and we had to join the exodus. We became exiles. My husband left Cuba three months before I did, and there were moments where I doubted I would ever see him again. Then after we got together, we realized we would have to forge ahead without looking back.

We lost everything. Even my mother's china had to be left behind. We arrived in this country as they say, "covering our nakedness with our bare hands" (una mano delante y otra detrás). My husband had had a good position in a bank. To think that he would take any old job in Miami was more than I could take; a man of his statute having to beg for a job in a hotel or a factory? It wasn't right!

Before her marriage Elvira had worked briefly as a secretary. As a middle-class wife and mother she was used to hiring at least one maid. Coming to the United States changed all that: "Something had to be done to keep the family together. So I looked around and finally found a job in a shirt factory in Hialeah. Manolo [her husband] joined a childhood friend and got a loan to start an export-import firm. All the time they were building the business, I was sewing. There were times when we wouldn't have been able to pay the bills without the money I brought in."

In her case, working outside the home was justified as a way to maintain the integrity of her family and as a means to support her husband's early incursions into the business world:

For six long years I worked in the factory, but when things got better financially, Manolo asked me to quit the job. He felt bad that I couldn't be at home all the time with the children. But it had to be done. There's no reason for women not to earn a living when necessary. But I tell my daughters that the strength of a family rests on the intelligence and work of women. It is foolish to give up your place as a mother and a wife only to take orders from men who aren't even part of the family. What's so liberated about that? It is better to see your husband succeed and to know you have supported one another.

Several points are worth noting in the experience of Cuban garment workers. Exile, for example, did not transform sexual roles; rather, it extended them in surprising ways. The high labor-force participation rates of Cuban women in the U.S. have been mentioned earlier. However, prior to their migration, only a small number of Cuban women had worked outside the home for any length of time. It was the need to maintain the integrity of their families and to achieve class-related ambitions that precipitated their entrance into the labor force of a foreign country.

As with Mexicans in southern California, Cuban women in Miami earned low wages in unskilled and semiskilled jobs. They too worked in environments devoid of union benefits. However, their membership in an economic enclave allowed them to see industrial homework as an expression of relative prosperity and as a means to achieve a supplementary income while minding domestic responsibilities.

Conclusions

The comparison between different experiences among Hispanic women in two distinct geographical locations shows that involvement in informal production can have entirely dissimilar meanings, depending on the type of incorporation into the broader economic context and on the interplay between sexual politics and household composition. In the case of Mexicans in southern California, proletarianization is related to a high number of female-headed households in which the earnings provided by women are indispensible for maintaining standards of modest subsistence. In the Cuban case, women's employment was a strategy for coping with the receiving environment and raising standards of living. This contrasting experience involving the relationships between households and labor markets occurred despite shared values regarding the family among Mexicans and Cubans. Both groups partake of similar mores regarding the roles of men and women; nevertheless, their actual experience has differed significantly.

This comparison of Mexican and Cuban experiences also shows that the meaning of women's participation in the labor force remains plagued by paradox. On the one hand, paid employment expands the potential for greater personal autonomy and financial independence. This should have a favorable impact upon women's capacity to negotiate an equitable position within the home and labor market. On the other hand, women's search for paid employment is frequently the consequence of severe economic need; it expresses vulnerability, not strength, within homes and in the marketplace. Under certain conditions, women's entry into the labor force also parallels the collapse of reciprocal exchanges between men and women.

While homework is perceived as a problem by observers and policy makers, our study suggests that an apparently identical outcome can have radically disparate meanings when actual processes are examined. This should lead to a reassessment of industrial homework as a highly diversified phenomenon rather than a secondary outcome resulting from the interaction of abstract economic factors.

NOTES

This chapter is based on findings from the research project titled "A Collaborative Study of Hispanic Women in Garment and Electronics Industries." Fieldwork in Southern California (Los Angeles, Orange and San Diego Counties) took place between 1984 and 1986. Preliminary research in Miami-Dade County, Florida, took place during the winters of 1985 and 1986. Funds for research in Southern California were provided by the Programs in Human Rights and Governance and in Urban Poverty at the Ford Foundation, and by the Tinker Foundation. Special thanks are due to Dr. William Diaz and Ms. Patricia Biggers for their faith and encouragement.

1. *Informalization* is understood in this chapter as a process leading to the expansion of industrial and service operations which do not comply with legislation regarding taxes, working conditions, licensing, wages, and other labor code requirements. For recent findings regarding the growth of the informal sector of underground economy in the United States see A. Portes and Saskia Sassen-Koob, "Making it Underground: Comparative Material on the Informal Sector in Western Market Economics," *American Journal of Sociology* 93 (July 1987): 30–61; see also Jonathan I. Gershuny, "The Informal Economy: Its Role in An Industrial Society," *Futures* 11 (February 1979): 3–16.

2. George J. Borgas and Marta Tienda, ed., *Hispanics in the U.S. Economy* (New York: Academic Press, 1985).

3. Ibid.

4. Figures abstracted from the U.S. Bureau of the Census, *1980 Census of Population* (Washington, D.C.: GPO, 1983).

5. Ibid.

6. Ibid. See also M. Patricia Fernández-Kelly and Anna M. García, "Informalization at the Core: Hispanic Women, Home Work and the Advanced Capitalist State," in *The Informal Economy: Studies in Advanced and Less Developed Countries,* ed. Alejandro Portes, Manuel Castells, and Lauren Benton (Baltimore: The Johns Hopkins University Press, 1989).

7. P. S. Taylor, "Mexican Women in Los Angeles Industry in 1928," *Aztlan: International Journal of Hispanic Research,* 11, no. 1 (Spring 1980): 99–129; M. Perlmutter, *The Rag Business* (Los Angeles, 1944); Commission on California State Government, Organization, and Economy, *Review of Selected Taxing and Enforcing Agencies' Programs to Control the Underground Economy* (Los Angeles: Commission on California State Government, Organization, and Economy, 1985).

8. School of Business Administration, University of Florida at Gainsville, *Florida Statistical Abstract, 1985.*

9. Perlmutter, *The Rag Business,* pp. 40–53; Taylor, "Mexican Women in Los Angeles Industry in 1928," pp. 91–129.

10. Alejandro Portes and Robert Bach, *Latin Journey* (Berkeley: University of California Press, 1985), p. 135.

11. Alejandro Portes, "The Social Origins of the Cuban Enclave Economy in Miami," *Sociological Perspectives,* 30 (October 1987): 340–72.

12. Ibid.

13. Within this context, *family* should be understood as an ideological concept defining an ideal form of kinship organization which may vary from culture to culture and from historical period to historical period. *Household,* on the other hand, refers to the actual manner in which individuals come together as part of domestic units pooling resources. Ideal notions of family organization are often at odds with the reality of household organization. See Rayna Rapp, "Family and Class in Contemporary America: Notes toward an Understanding of Ideology," in *Rethinking the Family,* ed. Barrie Thorne and Marilyn Yalom (New York: Longman, 1982).

14. In the following ethnographic accounts we have altered the names of firms and individuals for reasons of confidentiality. However, the situations are real.

15. For production and structures in electronics, see D. O'Connor, "Changing Patterns of International Production in the Semiconductor Industry: The Role of Transnational Corporations" (Paper prepared for the Conference on Microelectronics in Transition, University of California at Santa Cruz, May 12–15, 1983). For a succinct history of the electronics industry see Lenny Siegel, "Delicate Bonds: The Semiconductor Industry." (Mountain View, Calif.: Pacific Studies Center, 1984).

SECTION FOUR

———

The New Clerical and Professional Homework

———

9

Home-based Clerical Work: No Simple Truth, No Single Reality

KATHLEEN CHRISTENSEN

The simple truth about home-based clerical work is that it is not sim-ple. While working at home can enhance independence for some peo-ple, it can lead to abuses of others, particularly those fraudulently hired as self-employed independent contractors. Any meaningful discussion of clerical home-based work, therefore, must take into account the employment status of the workers. There are three major categories of home-based workers. First is the **home-based employee** who is on the company payroll and works at home in addition to some time in the office. Second is the self-employed **home-based business owner** who is genuinely self-employed and who for tax purposes might be listed as an independent contractor, sole proprietor, limited partnership, or incorporated business. Third is a category of some legal ambiguity—the self-employed **home-based independent contractor.** Some contrac-tors are genuinely self-employed, but others, in much more ambiguous circumstances, are expected to perform as employees with limited con-trol and autonomy but are not compensated as such in terms of salaries and benefits.

The purposes of this chapter are two-fold: to describe the broad picture of clerical home-based work and then to focus specifically on the most vulnerable group, those clerical workers who are questionably hired as independent contractors.

Statistics on Home-based Clerical Workers

1980 Census and Family Circle Survey Overviews

According to an analysis of the 1980 census, 1.1 percent of workers engaged in administrative support, including clerical occupations, worked at home. This means that in 1980 there was a home-based clerical labor force of approximately 181,000 people. The census analysis reveals further that home-based workers are predominantly white, self-employed (including sole proprietorships, limited partnerships, and incorporated businesses), and most likely to come from social groups which experience trouble being employed outside the home: mothers, the elderly, the disabled, and rural residents. More recent figures released by the Bureau of Labor Statistics found that in May 1985 there was a slightly larger home-based clerical workforce: 246,000 people worked eight hours or more as home-based secretaries, stenographers, and typists. Of this group 35,000 people worked thirty-five hours or more in these occupations.[1]

To present a more complete overview of clerical homework, I will examine the typical clerical homeworker, the role of technology in homework, and the prevailing employment arrangements by drawing on the results of a national survey I conducted under the auspices of the U.S. Department of Health and Human Services with the cooperation of *Family Circle Magazine.* The magazine published the National Survey on Women and Home-based Work in their January 15, 1985, issue as a public service.[2] Nearly 14,000 women responded, of whom 53 percent worked at home and 42 percent wanted to. Although the survey was not statistically random, the profile of the white-collar respondents to the *Family Circle* survey closely matched the U.S. census profile of white-collar home-based workers on several critical demographic variables (see table 1). As compared to the census profile, the *Family Circle* respondents are more apt to be married and self-employed but otherwise are very similar in race, age, and presence of pre-school children at home.

Subsequent to the survey, I interviewed over a hundred home-based professionals and clericals, including typists, medical transcribers, legal transcribers, data entry clerks, insurance raters, bookkeepers, and word processors in their homes in metropolitan and rural areas in New York, New Jersey, Illinois, and California.[3] Although the interview data provide important interpretive frameworks for the survey results, unless otherwise noted, the following figures refer only to the results of the national survey.

Typical Home-based Clerical Worker

According to our national survey, the typical home-based clerical worker is a self-employed married woman. On average, she works seventeen hours a week at home, is paid by the piece or hourly rates, and is covered by her husband's health insurance. She is slightly more likely

Table 1. Comparison of Profiles of White Collar Home-based Workers in 1980 Census and 1985 Family Circle Respondents Survey

Variable	1980 U.S. Census White-Collar Respondents[a]	Family Circle White-Collar Respondents[b]
Number	456,000	1084[c]
Percent		
White	96.1	97.0
Age (mean)	43.3	40.9
Married (or living with partner)	54.0	79.0
Preschool children at home	21.4	22.0
Self-employed or employee of own corporation	50.8	75.0

[a]Source: R. Kraut and P. Grambsch, "Home-based White Collar Employment: Lessons from 1980 Census," *Social Forces* 66, no. 4 (1987):410–26.
[b]Source: K. Christensen, "National Survey on Women and Home-based Work," *Family Circle Magazine,* January 15, 1985. White-collar occupations include professional, managers, technical, sales, and clerical.
[c]Random survey drawn from statistical purposes.

to have children under eighteen than not. In fact, only one out of every four of the women had preschool children. Perhaps the feature most commonly shared by the home-based clerical workers was that home-based clerical work represents an option of part-time work (see table 2).

Role of Technology

Much of the contemporary discussion on home-based work focuses on two terms—the *electronic cottage* and *telecommuting.* Implicit to both of these notions are the dual assumptions that computers somehow cause the decision to work at home and that homework cannot proceed without them. Our research questions the validity of those assumptions.

According to our survey results, approximately only one out of four (28 percent) of the clerical workers who currently work at home use any of the type of equipment—wordprocessor, personal computer, terminal hooked to mainframe, or modem—in their homework. The majority (72 percent) use typewriters, telephones, and pencils—the conventional tools of their trade. For most home-based clerical workers, therefore, their cottages were electronic only to the extent that they plug in their typewriters. Given these figures, we are prompted to question the role of technology in home employment.

Table 2. Characteristics of the Typical Home-based Clerical Worker

Married	77%
Children	55%
Under 18	
Pre-school (aged 5 and under)	25%
Self-Employed	72%
Payment Arrangements	35%
Piece Rate	
Hourly Rate	31%
Health Insurance	47%
Spouse's Coverage	
Average hours worked	17 hours

Source: The National Survey on Women and Home-based Work, *Family Circle,* January 1985.

Reasons for Home-based Work

Our research indicates that values related to family, work, and money— not technology—drive the initial decision to work at home. Survey respondents were asked why they started to work at home. The question had twelve response items, and the women were asked to check all that applied to them. When we computed the correlations between items, we found that for many of the respondents the initial decision to work at home was cognitively structured and coherent. Oblique factor analysis revealed four main factors in a respondent's reasoning:[4]

1. *Family reasons:* to care for her family and to ease her own conflicts between work and family.

2. *Job reasons:* to work in her own way, at her own pace; to increase her productivity; to minimize overhead, and to benefit from tax advantages of a home office. These items were all directed toward job achievement.

3. *Office avoidance reasons:* to avoid office politics; to save money on commuting and clothes; and to save time commuting. These items involve reactions to perceived hassles in an office environment.

4. *Financial reasons:* to earn extra money.

In other words, values, not computers, drive the initial decision to work at home. Let me play the devil's advocate on this point.

If the decision to work at home was in fact technologically determined, we would have no way of explaining why nearly three-quarters of the clerical homeworkers work at home. We would have to extend the notion of technology and say that typewriters and telephones cause people to work at home. What is critical to home-based work is not technology, despite all of the public attention to it. What is critical is employment status.

Employment Status of Home-based Workers

Will home-based work lead to exploitation of vulnerable workers or will it increase their flexibility and self-sufficiency? The question can be answered only if a fundamental distinction is made among the needs and circumstances of three types of home-based workers: company employees who retain all of the rights and privileges of being employees; genuinely self-employed business owners, and those self-employed independent contractors who work for only one company and whose employment status is highly questionable.[5] How workers are employed directly affects their autonomy, leverage, and security. Being a home-based employee can provide job security and advancement and a more flexible work style, while being a home-based business owner can enhance a worker's independence, earnings, and flexibility. But being an independent contractor under certain conditions can lead to exploitation—a fact verified by our research and by hearings on the pros and cons of home-based clerical work held by the Subcommittee of the Committee on Government Operations of the U.S. House of Representatives and documented in their 1986 report.[6] Yet the American economy is making contracting out an appealing hiring practice for many companies.

Home-Based Independent Contractors

American corporations are facing intense and increasing competition from abroad, forcing many of them to reduce their work forces through layoffs, attrition, and early retirement, so as to cut labor costs. As a corporation downsizes in this manner, it seeks a more flexible two-tiered labor force. The inner core of such a pool consists of salaried employees, but the outer rings consist of workers hired on part-time, temporary, or independent contracting bases.[7] From management's perspective, the flexibility of this two-tiered arrangement is very attractive because workers in the outside rings can be expanded, reduced, or redeployed according to demand. From the workers' side, the arrangement can be flexible, but it can also breed insecurity and limited opportunities for advancement or training. Workers in these outside rings are increasingly referred to as the contingent work force and evidence exists that a high proportion of them are women.[8]

In addition to the flexibility in staffing, employers can also save substantially on workers hired on contracted or temporary bases, saving anywhere from 30 to 40 percent on benefits as well as in their payment to the workers. Workers paid by a piece rate are paid only for the work done, not for any lag time between projects, thereby allowing the company to control the size of its work force as demand dictates without having to pay salaries for trough periods.

Although the data on clerical independent contracting are not systematic, our research indicates that the practice occurs across industries but is most evident in insurance claims rating, office correspondence, and medical and legal transcription. Corporations do not always directly hire the independent contractors. They often contract the work out to clerical services who hire women to do legal, medical, and insurance transcriptions as well as insurance coding, rating, and day-to-day office work in their homes.[9]

For example, several West Coast insurance companies contract out claims rating to a service that in turn contracts out the work to home-based claims raters, almost all of whom are mothers of young children. Other insurance companies, Blue Cross/Blue Shield of South Carolina being the most publicly noted, contract the work directly out to their home-based claims raters. Across the country small local typing services receive overflow work from local businesses who don't want to hire their own in-house secretarial staff; these services in turn contract the work out to women who sit in their homes and transcribe office correspondence and reports. In some suburban communities a neighborhood woman will begin to contract out this clerical piece work to fellow neighbor women. Court reporters and medical doctors also contract out transcription work, typically to home-based typists. Some of this home-based work may be vanishing due to automation. Women I have interviewed report, anecdotally, that court reporting and insurance claims rating are becoming increasingly automated and that they fear that their home-based jobs will eventually be phased out.[10]

These home-based independent contractors are often treated like, and expected to perform as, company employees. They receive work from only one company; they work on materials provided by that company; they are given turn-around times; and some are required to sign contracts stating that they will not take any similar kinds of work from competing companies. These contractors have very little independence; they are expected to behave as employees but have none of the benefits.

In fact, several corporations practice a form of place discrimination, altering the status of workers when they move from the office to the home. They switch them from being full-time salaried employees with benefits to independent contractors. One northeastern insurance company offered women home-based contracting in lieu of extended maternity leaves. In order to maintain their "employment" and work at home, they had to become contractors.[11]

These contractors trade the dependability of a salary for the undependability of an hourly or piece rate, often with no guarantee as to the number of hours or projects. They make less than they did when they worked in the office, doing the same work. They lose all employee benefits, including health care, pension plans, paid sick leaves, and vacations. They become responsible for paying their own social security (FICA) taxes. They operate entirely out of the mainstream of the company, so they are not in the pool of candidates considered for job advancement, skill upgrading, or retooling. They are not in touch with other contractors. As a result, they often work in both isolation and ignorance of other workers. They are rapidly becoming second-class corporate citizens.[12]

Not surprisingly, these women often think of themselves as employees. Some women told me that they did not even know they were hired as self-employed contractors until it was tax time. Moreover, there are legal questions as to whether the home-based clerical workers are contractors.[13] The confusion over employee status for the home-based clerical workers is tied to limitations in definitions and data collection regarding contractors versus employees.

Independent Contractors: Problems in Enumeration and Definition

The legal status of independent contracting is ambiguous, but the question of whether a worker is genuinely an *employee* or a *self-employed independent contractor* generally depends on the following related questions:[14]

- How much control does the worker have over the execution of the work?
- What is the worker's opportunity for profit and loss?
- Has the worker made a large investment in the enterprise? Does he or she have a place of business and offer services to the public?
- What is the worker's skill level?
- How permanent is the relationship?

A genuine independent contractor exercises control over the execution and timing of the work, has the opportunity to gain or lose, has made an investment in equipment or capital, has a skill that allows him or her to compete in the market place, and is not in an enduring relationship with the employer. The corollary holds true: if the worker has little control over work hours, priority, or pacing of the work, has no opportunity to gain or lose, uses materials, tools, or equipment from the employer, and has an on-going relationship with the company, then he or she is entitled to the rights and protections accorded by law to company employees. These include the right to unemployment insurance, workman's compensation, and employers' contributions to their social security (FICA) accounts.[15]

Our research reveals that according to common law many women working at home doing clerical work are being hired fraudulently as independent contractors. Some women themselves have come to recognize the inherent inequities of the arrangement. A case pending in the California courts challenges the corporate practice of contracting out work to home-based workers.

In 1982, California Western States Life Insurance Company offered some of its insurance claims processors the opportunity to work at home instead of in the office. They would become contractors, paid by a piece rate and given no benefits. The processors, most of them women with family responsibilities, saw it as an attractive option—at first. They could have more flexibility and save the money and time previously spent commuting. Most of them joined the program in 1983.

On December 1, 1985, eight of the women quit their jobs and filed a suit against the company, claiming that the independent contracting arrangement was simply a subterfuge to avoid paying them benefits. They also claimed that the company kept increasing their quotas, sometimes forcing them to work fifteen hours a day, eliminating any flexibility. Together, the women are seeking $250,000 in back benefits and at least $1 million in punitive damages. The women are claiming fraud on the part of the company. California Western's position is that the plaintiffs signed the contracts, knew what they were getting, and always had the right to quit.[16]

It seems clear that these home-based contractors are not self-employed in the way genuine contractors—business owners—with multiple choices are: these business owners exercise much more leverage and clout in the marketplace.

Home-based Business Owners

Although home-based business owners and independent contractors are both technically self-employed, a genuine business owner is in a very different economic picture than is a contractor. Home-based business owners often provide the same types of services as contractors, but they have multiple clients and contracting arrangements. As a result, they possess the autonomy to set their own rates according to what the market will bear and to recruit and monitor their flow of work. This autonomy leads many clerical business owners to think of themselves as professionals, even though the work they do would be considered clerical if done in a conventional office.

The home proves to be a very desirable workplace in which to incubate and shelter a home-based clerical business owner. She can write off her home office as well as her related business expenses. She can also minimize her monthly overhead by working at home rather than in a rented office.

Women are clearly partaking in the rise of such self-employment. From 1977 to 1982 the total number of sole proprietorships rose 21 percent, whereas the number of woman-owned-and-operated small businesses rose 46 percent.[17] Many women appear ready to strike out on their own for a variety of reasons. By starting their own businesses, some can re-enter the labor force after raising their children, circumventing the ageism and sexism they see in the corporate world. Others can leave the corporate world and, using the skills honed there, make more money.

Employment Status and Income

Based on a small sample we found that clerical independent contractors average $7.13 an hour (with a range between $4.50 and $13.50), whereas clerical business owners average $17.86 an hour (with a range between $6.00 and $30.00). These are before-tax figures and will be cut anywhere from 20 percent to 50 percent, depending on tax rates, FICA, and benefit coverages. It is possible that some independent contractors will end up with minimum wage or below by the time they finish. Why then, would a typist or transcriber want to be an independent contractor?

Homework and the Family

Clerical Independent Contracting and Motherhood

The answer is—she doesn't. Most home-based clerical independent contractors whose status is questionable are mothers of young children. They want to work at home: to have job security, to have a dependable competitive salary, to receive benefits that don't duplicate those of their husbands, and to have the potential to advance. In effect, they want the benefits of being an employee. They don't want to be business owners because they don't have the time or energy to work the twelve-hour days typical of those starting a business. These women are independent contractors by default. The marketplace offers them no other alternative.

They know that their "employers" are buying them cheaply. Yet they characterize the situation as a win-win. Their employers make money and the women get to be home with their children. Those without specialized education or training can actually take home more than they might if they worked outside and had to pay commuting and child-care costs.

But the situation is not so simple. Approximately two-thirds of all women with children under the age of eighteen work, but whether married or single, they face formidable challenges.[18] In addition to the demands of their jobs, they assume major responsibility for care of the children and house. They face severely limited opportunities for affordable, quality child care. And they often experience personal conflict and public criticism for leaving their young children in the care of others. In spite of these responsibilities, most of these women say they not only want to work, they need to work, and they need to find an arrangement for combining work and family.

Although home-based work appears to suit their needs, we must be circumspect about promoting it for all working mothers, particularly single parents. Moreover, the current corporate practice of independent contracting runs the risk of creating a second-class corporate citizenry, composed of women with limited options in the larger marketplace. When these women accept less than the market rate, they weaken their future bargaining positions if and when life circumstances necessitate that they earn more. Family situations change: husbands die or lose their jobs; marriages break up. Children get sick; medical bills mount. These women could find themselves in a position in which they need health benefits or more money but have weakened their leverage by accepting less than what the market would bear. From a wider perspective, the women who take a lower rate may do a disservice to other men or women who need to get a higher rate to support themselves and their families. In an unregulated and market-driven economy, the job obviously goes to the lowest bidder.

Homework as a Child Care Policy

Efforts to promote any form of home-employment as child care are premised on assumptions that are faulty. The first assumption is that a woman can simultaneously work and care for her children. The ad is familiar to us by now. It shows a woman working at her kitchen computer while her infant plays quietly behind her. Our survey shows that the ad does not describe the realities. The vast majority of women can not and do not try to work when their children are awake and around. Of clerical women with preschool children, about a fifth (17 percent) pay for child care, another fifth (19 percent) enlist their husbands or other family members to watch their children, and most of the rest work when their children are asleep.

Many women extend their day to accommodate their work. By rising well before the children awake and by working deep into the night, they obtain the quiet and concentration they need to work. The women often work split shifts and just as often put in a full "day's" work after the children go to bed. This type of work pattern affects the family: our in-person interviews reveal that it takes a toll on the woman's relationships with her husband *and* children.

The second assumption is that mothers like working at home. Well, they like working there better than not working. But of women who have primary responsibility for child care, most report the combination as stressful and isolating. They resent that when and how they work is constantly in response to the demands of others: their family or "employer."

Moreover, if the mother enjoyed working outside the home and made the decision as a compromise between family and earning extra money, she is likely to be less satisfied than mothers whose reasons were related to avoiding the office. For these women, home employment is much better than nonemployment, but it is far from ideal. They miss the office. They report stress at balancing work and family. They have a difficult time with loneliness. Often, these women view homework as a transitional stage in their lives. They want to work outside the home once their children are grown.

Overall, the mothers report satisfaction with home employment, but satisfaction must always be gauged in contrast to their existing options. The home as a workplace does not eliminate the juggling act every working mother knows about. For some women, the act becomes a bit easier because they have gained time. By not commuting, a woman can extend her work day to twenty-four hours, as opposed to eight, and she is more consistently, albeit indirectly, available to her children.

For others, the act gets harder. The worker is always reminded of what she's not doing. If she's working, she's not cleaning the house; if she's with her children, she's not working. The woman never gets away, since work is always there. One woman spoke longingly of her old commuter bus ride in rush-hour traffic. It was the only time she had to herself. Now when she walks out of her home office, she immediately picks up the laundry basket and becomes Mom.

For most, home employment is better than nonemployment but it is far from ideal. It is an option pursued within a society that offers working mothers few options for flexibility in combining work and family. Yet, it is an option that does allow them to oversee their children's critical first years, and the importance of that for many women cannot be underestimated.

Conclusions and Policy Recommendations

The realities of clerical homework are more complex than many would have us believe. Both protective and supportive legislation should be passed to ensure that clerical homeworkers can become strong competitive forces in the labor market.

To achieve this economic viability, the following issues should be addressed:

1. The definitions of employee versus self-employed independent contractors must be made explicit and consistent across federal and state agencies. Home-based workers who are expected to perform as employees should be defined as employees with full benefits. There should be consistency of definition across both the Internal Revenue Service and the Fair Labor Standards Law, as well as state laws. Employers should be held to these with tests, so that workers expected to perform as employees will be recompensed as such.
2. Medical and retirement benefits should be provided for home-based work pro-rated to wage earnings. In order to provide two-parent households with optimal coverage, a cafeteria approach to benefits could be undertaken. This would allow nontraditional benefits, such as child-care vouchers, to be available to these households. As I stressed before, over a third of the clerical homeworkers depend on some form of supplemental child care. In addition, retirement benefits should be provided for workers so they can take care of themselves in their old age.
3. Congress should support the creation of a national information center, as well as local support and referral systems, for women who work at home. The ignorance and isolation bred by the home as work place must be counteracted if homeworkers are to earn prevailing market rates.
4. Alternative forms of child care must be made available. People who work at home should have access to other forms of child care, so they can give full attention to both work and family and so that the decision to work at home is a choice freely made and not one forced by inadequate work-family alternatives.

5. Corporations cannot be allowed to discriminate according to place. Workers at home should be treated and paid in exactly the same fashion as those who work in the offices.
6. Families need flexible work arrangements, but home-based work should only be one type of work alternative. People who work at home should have the option of other flexible work alternatives, including job sharing, part-time work with benefits, flextime, and parental leave.

Home-based clerical workers should have a choice: either to work at home and become competitive in the marketplace or to work outside their homes. Everything must be done to provide these choices. To do otherwise is to undercut the financial security of these women and their families.

NOTES

This chapter is a revised version of testimony on the pros and cons of home-based clerical work, presented before the Subcommittee on Employment and Housing, Committee on Government Operations, U.S. House of Representatives, February 26, 1986.

1. The analysis of the home employment demographics in the 1980 U.S. census was conducted by R. Kraut and P. Grambsch, "Home-based White Collar Employment: Lessons from 1980 Census," *Social Forces* 66, no. 4 (1987): 410–26. See also F. Horvath, "Work at Home: New Findings from the Current Population Survey," *Monthly Labor Review* 109, no. 11 (November 1986): 31–35.

2. The Administration of Children, Youth, and Families, U.S. Department of Health and Human Services, sponsored the survey as part of "Impacts of Home-based work on Women and Their Families" (K. Christensen, Grant Number: 90-PD-86562). I want to thank Nava Lerer and Sheryl Meredith for their research assistance.

3. These in-depth interviews were conducted in the women's homes from September 1984 to May 1985. This research was sponsored by the Department of Health and Human Services (Grant 90-PD-86562) as well as by the Office of Technology Assessment, U.S. Congress (Agreement Number 433938.0), as part of their 1985 study, U.S. Congress, Office of Technology Assessment, *Automation of America's Offices*, OTA-CIT-287 (Washington, D.C.: 1985). The latter research is reported in K. Christensen, "Impacts of Computer-mediated Home-based Work on Women and Their Families," in *Office: Technology and People* 3 (1987): 211–30. Selected interviews constitute case studies in K. Christensen, *Women and Home-based Work: The Unspoken Contract* (New York: Henry Holt, 1988).

4. Detailed discussion of this factor analyses is provided in K. Christensen, N. Lerer, and R. Eichenstein, "Sources of Satisfaction for Women Working at Home" (unpublished manuscript, City University of New York, Graduate Center, August 1987).

5. See Christensen, "Impacts of Computer-mediated Home-based Work."

6. U.S. House of Representatives, Subcommittee of the Committee on Government Operations, *Home-based Clerical Workers: Are They Victims of Exploitation?* (Washington, D.C.: GPO, 1986).

7. E. Appelbaum, "Alternate Work Schedules of Women" (Paper prepared for the panel on Technology and Women's Employment Workshop, National Academy of Sciences, Washington, D.C., February 28–March 11, 1985).

8. See K. Christensen, "Women and Contingent Work," *Social Policy* 17, no. 4 (1987): 15–18. Also see U.S. Dept. of Labor, *Flexible Workstyles: A Look at Contingent Labor* (Washington: GPO, 1988), and K. Christensen, ed., *The New Era of Home-based Work: Directions and Policies* (Boulder, Colo.: Westview Press, 1988) for further analysis of the relationship of home-based work to trends in contingent labor.

9. I can't help but think that these services are forerunners of the emerging "employee leasing" firms. The obvious difference has to do with status. The services hire contractors paid by piece. The leasing firms hire salaried employees with benefits. But it would be very interesting to explore the latter from the pattern of the former, including the potential effects on occupation segregation and wage scales. See Jeff Day, "Employee Leasing" in *Flexible Workstyles: A Look at Contingent Labor.*

10. Systematic statistical data are not available, but see interview data presented in Christensen, *Women and Home-based Work.* Also see Vary Coates, "Office Automation and Contingent Work Modes" (Paper prepared for the Contingent Workplace Conference, cosponsored by U.S. Department of Labor and Graduate Center, City University of New York, New York City, January 15–16, 1987). An edited version is published in *Flexible Workstyles: A Look at Contingent Labor.*

11. Christensen, "Impacts of Computer-mediated Home-based Work."

12. Ibid.

13. See Internal Revenue Service, Advisory Memorandum no. 8451004, August, 1984. This 1984 Technical Advice Memorandum from the Internal Revenue Service may require companies and services to consider their contractors as employees for Social Security purposes.

14. The major difficulty encountered in trying to collect data on independent contractors is due to the lack of consistency in definition. For federal tax purposes, the Internal Revenue Service (IRS) relies on common law in determining who is an employee and draws on a substantial body of case law under the IRS code which supports that practice. Under the Fair Labor Standards Act (FLSA), U.S. Department of Labor (DOL) relies on a broader conception of employee status than that conveyed in common law. The Bureau of Labor Statistics (BLS) collects employment figures on three groups: self-employed, wage and salary earners (private and government), and unpaid family workers.

Independent contractors are technically self-employed and would fall under that category. When asked how BLS defines independent contractor, Ellie Abramson of their staff pointed out that they do not use such a term and it would be presumptuous to read the self-employment statistics as indicative of the number of independent contractors. Although the Fair Labor Standards Act (FLSA) of 1942 provides a broad definition of employee status, BLS does not currently collect such information.

The Internal Revenue Service (IRS), although concerned with independent contracting for tax purposes, does not have publicly available data on these workers. Norm Fox of the Examination Area of the IRS, which audits tax returns and is concerned with contractors for that reason, characterized independent contractors as people who do not have "withholding" taken from their salaries. He indicated that one way to find demographics on these workers would be to review the "1099" forms of Schedule Fees and the "530" tax forms. Both forms are used in addition to a "sole proprietorship" form by people who consider themselves independent contractors. See J. Simonson, "Protection of Clerical Homeworkers: From What? By Whom?" in *The New Era of Home-based Work: Directions and Policies*, ed. Christensen, pp. 157–67.

15. Correspondence from Ronald Moore, Chief Individual Income Tax Branch to Representative Barney Frack (D-Mass) CC: IND: J:1:1: - TR-38–30019–86. (1986).

16. K. Christensen, "Telecommuters Go to Court," *Across the Board* 29, no. 4: 20.

17. *The State of Small Businesses: A Report of the President to the Congress*, May 1985 (Washington, D.C.: 1985), p. 289.

18. U.S. Department of Labor, Women's Bureau, *20 Facts on Women Workers*, Fact Sheet no. 86.1 (1986).

10

The Clerical Homework Program at the Wisconsin Physicians Services Insurance Corporation

CYNTHIA B. COSTELLO

In the winter of 1980, the Wisconsin Physicians Services Insurance Corporation (WPS), a medium-sized insurance firm located in Madison, Wisconsin, began to recruit women to work part time processing insurance claims out of their homes. By 1984, the company had hired approximately a hundred women to work as clerical homeworkers. A senior vice-president of WPS told the *New York Times* that the homework program was initiated to "provide meaningful, gainful employment for the homebound."[1] Additional factors shaped the company's decision to hire homeworkers: as a cost-cutting initiative designed to increase managerial flexibility, the homework program also provided WPS management with a strategy for circumventing their in-company, unionized work force.

For homeworkers, employment with WPS offered an opportunity to combine wage-earning, household, and child-care responsibilities. Through homework, women sought to fulfill their family commitments while also retaining their ties to the labor market. Some women found, however, that the experience of homework fell short of their expectations. Confronted with the relative inflexibility of WPS managers and family members, homeworkers became dissatisfied with the arrangement.

Interviews I have conducted with homeworkers and managers employed by WPS, provide insights into the appeal as well as the limitations of home-based employment for working women, their motivations for seeking home-based employment, the interaction between homework and family life, the social networks and strategies the women forge and the contradictions they confront.[2] I shall discuss all of these here in this chapter.

Overview of the Clerical Homework Program at WPS

Several motivations shaped the decision by the Wisconsin Physicians Services Insurance Corporation to hire home-based women to work as typists, coders, and claims adjustors. First, the homeworkers provided a cost-effective method for adding staff to process high-volume medical and dental claims without having to expand the office space. A recent increase in business at the company put office space at a premium. Second, homeworkers provided a flexible work force for a company in an industry with peak and slack periods. WPS could hire part-time homeworkers and adjust their hours to the flow of insurance claims at the company. Third, homeworkers were less expensive than their in-company counterparts. Until 1984, the starting wage for homeworkers was $3.36 an hour, after which the starting wage increased to $3.75 an hour. By not paying for homeworkers' vacations, sick leave, or medical and pension benefits, the company saved additional costs as well.

Finally, the substitution of nonunion homeworkers for union employees allowed management to bypass the union. An acrimonious relationship between the company and the union had existed since 1976 when Local 1444 of the United Food and Commercial Workers organized the clerical work force. The conflict peaked in the fall of 1979, when the union employees voted to strike against WPS but later withdrew the threat when the company agreed to a contract with a union shop (that required all new, full-time clerical employees to join the union). However, the 1979 contract excluded part-time workers from the bargaining unit. In order to weaken the leverage of union employees, in 1980 WPS began to hire large numbers of part-time and temporary employees to work in the company offices, as well as homebound women to work at home. "There [was] never a good atmosphere at WPS in terms of union versus management," explained one former manager. "The idea [of the homework program] was to expand outside of the union . . . [to eliminate union] staff without having to go through all the hassles with the union."

The company recruited women with preschool or school-aged children to work as homeworkers. Women with clerical and medical experience were preferred, and the home environment of a potential homeworker was of special concern. "You looked to see that they took care of themselves and their house," explained one former supervisor, "and then they would take care of their work." The applicant's plan for accommodating mothering and homework responsibilities was also considered. Experience with homeworkers whose children "spilled [food] on the claims materials" made supervisors wary of women unable to separate their household from their homework tasks.

Once hired, homeworkers completed a two-week training program at the company. Supervisors instructed small groups of homeworkers in the skills of claims processing—the interpretation and coding of medical diagnoses and procedures, the application of insurance guidelines, and the determination of insurance payments. Homeworkers then returned home to begin their new jobs. Between 4 and 7 P.M. four days a week, a truck delivered a bucket of claims to the homeworker. The amount of work varied from day to day and week to week, depending on the work flow at WPS's main office buildings. The homeworker had twenty-four hours to complete the work, except in the case of the Thursday night delivery, which left the homeworker with the weekend.

Homeworkers performed different tasks. Some women addressed envelopes, pulled staples from insurance claims, and typed correspondence. The majority were either coders or adjustors. Both of these groups first counted the claims to ensure that the total matched the number listed on the invoice sheet. Coders then transferred the appropriate codes for medical diagnoses and procedures from insurance manuals to insurance claims. Homeworkers who adjusted insurance claims also checked the diagnosis for each claim to make sure it matched the medical procedure and consulted insurance manuals to determine the cost of the service performed. They then recorded onto a code sheet the appropriate codes for the medical diagnosis, the medical service performed (e.g., checkup, surgery, or x-ray), and the charge for the medical service. At the end of the day, the claims adjustors and the coders entered the total number of claims processed onto a ticket.

Until 1984, all of the homeworkers processed insurance claims manually. The only tools required for the job were code sheets, pencils, and calculators. Beginning in 1984, WPS began to provide personal computers to a handful of homeworkers. The delivery system didn't change, but some homeworkers received computer disks along with their insurance claims. Computer homeworkers entered data from insurance claims directly onto computer disks, thereby eliminating the intermediary step of transferring information from the insurance claim to the codesheet. Over the next two years, the company increased the number of computer homeworkers, but the majority of homeworkers continued to process claims manually. As a company that was automating its claims process very slowly, the distinction between manual coders and computer homeworkers paralleled the division between different groups of office workers who worked in WPS's main office buildings.

The homeworker had only sporadic contact with WPS management. After the initial training, homeworkers were instructed to call their supervisor between 10 A.M. and 1 P.M. as questions arose. Supervisors communicated with homeworkers through memos outlining any procedural changes. They also sent homeworkers monthly audits reporting their productivity and error rates. Personal contact with supervisors was rare. Periodically, supervisors called meetings to update homeworkers on new procedures for processing claims. And once or twice a year, supervisors visited the homeworker to evaluate her performance.

The maximum raise for homeworkers was 8 percent. Although homeworkers were not paid by the piece, their raises primarily depended on their productivity. Productivity was measured against the homeworkers' rate expectancies (RE's)—the number of claims homeworkers were expected to process in an hour. The homeworkers' attitudes and absenteeism also affected their raises. (Women who were frequently unavailable for homework received a high absenteeism score.) The highest paid homeworker had worked at home for five years and received $5.00 an hour. Most of the homeworkers earned $4.00 an hour or less.[3]

The Motivations of Homeworkers

Most homeworkers approached employment with WPS as a secondary activity that would allow them to fulfill their primary commitment to their families. All but one of the homeworkers were married. Their average age was thirty-one. All of the women had children: 58 percent had preschool-aged children, 19 percent had school-aged children, and 23 percent had children in both age groups.

It was against the backdrop of traditional values about women's roles that women sought employment as homeworkers. "It sounds old-fashioned, but women are still the ones who raise the children," stated one homeworker with strong religious commitments. "After that if a woman needs to get a job, preferably part-time, and if it is really necessary for a family, then that is alright. But I'm opposed when women get in and take jobs from men who really are the bread-winners. And I see men who can't get jobs . . . because affirmative action says you've got to hire this many women or blacks. Yet, I'm not opposed to working women. Women have to work. [But], the job is secondary to the family." And a second homeworker echoed, "I feel that women who are out there working don't have to be working. They are wanting more than they really need to live on. If they tone down their wants, they could make it without working. . . . I think that a woman with career aspirations should integrate that into her family life."

Additional motivations shaped the homeworkers' decision to apply for a job with WPS, as well. Many homeworkers needed the additional income. The yearly earnings of homeworkers ranged from $1000 to $4,450 a year, with an average of $2,380. While their income was minimal, homeworkers calculated the money saved on gas and clothing. "I wouldn't consider this gainful employment," stated one homeworker, "but if you have children at home, you can dress in rags all day . . . the work is brought right to your home and you don't have to spend money on gas or car insurance." The money saved on babysitters provided an additional incentive to work at home: "I thought that hiring a babysitter for the amount of money I could make [by working outside the home] would be just crazy because you would be paying out just about everything you earned for a sitter." The mean family income of homeworkers was $29,600, with a range from $12,000 to $50,000 a year. For women with lower family incomes, their earnings paid for groceries and rent while those from more affluent families invested in their children's education, family vacations, or household purchases.

Homeworkers also hoped that employment with WPS would offer an opportunity to retain their ties to the labor market. All of the homeworkers had high-school degrees, 60 percent had some college education in addition, and 28 percent held bachelor's or nursing degrees. Most homeworkers had previously worked in the white-collar and service sectors as waitresses, clerical workers, teachers, and health-care workers. Some of the women were ambivalent about leaving the labor force for children. "Work is important," asserted one homeworker, "and it is hard giving up a job. I had to decide if I would push my career or be with my children." Homework offered a means, some women thought, for preparing to re-enter the work force. Others hoped that the experience gained from adjusting claims at home might provide a route to job mobility. One woman underscored that she didn't want to start at the bottom again when she returned to the work force full time: "I didn't want people to think I have been sitting around eating potato chips and dip."

Finally, employment as homeworkers offered women an avenue for enhancing their self-esteem as well as their bargaining power with their husbands. Some women felt devalued in their status as housewives. "I was tired of everyone saying, 'Are you working now?' And I'd say, 'Yes, I work full-time. I'm home with my children.'" Homeworkers felt that WPS was placing a "value" on the housewife's time. "There was somebody out there who was willing to hire us," underscored one homeworker, "We're not just housewives—people with no minds—that are sitting home raising children. Somebody was giving us a chance to use our minds again and paying us to do it." Women also hoped that their homework income would increase their leverage with their husbands. As one woman explained, "I was always asking for money from my husband and I felt left out of everything. Then I thought, with homework, at least I'd have my own paycheck and I could do what I wanted to do with it."

Homework and Family Life

Women adapted their homes to the requirements of homework with varying degrees of success. Homeworkers with extra space transformed a spare bedroom or basement into a home office, sometimes with the help of husbands. Women with a separate room for claims adjusting could leave claims forms, calculators, and reference books out without worrying that a family member would disturb them. Others felt that the homework materials intruded into their household. Those with little space utilized a kitchen table to process claims, requiring the constant packing and unpacking of homework materials for meal preparation. "When I started out," stated one homeworker, "I had a little area where I worked and I could put work aside and leave it out. By the time I left, I had a large box full of information and paper. It was completely cluttered with all sorts of manuals and supplies. [It] was cluttering up the family environment."

Some homeworkers appreciated the solitude of the work, particularly at first. Working at home offered a "break" from the petty difficulties encountered in the office. "I like regulating my hours," reported one woman. "You do your work and nobody is hassling you or watching you." A second homeworker characterized the appeal of working at home: "Being able to do it at my own time, setting my own hours. No one was watching over me . . . over my shoulder all the time making sure I was doing it correctly." Another homeworker found that the arrangement allowed her to claim privacy in relation to her family: "I thought, this was one time of the day I can be alone, no one will bother me."

For other homeworkers, the feeling of detachment, of "being cut off from the mainstream," was disconcerting. Women missed the social interaction of the office and looked forward to returning to an organizational work setting. "The isolation was awful," reported one homeworker. "I had always worked with lots of people. I liked being out in the office. . . . I felt out of it. I was like a recluse. I didn't know how women were wearing their hair. . . . That part was real hard." A second homeworker agreed: "At first, it was great. I thought this is really it. This is fun. I can finally be home with my kids. And I enjoyed being a domestic person. . . . After awhile, I think I started talking like the kids. I missed the interactions with other people. I missed doing what I like doing best, that is being a secretary and being able to work with other people."

The invisibility of their work created problems for homeworkers. Friends and neighbors who presumed that homeworkers "weren't really working" didn't hesitate to call for a social chat, drop in for a visit, or send their children over to play. "Other women outside the home didn't look at you as working," reported one homeworker, "so they think of calling you any time of the day. It is so frustrating. . . . People think it isn't work, [but rather] a hobby." Even spouses sometimes failed to regard homework as "real work." "It is hard because [my husband] doesn't see it as a job because I am home," stated one homeworker, "A lot of men in this world think that just because you are at home, you aren't doing anything. I think they should have their heads looked at." In a few cases, homeworkers themselves downplayed their work. When friends asked her if she was working, one homeworker responded, "No." Despite the homeworker's desire for a work-based identity, the marginal nature of home-based employment made family members, neighbors, and even the homeworker herself unable to see it as a "real job."

Women differed as to the ease with which they juggled household, child care, and homework responsibilities. Some women integrated the homework into their lives with little difficulty. "I don't mind homework," one woman with a preschool daughter explained, "because when I'm home, I can have the laundry going when I am doing my homework." But other women encountered difficulties balancing the demands of homework and family. Some homeworkers received help from husbands who cleaned the house or cared for children so they could complete their claims adjusting. But most homeworkers retained primary responsibility for the household. The job of claims adjusting therefore was added onto women's housework and child-care tasks, resulting in a lengthened work day. Women with children in public school could complete most of their claims adjusting during school hours. Those with preschool children at home processed the simpler claims when children were awake, leaving the more difficult ones for nap time, evening, and early morning. One homeworker's allocation of her time typified their strategies: "When I get the claims at night, I try to put in an hour while the kids are watching t.v. Then I get up at 4:30 A.M. to work before the kids get up. It all depends on what the kids are doing. I work between 5:30 and 7:30 A.M. . . . It is easier when nobody is around so my mind isn't wandering. . . . During the day, I turn on the t.v. and tell my preschooler to watch. . . . Then, when she takes a nap, I can work."

Some homeworkers had no alternative but to let some of their housework go. "As far as housework, the house was never in such bad shape," reported one homeworker. For women whose primary identity was bound up with home and family, this caused distress. "The [homework] is always on my mind at home," reported another homeworker. "I think, 'Oh, I have that work; I have to get it done.' If I could go [out to work], it would be done and I could come home and not think about it. I would just think about work around the home. Doing homework is real difficult for me because I think I should be doing homework when I'm doing the laundry and then I think, 'No, this comes first.' "

In particular, many women found the demands of homework antithetical to the requirements of children. Claims adjusting requires concentration. Depending on their age and temperament, some children left their mothers alone to process insurance claims. Others did not. "I'd just get a claim done and [the baby] would get into something or he needed to be fed or held," stated one homeworker, "It is hard to hold a baby and do your work at the same time." Particularly frustrating for many homeworkers was the negative effect of children's interruptions on productivity. Minutes spent responding to children's needs cut into the time allotted for each claim. "You are working at home with small children," reported one homeworker, "and you are always interrupted for 'Mommy can I have a snack? Can I have this?' You have to write down the time you stop and the time you start up again. I have time sheets a foot long [at] times."

One of the ironies of homework was the cost it exacted on family relationships. Most homeworkers chose the work so they could care for their children. But to complete the work, they had to either keep their children occupied or ignore them. Over time, some homeworkers realized they were snapping at their kids and homework was cutting into their family time. One woman summed up the contradiction inherent in homework: "The advantage is being able to stay home and the disadvantage [is] not being able to keep up with your parenting responsibilities." In some cases, the homework contributed to conflict with spouses as well. Some husbands objected that homework interfered with their wive's availability for companionship; others resented their additional child-care responsibilities. "The money is not worth it," asserted one husband, "I can't stay down in the family room [with the children] one more night."

Job Satisfaction and Dissatisfaction

The womens' satisfaction with the home as a work environment was integrally tied to their assessment of the working conditions associated with the WPS homework program. Homeworkers expressed mixed feelings about the daily work of claims adjusting. Particularly in the beginning, many homeworkers enjoyed their work. "I like the work," stated one homeworker. "Sometimes there is variety. Some [claims] are easy and others are difficult." But after mastering the skill of the job, many homeworkers found the work monotonous. "Once you get it," stressed one homeworker, "it is like a factory or assembly line worker."

Many women felt they deserved higher wages. "For awhile, I rationalized [the low pay] by saying, 'I am saving money. They are saving money. It's a good deal for the company and it's a good deal for me so it balances out," related one woman. "But I really think the company does get the better end of the deal. They are saving a lot more money than I am saving by staying at home." The rate expectancies were another source of dissatisfaction. The expectancies varied, depending on the type of claim a homeworker processed. Some of the homeworkers had no problem meeting the rate, but others concluded that the rates were unfair. "They make it sound that it is the offer of a lifetime . . . ," explained one homeworker, "but after you're hired . . . they are going to squeeze everything out of you and then ask for more."

The requirement that women be home for the delivery truck created frustrations as well. Homeworkers were not paid for this waiting time. Although they could often predict the arrival time of the delivery truck, if it arrived late, the homeworker sometimes missed a family activity. The erratic amount of work caused additional problems. Some homeworkers received a consistent amount of work from week to week, but others did not. "If they got behind in-house, we went without work," stated one homeworker. "If they needed to get those claims it was always a call out . . . can we deliver some more? and they loaded us up." Under pressure to process all of the claims, homeworkers experienced stress. As one homeworker explained: "If you'd get six hours of work someday and you have two little kids at home and you only have three hours worth of t.v., when are you going to get the rest of the work done? And you may have made plans. One of the advantages of being at home was the flexibility. And yet, you weren't really flexible when you had planned on getting three hours of work and all of a sudden they gave you six hours of work. . . . That really limited your flexibility."

Homeworkers also found supervisors unnecessarily rigid. Some supervisors made adjustments for the homeworker's family responsibilities, but others expressed irritation with homeworkers whose children interfered with their work. At one point, WPS sent homeworkers a memo offering suggestions for the scheduling of household tasks around the requirements of homework. Only in an extreme emergency, the memo stated, should women return claims unprocessed. Supervisory pressure to complete the work added to the stress experienced by homeworkers; "You are always meeting the deadline," one homeworker concluded. "You cannot live your life that way if you've got kids. I mean they get sick or they want to do things. . . . It is very stressful because you have double duty. You have to take care of the kids and try to make these deadlines. . . . If you have more than one kid, it is incredible the pressure . . ."

Networks and Strategies

The company's recruitment strategy encouraged homeworkers to forge friendship networks. By targeting several Madison neighborhoods for recruitment, WPS often hired women who already knew each other. Moreover, WPS actively encouraged homeworkers to recommend friends and neighbors to the company. The majority of homeworkers gained employment in the homework program through friends and neighbors. "I was an Avon lady for a while," explained one woman, "and a lot of people I talked to in the neighborhood knew about the program because they had friends who did the work." WPS rarely needed to advertise for homeworkers because, according to one supervisor, "everyone in the homework program always knew somebody else (who wanted to work as a homeworker)."

The training program further contributed to the development of social ties among homeworkers. Homeworkers perceived the training program as inadequate and disorganized. Confused and overwhelmed at the end of the training, homeworkers exchanged phone numbers and addresses before they returned home. "We wanted contact with each other for moral support," explained one homeworker, "[since] we were sent out in total darkness."

Homeworkers sometimes arranged get-togethers over coffee breaks or lunch. They also met at the local YMCA, neighborhood church, or family sports event. There, women discussed new recruits to the homework program and exchanged information about wages, memos, and evaluations. A desire to break the isolation of homework, chat about their children, or request work-based advice also prompted homeworkers to communicate by phone. "You really get close to these girls," reported one woman. "If you have problems, instead of having to call work all the time, you call one of them. And it was really nice." A phone call to another homeworker also helped to relieve the pressure. "By Wednesday, we were burnt out, crying our heads off," reported one homeworker.

Communication among homeworkers increased prior to the periodic meetings called by WPS to update homeworkers about procedural changes. In anticipation of meetings, homeworkers discussed their grievances with each other. Many of the meetings turned into gripe sessions as women complained about the low pay and rigid procedures, as well as the intrusion of homework into their family lives. The response from management was less than satisfactory. "[Management] would claim that they would hear the complaints," explained one woman. "Instead, it was their running rough-shod over all the homeworkers." On the way home from the meetings, women stopped at McDonald's to gossip. "When we left," reported one woman, "we were always more disgusted than when we went to the meeting."

Interactions among homeworkers encouraged the women to develop an interpretation of fair wages and working conditions that differed from management's. Some managers thought that homeworkers were underpaid, but others viewed them as secondary wage-earners from middle-class households. "Mostly, women were looking for a second income or something to do," stated one former manager. "They were bored. Most were middle to upper class. They did not need the money. Salary was not the issue." Compared to the in-company work force which, according to WPS managers, was "lower class" and "less educated," the homeworkers represented a middle-class labor pool. But the homeworkers offered a different view of the company's policies. "They are getting homeworkers to do the work that they have to pay union workers more money for and they are getting cheap labor," asserted one homeworker. Many women felt they deserved higher raises for the skill and effort exercised in their jobs. One woman summed up the views of many of her coworkers: "What you needed to perform your jobs would have qualified you to make a lot more money." Homeworkers also took issue with their lack of influence over company policy. WPS could change the rules and the homeworker had no recourse. "If the company says your performance must be higher to get a raise, you have no input into that," reported one homeworker. "You are totally out of the decision-making process." For many homeworkers, their grievances boiled down to a lack of respect. "That's one thing we don't really feel, that we are respected," emphasized one homeworker. "It's like they are doing you a favor by giving you this job and if you are not going to fill it, there is another woman out there who will take it."

Homeworkers devised a myriad of strategies for dealing with their working conditions. Many responded by "biting the bullet." "There were times when it was very stressful," stated one homeworker, "when I just wanted to throw that work right out the window. And then I'd say to myself, 'Just do it, it's just a job, earn the money, it's not worth worrying about. . . . By taking the attitude that it's just a job, that's how I made it through." Although many homeworkers felt that their working conditions were unfair, few felt in a position to "create waves about it." Homeworkers therefore encouraged each other to "hang tough" with the admonishment, "It's just a job, you can put up with it."

Homeworkers did circumvent WPS's policies, however. The constant interaction among homeworkers ran counter to company policy. Homeworkers took additional part-time jobs, despite the directive not to. And rather than adapt to the unpredictability of the daily work load, homeworkers chose to regulate their own hours. Some women refused to process more claims than they could handle; and others extended their hours beyond the nineteen-and-three-quarter maximum. Although the company didn't like the practice, WPS paid the homeworkers for the additional time.

Other initiatives focused on the rate expectancies. In order to improve their productivity, some homeworkers processed the easiest claims first and left the difficult ones to the end of the day. If the more challenging claims were returned unprocessed, so much the better for the homeworker. Other women paced themselves to extend their hours and prevent the company from raising the rate expectancies. "It wasn't to your benefit to do sixty an hour if the expectancy was thirty," explained one homeworker, "because then they would raise the expectancy and everybody would be expected to do it." Homeworkers also shortcircuited the steps involved in claims processing. Since WPS management emphasized quantity, homeworkers decided that accuracy could be ignored. And in a few cases, women overreported their hours.

On multiple occasions, homeworkers individually registered their dissatisfactions with supervisors. Some complaints brought results. The production requirement was lowered in one case; a homeworker's raise was adjusted in another. But in many instances, the homeworker's grievance was ignored. Management responded that if the woman disagreed with company policy, she could quit. A homeworker who complained was in a particularly vulnerable position. "The homeworkers aren't protected by any rules," explained one woman. "You are [therefore] at the company's mercy." Only one homeworker had been fired, but other homeworkers who challenged management authority were patronized, reprimanded, or denied work.

The examples of collective initiatives among homeworkers revealed the limitations to group action among isolated employees. In a few instances, collective efforts were effective. When a group of homeworkers complained at a meeting about the rate expectancies, for example, the supervisor lifted their quotas. For the most part, however, homeworkers' collective initiatives were unsuccessful. In one case, a homeworker tried to organize her coworkers to demand higher wages. "I said," this homeworker reported, " 'Let's all get together and say we have to get more money because we do all this work and it is [worth] good money.' " But her coworkers were unwilling to present a united front. In a second case, conflict arose after a CBS news story revealed that homeworkers were paid less than their in-company counterparts. Supervisors diffused the homeworkers' grievance by stressing that in-company employees paid for clothing, gas, and babysitters. And in a third case, several homeworkers voiced dissatisfactions when they learned that the company had hired new recruits at a higher wage than longer-term homeworkers. Although many of the homeworkers were angry, few were willing to confront the company.

What prevented the homeworkers from mounting an effective, collective challenge to managerial policies at WPS? In part, the homeworkers' family commitments and temporary status weakened their identification with "working women's rights." Many homeworkers did express a consciousness about the problems with the homework program at WPS and a few evidenced a strong commitment to feminist values, particularly to equal opportunity and pay equity. Most of the homeworkers, however, viewed their WPS employment as temporary and subordinate to their family commitments. Had the WPS homeworkers intended to work as homeworkers indefinitely, their accumulated grievances might have catalyzed a collective organizing effort. But as it was, the transitory nature of the homeworker's employment reduced their motivation to act.

A second barrier to collective action for the homeworkers was their isolation. The geographic proximity of homeworkers facilitated the formation of friendships which helped to foster a critical assessment of the homeworkers' working conditions. But to organize the home work force at WPS would have required the development of broad social ties across the multiple small groups of homeworkers who knew each other. The high turnover among homeworkers undermined this possibility. And the two factors which typically encourage the development of strong ties of solidarity among workers—a central work setting that provides opportunities for workers to communicate with each other and a labor union with resources to underwrite workers' organization—were absent.

The labor union that represented the in-office work force—Local 1444 of the United Food and Commercial Workers—did make preliminary attempts to organize the homeworkers. But the company did everything it could to block the union's efforts. During training sessions supervisors warned homeworkers that union employees resented them for taking their work away. They also kept homeworkers out of the cafeteria to avoid any contact with union employees. To further "protect" homeworkers from their unionized night-shift counterparts, WPS convened evening meetings outside the company premises. While managers did not explicitly forbid homeworkers from interacting with union employees, they underscored the negative repercussions that could follow from unionization. The company's tactics, together with the high turnover and relative isolation of homeworkers, made union attempts to organize homeworkers unsuccessful.

Despite the obstacles to collective organization, some homeworkers expressed an openess to labor unions that was surprising. One group of homeworkers talked seriously among themselves of their need for a union. "It was always a joke that we were going to form a union and really get after them for some of these breaches," emphasized one woman. "[But] sometimes it wasn't 'real jokey' when the women talked about forming a union. . . . We talked about [unionization] a lot. We didn't have any control over anything. . . . As far as getting our raises and things like that, we just thought, "Well, if all the homeworkers were united, we could work it all out." However, the threat of management retaliation deterred the women from organizing. "I don't see how we could make demands for greater benefits and wages," underscored one homeworker. "We would be fired. If you questioned what they do, they would find some way to fire you."

Quitting offered a more expedient response to job dissatisfaction. Low wages, poor communication with supervisors, erratic work, and conflict with family roles led most homeworkers to leave their jobs before their second-year anniversary. "The way WPS was set up when I was there," stated one woman, "there was no encouragement for you to stay there after you were no longer homebound. And they knew that . . . when you had the opportunity to get out and get a job that paid more, you were going to quit." The discrepancy between the expectations and the reality of homework provided a common motivation for leaving. "Initially at the time that I got the position," concluded one woman, "I was very happy about it because I had the job and I would be able to be home. . . . But that changed in the second year when I found my frustration level increasing and I found that it just wasn't worth it any more trying to fight the group that was controlling us."

Conclusion

This account of the motivations, experience, and behavior of WPS homeworkers offers a complex portrait of women caught in a web of contradictions. On the one hand, these homeworkers accepted their place in a traditional sexual division of labor that assigns to women exclusive responsibility for the household and child care. Against the backdrop of a strong commitment to their family roles, homeworkers sought a source of secondary income. At the same time, however, homeworkers recognized the limitations of their family status and sought to increase their options. Employment with WPS offered an opportunity to enhance their feelings of self-worth, their power in relation to their husbands, and their future possibilities in the labor market. More than a means for coordinating their multiple responsibilities, homework promised an avenue for expanding women's alternatives.

For many women, the reality of homework departed from their expectations as the home proved to be a less than satisfactory work place. Instead of a flexible work arrangement, homeworkers encountered rigid company procedures, erratic work loads, and unsympathetic supervisors. As women attempted to adjust their family lives to the requirements of their homework schedules, children and husbands sometimes protested. Homeworkers found themselves caught between their family obligations and their homework deadlines. Nor did homework fulfill its other promises. The income earned from homework helped to provide women with an independent identity, but the marginal nature of the work reinforced its invisibility. With time, it became evident that homework would not provide a stepping stone into more highly skilled and renumerated positions.

The common experience of homework provided a basis for the development of social ties among homeworkers. The extent of these friendship networks was unusual among homeworkers, who are typically isolated from other women in similar situations. Ironically, the recruitment policies and training programs of WPS inadvertently fostered homeworkers' friendships as an outlet for their isolation and a source of advice for work-related problems.

Women's social ties also encouraged a collective assessment about working conditions and provided a resource for developing work-based strategies.[4] Yet in only a few instances did homeworkers systematically challenge their supervisors. The transitional nature of their employment, together with their vulnerability to management retaliation and the inaccessibility of labor resources, undermined the homeworkers' capacity to act collectively.[5] Homeworkers did, however, employ informal strategies, which ranged from setting their own work pace to quitting—for negotiating with managerial policies. With a large pool of homebound women eagerly awaiting the positions vacated by dissatisfied homeworkers, these initiatives posed little threat to managerial prerogatives at WPS. They nevertheless demonstrated that these homeworkers were actors who shaped their own responses to the constraints of work and family.

Home-based clerical employment is unlikely to resolve the tension between women's wage-earning and family responsibilities. Most women today expect to work in the paid labor force for most of their adult lives, while also retaining primary responsibility for the household and child care. Caught between their two roles, women seek flexible work arrangements. In the absence of high-quality, inexpensive child care and after-school care, homework represents an enticing option. But as the WPS case illustrates, homework offers an illusionary flexibility.

NOTES

The research for this article was supported by the Russell Sage Foundation. I wish to express my appreciation to Cynthia Fuchs Epstein, Patricia Gurin, and Joanne Miller for comments on an earlier version of this paper. I am also grateful to Susan Adams and Harold Bitters for generously providing records and documents from Local 1444 of the United Food and Commercial Workers. Special thanks are due to Harold Benenson and Eileen Boris for their lucid comments.

1. Bill Keller, "At the Center of the New Fight: Home Work," *New York Times*, May 20, 1984, I-1, 32.

2. Most of the data for this essay is based on interviews with five current homeworkers, twenty-one former homeworkers, and three former managers involved in the clerical homework program at the Wisconsin Physicians Services Insurance Corporation (WPS). Since homeworkers were contacted through newspaper ads and recommendations from other homeworkers and paid by the hour for their interview time, the data is undoubtedly somewhat biased. The open-ended interviews with homeworkers covered the following topics: work history, motivations for seeking employment as homeworkers, attitudes toward work and family, experience of working as homeworkers, friendship networks, attitudes about the homework program, and strategies for responding to their work and family situations. The interviews with former managers included questions on managerial responsibility for the homework program, advantages and disadvantages of homework from the managerial perspective, and perceptions of management-union relations. Additional materials for this article (e.g. legal documents and labor contracts) were supplied by Local 1444 of the United Food and Commercial Workers Union.

3. Unfortunately, comparative data is unavailable on the wages of full-time, in-company clerical workers with similar responsibilities and job tenure at WPS. Because the full-time, in-company employees were also low paid, the receipt of medical and pension benefits, vacation time, and sick leave represented the principle difference between their situation and the homeworkers'.

4. Several feminist scholars have recently analyzed cases in which women's shared domestic responsibilities nurtured networks that provided resources for collective action. See Temma Kaplan, "Female Consciousness and Collective Action: The Case of Barcelona, 1910–1918," *Signs* 7 (Spring 1982): 545–66, and Ardis Cameron, "Bread and Roses Revisited: Women's Culture and Working-Class Activism in the Lawrence Strike of 1912," in *Women, Work, and Protest: A Century of U.S. Women's Labor History*, ed. Ruth Milkman (Boston: Routledge and Kegan Paul, 1985), pp. 42–61.

5. For a more elaborate discussion of the preconditions for work-based collective action, see Cynthia B. Costello, "WEA're Worth It!" Work Culture and Conflict at the Wisconsin Education Association Insurance Trust," *Feminist Studies* 11 (Fall 1985): 497–518. See also Louise A. Tilly, "Paths of Proletarianization: Organization of Production, Sexual Division of Labor, and Women's Collective Action," *SIGNS* 7 (Winter 1981): 400–417.

11

Organizational Barriers to Professional Telework

MARGRETHE H. OLSON

The development of computer technologies for office work has led to popular speculation about the growth of "telework" as an alternative to office-based work for professionals. Images of highly paid computer professionals "logging in" at their leisure from their home-based work places are common in futuristic articles about computer-based work. But what are the real possibilities for the development of telework as an employee work option? We can address that question by examining the current controversy surrounding telework: Who now does computer-based work at home? For what reasons and under what circumstances do professional employees work at home? What are corporate management's views on computer-based work at home? Through an examination of these questions, I will assess the current status of telework in information-intensive industries and will make some predictions regarding the future of telework and the forms it will take.

What Is Telework?

The term *telework* here refers to *organizational work performed outside of the normal organizational confines of space and time, augmented by computer and communications technology.* The work is not necessarily performed in the home, but the home is the most common location and the one that is the primary focus of this essay. Because of the role of information technology, telework is generally confined to work that would otherwise be performed in an office, as opposed to industrial work. A formal definition of *telecommuting* is *the use of computer and communications technology to transport work to the worker as a substitute for physical transportation of the worker to the location of the work.* Thus telecommuting implies the work is done in or near the home. The terms *telework* and *telecommuting* will be used interchangeably here and, unless otherwise specified, will refer to work done in the home. A generally confused notion of who works at home, under what circumstances, and for what reasons fuels much of the controversy about telecommuting.

Where is Telework Performed?

In the broadest sense, telework includes any situation where the employee is physically separate from the employer. This could include physical decentralization of functional units as well as "off-shore" work. Both of these phenomena have been common with industrial work and are now becoming more common with office work, as in back-office decentralization and off-shore data entry. Two more innovative options which take advantage of the potential of information technology are satellite work centers and neighborhood work centers, but neither of these is in common use in the United States today.[1]

A more informal category of telework is occasional work away from the office, such as in a hotel room or in transit (e.g., airplane, train, automobile). A considerable amount of technology has been applied to this type of telework; video conferencing, lap-top computers, and automobile telephones are examples. The emphasis is primarily in permitting a traveling employee to keep in touch with the office. But the home remains the most common telework location.

Who Performs Telework and When?

Teleworkers consist primarily of three groups:

1. Self-employed people working exclusively in or out of their homes.

2. Employees (full-time) who work in their homes from one to five days a week as a substitute for going to the office.

3. Employees (full-time) who work at home in addition to going to the office.

The first category further encompasses a wide range of work, from word processing on piece rates (e.g., paid by the page) to free-lance writers to management consultants. Elsewhere this book discusses issues with respect to piece rates, employment status, and potential abuses of home workers doing primarily clerical work. This essay focuses on professional consultants or self-employed business people, running their businesses out of their homes, who use computers at home in their businesses. It also focuses on professionals in the second and third categories. These workers receive a full-time salary and benefits from their employer; they also do *not* receive compensation for work performed overtime. Unlike other homeworkers discussed in this volume, most of these are male professionals who work at home out of professional considerations. The conflict between work and home responsibilities seems not to be central to their choice.

Current Interest in Telework in the United States

If telework is not a new phenomenon, why is it creating so much interest (and controversy) today? This section discusses some of the social and economic forces affecting individuals and organizations in the U.S., placing in perspective the role of information technology with respect to work at home.

Why Do People Want to Work at Home?

In preliminary surveys and interviews with people who work at home, I identified several recurrent issues with respect to people's interest in work at home.[2] Since they are discussed adequately in other essays in this book, they are only described briefly here.

With over 70 percent of women, and over fifty percent of mothers of small children, holding permanent jobs, the amount of conflict between work and nonwork demands for both men and women has increased substantially. Workers search for any kind of work situation that gives them flexibility in their schedule, and work at home appears to provide that flexibility. Also, the number of people who choose autonomy over job security in their work lives appears to be increasing. The desire to set up arrangements which provide more autonomy may explain the apparent growth of self-employed teleworkers. Many workers find the tolls of commuting to and from work—in terms of stress and physical health as well as time and cost—to be considerable. Though few have recognized the negative effect of commuting stress on productivity, it is possible that many spend at least the first half hour of the day simply recovering from getting to work.[3]

For a small number of people whose skills are in demand, work at home is a convenience and a privilege. They choose to live at a distance that precludes commuting or simply prefer to stay home, and the company tolerates it because of their valued skills. Scholars and journalists have given a disproportionate amount of attention to people in this situation, such as wealthy stockbrokers and specialized computer "hackers."[4]

Why Do Organizations Want People to Work at Home?
Organizational interest in telework is spurred primarily by short-term needs, and the most pressing need is to attract and/or retain qualified employees. Shortages of qualified employees are particularly acute in the data-processing profession, a primary reason why many company experiments in telework originate in data-processing departments. Sometimes an experiment derives from an immediate situation and a need to respond; one company began an experiment because the department was relocating and management wanted ways to retain key employees who threatened to leave because of long commute times. More often, the experiment is a way to demonstrate that telework is feasible; the next stage is presumably to hire new employees who are highly qualified but would be unavailable to the firm without the arrangement.

A second organizational interest is productivity improvement. Although most managers are concerned only that productivity does not decrease while the employee is at home, others recognize that significant productivity gains are feasible. There are several possible reasons. The one most commonly cited is fewer distractions. The employee may work longer hours. Most likely, the employee counts only the time he or she is working. Breaks to do the dishes do not count as work time, whereas in the office informal breaks are part of the work day.

A third reason for organizational interest in telework is simply faddism. With the press focusing on telework, a company may receive favorable publicity for its "enlightened" work style. One company hired twelve physically home-bound disabled persons at considerable expense and benefited from the publicity. Others are concerned that if the option does prove to be widespread, they need to be ready. Personnel departments generally view telework as another interesting work option to be studied.

When discussing telework, management often describes long-term scenarios. They envision significant savings in indirect costs, such as space, cafeteria service, parking. They presume that, if telework is feasible for large numbers of workers, then the organization can enjoy significant savings by reducing many kinds of overhead, including, but not limited to, facilities to support full-time employees at a work site. It is clear that such savings would only be realized if a significant percent of the employee population were shifted permanently into their homes.

Despite short- and long-term justifications, managers are generally reluctant to have employees work at home. They resist having to manage employees they cannot "see." In the view of most managers of professional workers, when output is not easily measurable, only highly trusted, proven employees should be "allowed" to work at home as a substitute for coming to the office, where they can be seen.[5]

What Is the Role of Information Technology

Information (i.e., computer and communications) technology plays a significant role in the phenomenon of telecommuting. However, it is not the driving force. Information technology facilitates new forms of work organization, of which telework is only one example, but organizational culture and individual needs play a much more significant role in determining what new forms will be adopted.

The primary tools required to perform office work are changing from paper, pens, telephones, calculators, and typewriters to personal computers. If a person's primary tools are a personal computer, a modem, and a telephone, the person can use that equipment at home with relative ease. However, business has not achieved the level of penetration of information technology into basic office work that would really relax the constraints on work in space and time. While personal computers proliferate, they have not yet become a basic office support tool of the stature of a typewriter or telephone. While substitution of electronic for other forms of communication is a key requirement for widespread telework (a person working remotely must be able to keep in touch with all significant others), most organizations today do not commonly use electronic mail or equivalent tools for work-related communication.[6]

Research on Current Telework Trends
in the United States

The current body of research on actual telework trends in the U.S. is relatively small, particularly when compared to the plethora of speculative or anecdotal articles on the subject. A significant body of research took place in the mid-1970s, partly in response to the then pressing energy crisis. This work argued that, since telecommunications can substitute for transportation of the worker (thus "telework"), significant savings in energy costs can be ensured if steps are taken to facilitate this substitution.[7]

This work generally assumed technological determinism. For example, the study by Harkness *et al.* emphasized technological potential by contending that if 50 percent of all office workers worked in or near their homes six out of every seven working days the savings in fuel consumption from reduced commuting would be about 240,000 barrels of gasoline daily in 1985. A more appropriate view is one of contingencies. As Thomas Mandeville has explained: "The conclusion from comparing many studies is that information technologies can indeed encourage and also substitute for the physical movement of goods and people, with consequences for centralization and decentralization. Which of the two effects will appear in any given case appears to depend more on factors other than the choice of technology."[8]

One issue of continuing uncertainty is the lack of accurate figures on how many people work at home as telecommuters as well as how many work at home under any conditions. Census figures give no evidence of a significant growth of home workers using information technology. One frequently cited estimate holds that there are currently ten thousand teleworkers in the United States.[9] This estimate may appear low until one considers that the implied definition of teleworker is the restricted one of employees working at home with information technology on a regular basis as a substitute for commuting to the office.

A small amount of research on use of personal computers in the home is relevant to telework. In a survey of 282 home computer users, Vitalari et al. found that approximately 45 percent of computer use in the home is spent on work-related activities. They conclude that "home computers engender a shift from recreational or pleasure-oriented activities (e.g., television watching) to task-oriented activities. . . . The household of the future may be the site of more task-oriented behaviors." Drawn from computer clubs, their sample was heavily oriented toward early adopters and those in technical professions; these people may have had more justification for a personal computer based on task-oriented needs and thus were motivated to purchase one sooner than the rest of the population.[10] In a similar vein, Horowitz concludes from her research on computer use in the home that there is a preliminary trend to seeing the household as an income-producing unit.[11]

A few studies have focused on the relationship between the employee and the employer and the feasibility of telecommuting as a permanent employee work arrangement. McClintock interviewed twenty telecommuters to determine the effects of their work arrangement on their productivity. He found they experienced greater productivity on routine tasks, primarily because of access to an electronic mail system. His respondents also felt they increased their effectiveness on complex tasks because of fewer interruptions. They felt, somewhat surprisingly, that they had greater interdependence with coworkers and more effective use of face-to-face contact as a result of their homework arrangement.[12]

In my own survey, I interviewed ten employees who were geographically separated from their managers at least part of the week; I also interviewed their managers. All the employees were professionals working on long-term deliverables. I found a tendency to formalize supervision of the remote employee, possibly representing differential treatment. Managers acknowledged that remote supervision was more time-consuming; they also depended on selection of employees, already highly motivated and self-disciplined, that the manager could trust to be productive. Even so, managers admitted to being uncomfortable not being able to see their employees working.[13]

Other studies report on particular companies or experiments. Robert Kraut conducted a survey of professionals at Bell Communications Research and concluded that "overall, the time people spend working at home is independent of the time they spend working in the office." He concludes that telecommuting is not a significant phenomenon, the primary reason being "incompatibility with the current work ethos."[14]

In longitudinal evaluations of three corporate telecommuting experiments, I found noticeable differences between employees and managers in their perceptions of the effect of telecommuting on work performance. In general, employees felt that the opportunity to work at home several days a week enhanced their work performance, improved their personal job satisfaction, and had no negative effect on their chance for promotion or their relationship with their supervisors. Managers, on the other hand, were considerably more conservative about the effect of the arrangement on employee productivity. They generally felt that the arrangement was not detrimental to performance but that it entailed significantly more work for them in terms of preparing work assignments and monitoring progress. They considered the work arrangement necessary or tolerable but in virtually all cases would have preferred to have the employee on-site full time if possible.[15]

In a recent survey of 210 life insurance companies, Moore shows that only a handful are currently involved in telecommuting. Most reported cases are in addition to regular work hours, most are informal, and companies have no formal policy regarding telecommuting as an employee work option.[16] A recent survey of Canadian companies shows that, although they recognize the need to provide employees with flexible work scheduling alternatives, only 4.5 percent of those responding had any kind of home work program.[17]

Based on the research reviewed in this section, the question of whether telecommuting is a significant phenomenon today certainly cannot be answered clearly in the affirmative. One point is certain: information technology is not the driving force. Information technology may make new forms of work organization possible, but organizational culture as well as economic and social concerns of employees and employers have a stronger influence over what choices are actually made.

A second point is also clear: telecommuting is not necessarily favored by management. In fact, it is quite the opposite: most managers, given the choice, prefer to "see" their employees, and for them telecommuting is more of a hassle than a benefit.

A Demographic Survey of Teleworkers

In documenting more fully the extent of the trend to telework in a population of presumable teleworkers, I decided not to attempt a random sample of U.S. households or U.S. office workers. Instead, I targeted two trade magazines whose readership best fits those who appear to be telecommuters under the best of circumstances—one for computer professionals and one on personal computing for general professionals. The survey was sent by mail to a random sample of 5,000 subscribers to each magazine. The results from the combined sample are summarized here.[18]

The 807 respondents form a homogeneous group. Most are male (84 percent) and married (83 percent); no data were collected about spouse's occupation. Their average age is 42.5 years, and they have an average of 2.1 children. Eighty-five percent earn at least $30,000 per year (although the question was stated in terms of household income, which also includes spouse's income); 31 percent earn over $60,000 (see tables 1 and 2).

Is telework a significant departure from the daily commute to a nine-to-five workplace? The data shows that the respondents, like others in similar professions, work long hours. Although the average number of hours worked at home is equivalent to nearly two work days, most

Table 1. Homeworkers' Employment Status

	Frequency	Percent
Employed by a company or another person	342	42.4
Self-employed	351	43.5
Other	114	14.1

Table 2. Average Number of Hours Worked

Total hours worked per week	50.6
Total hours worked at home	14.7

Table 3. Hours Worked at Home

	Frequency	Percent
In addition to regular work hours	469	58.1
Occasional substitute for work at another location	97	12.0
Regular substitute for work at another location	95	11.8
All the paid work done	87	10.8
Other/no response	59	7.3

them appear to be worked *in addition to* regular work hours. The one significant change in work habits is that now an employee can perform (unpaid) overtime work in the convenience of the home, surrounded by the family, instead of having to stay long hours at the office in order to have access to equipment (see table 3).

Why did they decide to work at home? Clearly this group is motivated to increase their productivity. Whether they find the office too distracting or are worried about not getting enough work done or are constantly under deadlines, they choose to extend their work day into their home life in order to get more work accomplished. For the most part they are not compensated directly by employers (i.e., overtime) for the work they do at home. They are also not motivated by family considerations, although many seem to feel that it is a better choice to be near one's family while working than spending longer hours at the office.[19] They may feel that this way they can share regular meals with their families and be physically present in the evening hours, even though they might be off in a separate room toiling over their terminals while the rest of the family watches television (see tables 4 and 5).

How do they like working at home? Clearly, many feel that they accomplish their goal of increasing their productivity. Of course this result must be considered with caution, since strictly speaking productivity is output per unit of input (hours worked), and they may be simply extending their hours rather than increasing their output per hour. However, interviews with people who work at home show they do feel that their actual productivity has increased, due to the relative

Table 4. Satisfaction with Homework

	Frequency	Percent
Very satisfied	407	50.4
Somewhat satisfied	282	35.0
Somewhat dissatisfied	43	5.3
Very dissatisfied	4	0.5
No response	71	8.8

Table 5. Reasons for First Deciding to Work at Home*

	Frequency	Percent
To increase my productivity	414	51.3
To work in my own way, at my own pace	390	48.3
To earn extra money	266	33.0
To save time commuting	160	19.8
Tax benefits	129	16.0
Low overhead	124	15.4
Other	124	15.4
To ease conflicts between work and family	110	13.6
To take care of family	63	7.8
To avoid office politics	61	7.6

*Respondents gave multiple answers.

lack of distractions and interruptions in the home environment (see table 6).[20]

Telework is not ideal. The most frequently cited disadvantage is lack of interaction with coworkers. This is a particularly interesting result, given that readers of one of the magazines are computer professionals. The stereotypical programmers are solitary types, preferring their terminals to people. Since most do not work exclusively in the home, the disadvantage of lack of interaction with coworkers is probably not critical. However, having access to equipment and work-related materials in the home may encourage them to work too much. Indeed, they work long hours and otherwise show signs of being "workaholics" (see table 7).

Secondly, at least some of this group recognize in interviews that the convenience of having the equipment in the home is countered by the disadvantage that they tend to use it, sometimes causing family conflict. With the terminal or computer so close and inviting, it is

Table 6. Advantages of Working at Home*

	Frequency	Percent
More productivity	499	61.8
More time with my family	290	35.9
More time to myself	263	32.6
More money	223	27.6
Increased career opportunities	185	22.9
Less personal conflict	116	14.4
No advantages	18	2.2

*Respondents gave multiple answers.

Table 7. Disadvantages of Working at Home*

	Frequency	Percent
Lack of interaction with co-workers	269	33.3
Work too much	258	32.0
Less time to myself	134	16.6
Less time with my family	82	10.2
Resentment of my spouse	69	8.6
Increased stress	63	7.8
No disadvantages	151	18.7

*Respondents gave multiple answers.

tempting (particularly with electronic mail) to just sign on and "check my mail" or "see who else is on the system," and then to keep on working.[21]

Overall, however, teleworkers who responded to this survey seem to feel that the advantages outweigh the disadvantages. Over 85 percent reported being at least somewhat satisfied with the opportunity to work at home. They do not want to work at home full time. The overwhelming majority favor the flexibility to be able to work at home part of the time but still have a regular workplace outside of the home.

Clearly, no dramatic shift has transformed work location from central offices to "electronic cottages." Instead, information technology has made it easier to increase the total number of hours worked by allowing telework to substitute for what might have been longer hours in the office.

Certainly, the respondents to this survey are a privileged group in terms of employment status. The jobs they do at home are those that generally bring a significant degree of autonomy and have been performed at least partly in the home without technological support. Those who work at home, even in addition to regular work hours rather than as a substitute, choose to do so because of the autonomy to work at one's own pace and to thus benefit from increased productivity. The large majority have spouses who live with them, and although I did not ask if the spouses work outside of the home, it is clear that only a very small percentage of the respondents work at home to help with child care.

Future Developments

Based on existing research, we cannot predict that telework, as defined and practiced today, will become a prevalent form of work organization in the future. While telework may be technologically feasible in the near future, it is not technologically driven. Indeed, organizational culture and traditional bureaucratic structure strongly inhibit its development. But, in the long run, a combination of technological, economic, and social forces may bring about significant changes in organizational structure and culture, which may in turn lead to new work organizations, including remote collaboration and remote supervision.

First, as this essay has pointed out, the current state of technology constrains, rather than facilitates, telework, primarily because the use of information technology for interpersonal communication is not widespread in organizations today. However, significant developments in the use of technology to support and add value to interpersonal communication, particularly in work-related communication and collaboration, will occur in the near future. Computer science research labs and universities are beginning to develop computer-based tools for work groups.[22]

As such tools become cost effective and as the costs of telecommunications to support wideband communications decrease, *remote collaboration* will become commonplace. It will become relatively easy for professionals to work together even when they are not co-located. Organizations, particularly those which are already physically decentralized, will quickly take advantage of the opportunity to utilize scarce specialized human resources effectively without incurring travel expenses. Clearly, remote collaboration also requires *remote supervision.* To date, neither computer science nor management researchers have addressed issues involving the process of remote supervision (e.g., training) and technological support for it (e.g., work measurement, communication support). However, when the technology to support remote collaboration and remote supervision are in place, will it matter where people work? Will most of them be at home? In my opinion, telework will be more feasible than it is with today's technology, but organizational and social forces will work against it.

Second, organizational forces both encourage and impede such telework. The economics of environmental uncertainty and competitive pressure will continue to force organizations to look for ways to respond quickly to changes in demand for products and services. This means finding ways to quickly expand and contract output, and an important factor will be the ability to quickly expand and contract the labor force. This can be accomplished most efficiently through an increase in contract work, particularly as information technology reduces transaction costs for acquiring contracts, distributing work, and measuring output.[23] Therefore, organizations are likely to increase the substitution of contract labor for full-time employment in more and more domains of office work, professional as well as clerical. This trend alone may signify an increase in telework, since the employer does not bear the cost of space to perform the work. As noted below, protection of contract labor will become a significant issue requiring immediate attention.

Organizations will also continue a trend to physical decentralization, facilitated, but not driven, by lowered costs of telecommunications. Facilities location is now dictated by costs of real estate and energy as well as by location of an adequate work force. In the U.S., continued "suburbanization" of back-office facilities as well as "off-shore" work should be expected.[24] In many cases today, location of a facility in a suburb with an adequate population of skilled employees (primarily full-time homemakers with few or no alternative work options) solves the problems of shortages of skilled employees at least temporarily and renders telework as an employee work option unnecessary.

Third, social and psychological forces will shape the extent of telework. Employees will increase their demands for flexibility in their work lives in order to accommodate nonwork demands. Many writers have speculated on the social isolation of people working at home; evidence shows that this problem is much less important than the significant strains produced from trying to work and take care of children simultaneously. But employee demands for flexibility will only be heeded if their skills are in sufficiently short supply that organizations have no alternative.

The one social force which is and will continue to be a major barrier to telework is organizational culture, in particular, management style.

Managers do not like telework; they want to see their employees. Over and over again I have heard the complaint "How can I manage someone I can't see?" Having an employee work effectively at home requires management skills such as trust and confidence in the employee's abilities—skills which represent good management in any case. A bad manager does not want his or her inadequacies exposed, and having an employee working at home increases the manager's vulnerability to exposure of poor general management practices.

Furthermore, organizational culture dictates a commitment to the organization as a *place*. Companies incur tremendous expense providing facilities in which an employee can feel a sense of belonging and safety, with health facilities, libraries, natural surroundings, as well as cafeterias and parking lots. Such trappings are designed to keep employees "in"; once they walk over the threshold they "belong" to the organization until they leave. Employee productivity, particularly of professional workers, is often measured by "time in" rather than output. Signs of status abound, from the size of one's office to whom one speaks to in the elevator. Promotability is related above all else to visibility, not to performance on some objective criteria. While this approach to employee performance and control may appear on the surface to be inefficient, it is entrenched in most bureaucracies and changes slowly. In all respects, the notion of an employee working at home when and where he or she wants flies in the face of this corporate culture.

Conclusions

There are many arguments against telework, primarily in terms of its potential to be used to exploit workers. In these arguments, organizations are usually described as poised and ready to implement telework in exploitative ways as soon as certain legal barriers are removed. As we have seen, this is simply not the case. Organizations are *not* particularly interested in telework as an employee work option, particularly for professional employees. Furthermore, since the necessary technology has not been fully developed, from a technical standpoint telework is still difficult for most professional jobs.

As technical developments encourage remote collaboration and remote supervision, telework will take on a different meaning, not focused on work location "in or out" of the organization. Physical organizational boundaries will become less clearly defined in a general way. The definition of "employment" will also become less clear as part-time and contract work become commonplace. These trends will override telework. Two issues of paramount importance in the United States, regardless of whether they result in an increase in telework, will shape its meaning: improvements in affordable, adequate day care alternatives and protections for work under independent contractor status. Without either, telework may place greater demands on professionals rather than fulfill its promise of increased flexibility and autonomy.

NOTES

1. J. M. Nilles, F. R. Carlson, P. Gray, and G. G. Hanneman, *The Telecommunications-Transportation Tradeoff* (New York: John Wiley and Sons, 1976).

2. M. H. Olson, "Remote Office Work: Changing Work Patterns in Space and Time," *Communications of the ACM* 26, no. 3 (March 1983): 182–87; see also M. H. Olson, and S. B. Primps, "Working at Home with Computers: Work and Nonwork Issues," *Journal of Social Issues* 40, no. 3 (1984): 97–112.

3. Gerald Manners, "The Office in Metropolis: An Opportunity for Shaping Metropolitan America," *Economic Geography* 50, no. 2 (April 1974): 93–110.

4. See, for example, Enid Nemy, "New Yorkers, etc.: Intruding on Those Working at Home," *New York Times,* March 15, 1987, C-57. One of the first popular articles on telework was "Rising Trend in the Computer Age: Employees Who Work at Home," *New York Times,* March 12, 1981, A-1, D-6.

5. M. H. Olson "The Potential of Remote Work for Professionals," *Office Workstations in the Home,* (Washington, D.C.: National Academy Press, 1985), pp. 125–32; see also M. H. Olson "Corporate Culture and the Home Worker," in *The New Era of Home-Based Work: Directions and Policies,* ed. K. Christensen (Boulder, Colo.: Westview Press, 1988), pp. 126–34.

6. Two recent studies of electronic mail use in organizations are M. Feldman, "Electronic Mail and Weak Ties in Organizations," and J. D. Eveland and T. K. Bikson, "Evolving Electronic Communication Networks: An Empirical Assessment," *Office: Technology and People* 3 (August 1987): 83–101, 103–28.

7. Nilles et al., *The Telecommunications-Transportation Tradeoff;* R. C. Harkness, *Technology Assessment of Telecommunications/Transportation Interactions* (Menlo Park, Cal.: SRI International, 1977). A retrospective view of this work and its influence is found in K. L. Kraemer, "Telecommunications—Transportation Substitution and Energy Productivity: A Re-Examination," *Telecommunications Policy* 6, no. 1 (March 1982): 39–59, and 6, no. 2 (June 1982): 87–99.

8. Thomas Mandeville, "The Spatial Effects of Information Technology: Some Literature," *Futures,* February 1983.

9. Electronic Services Unlimited, *Telework: A Multi-Client Study* (New York, 1984). The basis for the estimate is not given in the report. See also Robert E. Kraut, "Telework: Cautious Pessimism," in *Technology and the Transformation of White-Collar Work,* ed. R. Kraut (Hillsdale, N.J.: Erlbaum, 1986),

pp. 135–52; J. H. Pratt and J. A. Davis, *Measurement and Evaluation of Family-Owned and Home-Based Businesses,* (Springfield, Va.: U.S. Department of Commerce, National Technical Information Service, July 1986).

10. N. P. Vitalari, A. Venkatesh, and K. Gronhaug, "Computing in the Home: Shifts in the Time Allocation Patterns of Households," *Communications of the ACM* 28, no. 5 (May 1985): 512–22.

11. Jamie Horowitz, "Working at Home and Being at Home: The Interaction of Microcomputers and the Social Life of Households," (Ph.D. diss., City University of New York, 1986).

12. C. C. McClintock, "Working Alone Together: Managing Telecommuting," Proceedings of the National Telecommunications Conference, December 1981.

13. M. H. Olson, "New Information Technology and Organization Culture," *Management Information Systems Quarterly* 6, no. 5 (December 1982): 71–92.

14. Kraut, "Telework: Cautious Pessimism."

15. M. H. Olson, Final Project Report, NSF Grant No. IST-8208451, 7/182-3/3/83, March 1983.

16. Kay Moore, *1986 Personnel Policies And Practices Survey* (Atlanta: Life Office Management Associate, 1986).

17. Laura C. Johnson, *Working Families: Workplace Supports for Families,* (Toronto: Social Metropolitan Planning Council, Canada, 1986).

18. See M. H. Olson, "Do You Telecommute?" *Datamation,* October 1985; see also *Personal Computing,* June 1985.

19. The author is currently working with Kathleen Christensen, who developed the original questionnaire, to compare this sample with a sample from *Family Circle Magazine,* whose readership is primarily women earning second incomes. The differences between the two samples are expected to be dramatic.

20. M. H. Olson, "Remote Office Work: Changing Work Patterns in Space and Time," *Communications of the ACM* 26, no. 3 (1988): 182–87.

21. Ibid.; see also Olson and Primps, "Working at Home with Computers."

22. A recent significant event was the Conference on Computer Support for Cooperative Work, held in Austin, Texas, in December 1986.

23. O. E. Williamson, *Markets and Hierarchies: Analysis and Antitrust Implications* (New York: Free Press, 1975).

24. Kristin Nelson, "Automation, Skill, and Back-Office Location" (Paper presented to the Association of American Geographers, Minneapolis, Minn. May 1986).

SECTION FIVE

The Politics of Homework

12

Homework and Women's Rights: The Case of the Vermont Knitters, 1980–85

EILEEN BORIS

Picture Mrs. Audrey Pudvah as the *New York Times* described her in March 1981, "working at her knitting machine in a quiet room looking out on snow covered fields, tall trees, and craggy hills. "While earning nearly four dollars an hour, more than the minimum wage, she also "can keep an eye on her two young children and keep the woodburning stove stoked and the house spotless." Mrs. Pudvah's knitting, however, was then illegal. It violated a 1942 administrative ruling under the Fair Labor Standards Act (FLSA) that banned industrial homework in knitted outerwear. Yet she claimed not to "feel the least bit exploited ... she thinks that her job knitting ski hats in her own pleasant log home at her own pace is a pretty good deal."[1]

In the early 1980s, the plight of Audrey Pudvah and other New England knitters became a cause célèbre among free market conservatives who argued for lifting the homework ban because it deprived workers of their constitutional "right to work." For the Reagan administration, ending the ban fitted nicely into its plans to deregulate the economy.[2] But Audrey Pudvah herself offered another set of reasons for homework: "All the time the Government says to be more family-oriented and spend time with your children and to save energy," she explained. "That's what I am doing. I don't have money for an extra vehicle, extra clothes, or for baby sitters that I would need to go out to work."[3] Given her responsibilities for children and household, and given the low wages available to women in the workplace, homework made sense.

While the media portrayed the homeworkers as mothers challenging the Goliath of big government, the knitters presented themselves as craftswomen, "worksteaders," and pioneers of "the American cottage industry" who also cared for children and tended wood furnaces. Though they saw themselves as controlling their own labor, these women were not independent contractors in the legal sense but employees—industrial homeworkers paid by the piece and thus subject to FLSA. Their fight to knit ski caps and sweaters at home began in the partisan pre-election atmosphere of 1980 as a routine labor department suit against homework wage and hour violations. It ended in late 1985 when the Department of Labor, after a four-year battle with the International Ladies' Garment Workers' Union (ILGWU), rescinded the rule prohibiting industrial homework in knitted outerwear but instituted an employer certification program that would comply with FLSA.[4] The public debate that occurred in the course of changing the knitwear regulations questioned the exploitative nature of home labor and the "fairness" of labor standards legislation toward women—both assumptions underlying the homework ban. From the perspective of the knitters, the regulatory state seemed to ignore women's dual role as family nurturers and wage earners in its attempt to protect workers by disallowing homework.

This recent controversy marks a profound shift in the decades-old debate surrounding homework. Since the New Deal, defenders of homework have pointed out its advantages for women who must work and care for their children at the same time. Advocates of the Vermont knitters, most of whom identify themselves as political conservatives, added to this defense a critique of protective legislation that echoed feminist demands for equal rights: they claimed laws that ostensibly "protect" women from poor wages and long hours actually intensify employer discrimination against women by making women as expensive to hire as men and thus limiting women's opportunities in the labor market.[5]

The homework advocates' arguments rely on the major tenets of classical liberalism: equal rights, equal opportunity, the separation of the private from the public, and the right to work. Using the rhetoric of sex equity, defenders of homework have labeled a homework ban discriminatory because it bars women from sewing or knitting at home while permitting men to work at carpentry or other home-based labor. Such gender classification in the homework restrictions, Ruth Yudenfriend of the National Center on Labor Policy argued, fails to meet the Supreme Court's test of serving "important government objectives" and thus "discriminate[s] against women by eliminating their rights to raise their children and earn a living at the same time." "Prohibitions against industrial homework disenfranchise women from the workplace," reiterated Mark A. de Bernardo of the U.S. Chamber of Commerce. "It is therefore a women's issue."[6] Feminist rhetoric has found a particularly strange home in the voice of New Right conservatives like Senator Orrin Hatch (R-Utah), who equates "right to work" with "rights of women . . . the right to be able to support your family . . . in the privacy of your home."[7] Thus, homework regulation, historically supported by labor unions, restricts the "right to work," long associated with business's defense of the open shop. For some conservatives, a pro-homework stance complements their assault on government regulation of industry, union power, and the welfare state because it characterizes labor as an individualized, rather than a collective, experience. Such conservatives have extended "right to work" as a woman's right to maintaining women's place within a male-dominated society: at home, earning wages, while caring for children. Capitalism and patriarchy have joined forces for their mutual benefit.

Opponents of homework also have shifted their arguments from the historical stance of women reformers, labor unions, and New Dealers, who advocated mother care of children and prophesied the downfall of domestic life if work for pay was introduced into the home. Today, opponents assert the adverse impact of homework on wage standards for women in the workplace, and most advocate day care for women who work outside the home. However, they continue to present the homeworker as a victim of unscrupulous employers, who is without the economic, political, and legal resources needed to defend herself. Jay Mazur, the current president of the ILGWU, has argued, "To license industrial homework is to license exploitation." Yet he and other opponents of homework fail to address the social and cultural conditions affecting all women that make homework a solution to some women's double day. By maintaining a separation between home and work, anti-homework liberals keep the home free from homework but not from the unwaged labor that is the cornerstone of power inequities between men and women.[8] The gender economy, however, intertwines with the political economy. Homework not only belies any separation between family and economy, it also forces us to rethink their connection.

The debate over industrial homework appears to have only two sides: rescind the 1940s prohibitions against homework in the garment-related industries or maintain them. Yet despite the "prohibitions," homework in most industries is legal as long as employers comply with the wage, hour, child labor, and record-keeping provisions of FLSA. Opponents of homework question the effectiveness of this or any regulation, because the wage and hour administration lacks the funds needed to enforce certification and record-keeping systems of employers and because historically, at least, it has been impossible to monitor whether homeworkers are receiving fair piece rates. In fact, reformers in the 1930s suggested regulation as a form of prohibition because they understood that if employers paid minimum wages to homeworkers, the cost-cutting advantage of this system would be lost, leading to a decline in homework in most trades. Indeed, until the 1970s this strategy (along with unionization) seemed to have worked.[9]

It's time to take the debate over homework regulation beyond these simple dichotomies. A feminist analysis recognizes the complexity of the fact that while some individual women consider homework their best option, homework may not be beneficial for women as a group. Such an analysis recognizes that unwaged labor in the home (women's responsibility for nurturing and housekeeping) supports the traditional division of labor in the marketplace. Thus, although homework has been a strategy for individual women to cope with limited opportunities in the workplace, it has also reinforced the subordinate position of women as a group in the economy and perhaps also in the family. To fully understand homework, then, we need to explore the interaction of social, economic, and cultural forces that make homework both appealing and exploitive, and we need to listen to the voices of homeworkers themselves, both in the past and in the present. Only then can we get beyond current policy options to imagine those social conditions (such as accessible, affordable dependent care or community-located workshops) that would enable women truly to choose between working within or outside of the home.

The History of Homework Legislation

In their defense of homework, the Vermont knitters challenged arguments against homework that originated nearly a century ago. In the chaos of rapid industrialization, reformers fought to regulate homework as part of a larger quest for labor standards for all workers, protective legislation for women, and maintenance of the family wage. These reformers, especially the women of the National Consumers' League and the Women's Trade Union League, sought maximum hours, minimum wages, child labor regulations, and workplace safety measures to protect the health of young female industrial workers, whom they saw as potential mothers. Such measures, however, also would increase the cost to businesses of employing women. Some employers, consequently, forced women out of the workplace. Reformers believed that the laws, along with improved wages for men gained through unionization, would allow wives and children to remain at home or at school, with husbands in the work force supporting them. The prohibition of homework, with its long hours and low wages that undercut male workers' demands for better working conditions and higher wages, was essential to their plans. Homework regulation was thus a form of protective legislation that assumed the separation of home and work. Mothers did not belong in the waged work force, a point that reformers dramatized through a portrait, mockingly entitled "Sacred Motherhood," of a haggard woman suckling an infant as she worked at her foot-powered sewing machine.[10]

Since the mid-nineteenth century, women who stayed at home because of their cultural traditions or family responsibilities had taken in homework. These women, most of whom were married, worked because their men held seasonal, casual jobs and earned too little to sustain their families. (To a lesser extent the old and disabled also became homeworkers.) They included rural women who lacked other means to earn wages and immigrant women in the Italian, Jewish, and Spanish-speaking districts of northeastern, midwestern, and southwestern cities.[11] These women shared with reformers the belief that mothers should stay at home with children. Unable to live on the income of husbands or other family members, or on charity, such women took in homework, despite its exploitative conditions, because it was necessary for family survival.

Like the Vermont knitters, most homeworkers who answered government queries in the 1920s and 1930s cited care of children and household responsibilities as the major reasons for doing homework. Respondents also listed physical disability and old age. A few preferred homework because they could set their own pace, determine their own hours, and still earn the same wages as they would in a factory. A few felt that it was beneath them to work in a factory, and others believed that it was impossible to find factory or office work due to their lack of English skills or to general economic conditions. Still others combined homework with caring for sick relatives or taking in boarders. For the most part, then, unwaged family labor, custom, and limited economic opportunities kept them at homework. Yet when faced with a homework ban in 1933–35, 60 percent of such women took factory jobs. Of those who accepted factory positions, 83 percent were able to make alternative child-care arrangements. Only 15 percent wished they could return to homework.[12]

Regulation of homework began in the late nineteenth century as a crusade against tenement-made goods that middle-class consumers feared were contaminated by tuberculosis, vermin, and filth. Beginning with the 1892 New York State Tenement House Law, regulations were proposed to protect the consumer through licensing that prohibited certain items. Reformers also emphasized the demoralizing environment of the home as a workplace in ways that sustained the public/ private dichotomy central to the gender stratification of labor. As Annie S. Daniel of the New York Infirmary for Women and Children put it, "Absolutely no home life is possible in a tenement workroom." Or, as one factory inspector explained, "privacy of the home" succumbed to a "stronger duty," the public interest, which would "rescue . . . all homes, and make the necessary division between home and workplace." Middle-class reformers desired to make working-class homes conform to their own image of domesticity.[13] At the same time, union agreements in the garment trades attempted to stamp out homework.[14]

With the New Deal, under which women reformers played a key role in shaping social welfare and labor policy, homework became federally regulated. The 1933 National Recovery Administration (NRA) established codes of fair competition that prohibited homework in over one hundred industries. When the Supreme Court declared the NRA unconstitutional in 1935, women reformers combined their efforts to win passage of the FLSA in 1938. Viewing an administrative ban on homework as crucial for carrying out the provisions of this act, the Department of Labor instituted special record-keeping requirements for employers of homeworkers to establish that FLSA could never be enforced for homework. By 1939 seventeen states also had laws regulating homework, though none was able to enforce them fully.[15]

Participants in the debate over homework during the thirties shared a common conception of womanhood that equated women with mothers and mothers with the home. The small-business community's reason for permitting homework—that mothers could earn wages and still watch children—suggested the very circumstances under which their opponents rejected homework: a mother could not properly care for children while engaged in the low-wage piecework of sewing dresses, knitting sweaters, or soldering jewelry. As Clara Beyer of the Division of Labor Standards asked, "Is it socially desirable for a mother with a four months old baby and three other children under 6 to work 33 hours a week for $1.75; or for a mother with 4 children under 5 to work an average of 4 hours a day and receive 63 cents for her week's work?"[16] Women reformers and organized labor opposed homework for its effect on labor standards and interference with union organizing, but protection of the working-class family and the male wage lay at the center of these concerns. Women's Bureau head Mary Anderson reflected the prevailing sentiment when she argued, "The only thing to do about homework is to abolish it and to arrange for higher wages for the breadwinner in a family so that his wife and children do not have to supplement the family income by doing homework, or, if there is no regular breadwinner, to provide pensions or relief."[17]

In the late thirties, FLSA discouraged urban employers from sending work across state lines into rural districts to avoid paying the minimum wage required by their own states. At the same time, federal courts disallowed buy-back schemes of employer-controlled rural cooperatives, according to which employers would sell materials to homeworkers and then "buy" the finished product. Homework, however, persisted in rural areas, especially in the business of hand-knitted outerwear, in which throughout the depression women had contracted for knitting from different firms under four or five names. As one woman had complained, "None of the people that do this work do it for pleasure . . . it is for the money. They must have to live and try to keep or help keep up taxes on their little homes. . . . Why should our women . . . be obliged to work at such wages? Is there any way of making things different and women as well as men get living wages?"[18] Though the number of homeworkers in this industry decreased from 20,300 in 1935 to an estimated 6,000 to 8,000 in 1941, the latter figure still constituted 28 percent of the industry. In the early 1940s, wage and hour administrators found widespread violations in the payment of homeworkers of knitted outerwear and, thus, prohibited homework.[19] The Supreme Court upheld this ruling, applied also to six other industries, in Gemsco v. Walling (1945). In 1949 Congress incorporated the prohibitions into the FLSA.[20]

Following World War II, in response to the apparent consensus on the need for prohibition, industrial homework became less common. Some industries' use of cheap labor abroad or profit from economies of scale also made the use of homeworkers less attractive. The number of homeworkers in knitted outerwear had dwindled to about one thousand by 1981, constituting about 6.3 percent of the industry's work force. This figure, though representing a drastic decline from earlier years, also represents the beginning of a resurgence in homework (both in old industries, such as knitted outerwear, and in new ones, such as microcomputer assembly and word processing), which issues from the unstable economy of the 1970s. As the garment unions weakened and economic and political refugees from the Americas and Asia entered the work force in increasing numbers, garment manufacturers and their contractors began to pay less for homework, much of which had been taken on by the new immigrants. Meanwhile, industries faced with increasing competition promoted the deregulation of industry and joined ideological supporters of "free enterprise" and "the right to work" to dismantle homework regulations. Indeed, as one of Senator Hatch's aides, who asked not to be named, commented, the desire to make American industry more competitive by cutting labor costs and ending government protection of organized labor informed his pro-homework Freedom of the Workplace Act as much as the desire to appeal to women who wanted to work at home.[21]

Homework and Motherhood in the 1980s

Opponents of homework today address the issue without the "sacred motherhood" rhetoric of the past. These labor liberals contend that homework undermines labor standards (health and safety, minimum wage, maximum hours, etc.), encourages employers and employees not to accurately report wages or hours to the Internal Revenue Service, tramples the rights of undocumented workers, and condones competition that is unfair to law-abiding businesses and unions. They call for child care in the workplace so that mothers can go to work "in decent places" instead of being forced to take work into their homes because they lack such care.[22] Proponents of homework, in contrast, argue as they have in the past that women should have the right to work at home while also caring for their children.

Homework defenders still associate homeworkers with motherhood. Before hearings in 1981 to rescind the outerwear prohibition, Vermont entrepreneur C. B. Vaughan urged that "we work together to enable the mothers of small children to stay at home to care for their children and at the same time have the opportunity to earn income." In a resolution supporting homework in 1984, the Iowa Senate argued that "no rational legislative objective is served by effectively forcing mothers out of the home and into the factory." Vermonters, the state's secretary of labor, Joel Cherington, asserted, prefer mother care to day care because they value "the family as a building block in our society, and because of the costs associated with child care."[23] As the Center on National Labor Policy (counsel for many of the Vermont knitters) argued in one brief filed with the Department of Labor, "The children know their mother is home with them and she can teach them the skills and values which would otherwise go untaught." The knitters themselves constantly attacked day care out of the belief that "it is important that preschool children be with their mothers," although a few complained about lack of available services in their rural regions.

Others recognized that the cost of child care would consume so much of their wages that it would not be worth working outside the home.[24]

Yet in the debate about the Vermont knitters, even the most diehard supporters of motherhood as woman's noblest profession, like Senator Jeremiah Denton (R-Ala), recognized the economic necessity for two-earner families and thus viewed homework as a necessary compromise between economic reality and cultural preferences. Acknowledging the entrance of married women with small children into the official labor force, the Heritage Foundation supported letting Americans work out of their homes. Moreover, the Center on National Labor Policy claimed that such homework offers a huge "non-monetary advantage" to society. Because of its flexible hours, homework gives women more time than a factory or office job to do nonpaid work, such as volunteer work, nurturing activities, and other traditional women's tasks.[25]

In the rhetoric of deregulators, welfare and dependence stand in opposition to homework and independence. The Heritage Foundation argued that prohibiting homework "would be a serious blow to thousands of women seeking financial independence." Similarly, Senator Orrin Hatch introduced the Freedom of the Workplace Act as part of "a comprehensive initiative aimed at removing the barriers [that] prevent families and women in transition [female heads of households] from reaching their potential and achieving economic self-sufficiency." Appropriating the phrase "feminization of poverty," Hatch perceived homework to be one tool—along with various workfare schemes and private sector training programs—that would take women off welfare and make poor women "independent." Moreover, it would allow them to work at home and care for small children.[26]

Homeworkers themselves also associated their work with autonomy, self-sufficiency, and independence, which were otherwise difficult for them to achieve in the economy of rural New England. No precise statistical profile of the knitters and other homeworkers in Vermont and the New England states is possible; but their letters and comments reflect a range of economic and social situations, including divorced heads of households on welfare, retired couples on social security, and college-educated, home-owning, dual-earner families. Like rural homeworkers in the past, the Vermont knitters were primarily female, white, native born, either mothers of young children or older women. Whether working class or middle class, all faced a labor market in which jobs for women consisted of part-time work or of low-paying service, retail, or manufacturing jobs. Economic pressure in the stagnated economy of the late 1970s encouraged them to earn wages; in an economy in which women were paid three-fifths what men were paid, homework appeared to be a viable alternative to pink-collar jobs that included the hidden costs of child care, transportation, and wardrobe.[27]

As Violet Jones of Hardwick, Vermont, a divorced mother of two preteen boys, wrote to the wage and hour administrator, home knitting "gives me the opportunity to become self supportive and get off of state aid." A Maine woman commented on the proposed deregulation of homework, "It just doesn't make sense to ban homeknitting when it is helping people to help themselves and helping the economy at the same time." A Massachusetts woman poignantly combined her feelings about traditional mothering, her distaste for dependence on the state, and her need for "productive" labor:

> Children need a home life, and . . . I am now able to stay home and nurture my own children not rely on others for their child care. My husband is under medical care for a pre-ulcer condition and because I can knit at home I can relieve him of some of the burden of our financial support. There are many women like me. We want to be productive not just reproductive. Many of us do not want to be on welfare and food stamps and medicaid. Some of us don't want full time careers and "latch-key" children. We just want to help out, but not at the expense of our children. We need our "at home" jobs. Please help us!

Although perceiving her labor as supplementary, as the majority of homeworkers do, this Massachusetts woman found satisfaction in being able to maintain her web of familial interdependence through homework.[28]

Many women have internalized the criterion of worth that undervalues bearing children and the tasks related to nurturing them. Yet, at the same time, many of these women criticize the organization of factory labor that interferes with their ability to care for dependents. A Norridgewock, Maine, woman protested that working in a factory was not worth the sacrifice:

> I have worked for minimum wage in mills and factories in Maine and Massachusetts in the woolen, paper, plastic and shoe industries. I know what the conditions in factories like those are and what the workers have to tolerate in the way of noise pollution, air pollution and other poor working conditions. I know what working seven to three is like; getting to work when the sun is just rising in the morning, getting home just as it is going down, not seeing the sunshine for five days a week. I know mothers and fathers who only see their babies when they are asleep in their cribs. Believe me, "minimum wage" doesn't begin to cover it.

Since the New Deal, labor legislation has regulated but hardly transformed the deadening experience of most factory work. The Vermont knitters, claiming that "working in a factory is demeaning, and working at home has dignity," have taken factory conditions to task. Although during hearings in Burlington, Vermont, and Washington, D.C., the ILGWU constantly linked homework with sweatshops, the knitters imagined the home as a place of rest and took offense that anyone could call their well-maintained houses sweatshops.[29]

Homework, the knitters believed, fosters independence not only because it allows them to earn money but also because they perceive themselves in control of their labor. Virginia Gray of Greensboro, Vermont, testified, "Factory work with straight time, two fifteen minute breaks and at lunch is boring. I know. I believe that I can get done more at home with the freedom to do anything as I want to and to knit during the day and in the evenings if I wish to. I like a chance to do different things and that being home lets me do." Another woman wrote, "I enjoy being at home, and not having someone looking over my shoulder while I work." Lacking direct supervision, having no card to punch or bell to obey, these homeworkers report a relative autonomy over their work. They think of themselves not as laborers but as artisans, as skilled workers, making arts and crafts rather than mass-produced products.[30]

However, the control the knitters actually have over their labor varies considerably, depending on whether they design the hats or sweaters they knit, whether they choose colors and yarn, and whether they are truly independent contractors. While most own their knitting machines (which are hand-operated shuttle types that have a row of little teeth resembling knitting needle tips along the top), many have purchased them and taken lessons from the "manufacturer" who is their major source of orders. If a knitter buys supplies, especially yarn, from this manufacturer and the finished product goes back to that same person for marketing, then FLSA considers the knitter an employee, even if the "employer" did not instruct on colors and design.[31]

Moreover, most of the knitters followed patterns determined by manufacturers. For example, the Stowe Woolens receipt and order sheet for Gene Gray reveals handwritten notes: "The little border just before and after the reindeers is the only navy in those sweaters. The flakes and the reindeers itself is white. Thank you. Please do these sweaters last." Certainly the descriptions provided by knitters suggest a predetermined quality to the work, albeit of a skilled kind. While the knitter sets up the machine by pushing out the of needles the work process itself consists simply of moving the shuttle back and forth except when finishing or beginning an item. Moreover, the knitters rely on punch cards, eliminating the need to manually change needle lengths per row. For some machines, the design comes on computer-programmed cards that further eliminate the need for skill or creativity.[32]

Even though the knitters are not considered independent contractors and lack the autonomy or artistry of the true craftswoman, they do sometimes finish their work by hand, and they certainly control their work pace to a greater degree than factory workers or many other kinds of garment homeworkers. The Vermont women knit between ten and thirty hours each week and choose how much work to accept over a two-week period or whether to knit at all that week. Many knitters expressed the sentiments of Jan Kuhn of Johnson, Vermont, who wrote, "Although my working conditions, i.e., small children constantly present, make it difficult to compute my hourly wage exactly, I estimate my earnings to be $5.00 per hour. Even days when my knitting develops problems or the children are difficult I still earn the minimum wage."[33] Working at home means interrupted labor, phones to answer, and clothes to wash, a style of work familiar to many women with small children. If such patterns curtail production and ultimately decrease the number of hours devoted to knitting, the knitters seem less concerned with such factory-imposed criteria than with controlling the quality and distribution of their time.

The Vermont knitters' concern for control over their own labor acknowledges a connection between women's rights and the right to work that is hardly surprising, given the origins of each in classical liberalism. These terms were not often drawn together in the past because of the residue of patriarchal thinking within liberalism itself that regarded women as dependents. Because liberalism divided social life into private and public, family and state, women and men, because its generic individual was the man who was associated with the market and the polity, its concepts of choice, opportunity, and rights applied to only one sex. Connected to nature rather than culture, women were controlled by biology and thus belonged to the private realm of the family.[34]

Women were thought of as children, "wards of the state," requiring state protection. Thus in Commonwealth v. Hamilton Manufacturing (1876), one of the first rulings on protective legislation, the Massachusetts high court rejected wage and hour laws for men because such legislation interfered with so-called sanctity of contract. However, the same freedom of contract, the judges reasoned, could hardly apply to women in their condition of dependency. Later, social reformers argued for the prohibition of homework and other labor legislation on the basis of the state's right to exercise its police powers to protect potential as well as actual mothers; the courts concurred. (A notable exception was the conservative Supreme Court decision Adkins v. Children's Hospital of 1923, which struck down the Washington, D.C., minimum wage law for women. There the justices argued that women's newly enfranchised status made them equal to men and that they too had the right to compete in the marketplace free from "protective" legislation.)[35]

Today some of the most outspoken homeworkers have taken up this notion of women's rights, declaring with Mary Clement of Ripon, Wisconsin, "I am tired of the antiquated idea that women must be taken care of." Many knitters reject the concept of government "protection" with the bitter comment that such protection is depriving them of their work.[36] This rejection of "protective legislation" echoes the sentiments of Alice Paul and other ERA supporters in the 1920s, who were backed by the National Manufacturers Association but opposed by women reformers fighting for homework prohibition and other labor laws.[37] Nevertheless, few homeworkers identify themselves as feminists, even when drawing on an ideology of rights. Mary Louise Norman from Denver wrote to the Department of Labor, "Not every woman is inclined to march for equal rights. Many of us prefer to stay at home with husband and children and WORK for equal rights. We believe in FREEDOM OF CHOICE. I can knit, be at home when my two teenagers need me, bake a chocolate cake, collect my neighbors' UPS packages and deliveries, keep an eye on the neighborhood for vandals ... *and* provide city and state with taxes all at the same time. This makes me something of a Wonder Woman compared to my 'sister' marchers." While evidence suggests that knitters draw on existing kinship and women's friendship networks (e.g., Audrey Pudvah and her sister knitted for the same firm), they belong to a woman-centered, but rarely feminist, culture. Yet, one woman who sold knitting machines and had hired homeworkers in the past declared that the practice allowed women who cared for their families to feel "some independence from their husbands."[38] Although the meagerness of homework wages limited women's financial autonomy and certainly never led to complete economic independence from their spouses, homework income did supplement men's earnings and provided a check on men's absolute power over family finances.

Kathy Hobart was one of the most combative of the Vermont women. Identifying herself as a feminist, she declared, "I don't believe that a woman should be home, that she needs to be home with her children. The only reason that I choose to be home is because it keeps me from getting an ulcer." Yet even she admitted, "My children benefit most by my staying at home, I think I have a right and my children have a right to have me home with them." Hobart's stance in favor of both women's responsibility as mothers and women's right to work and be economically independent reflects the complexity of the homework dilemma: "I look at this as a women's issue because I just think women have been forced to choose ... [between] being full-time mothers or workers finding work in the workplace, and I think for those of us who have found an alternative measure to both and can get them to work together, we should be encouraged rather than discouraged. I think this is a real struggle, and in these two identities of being a worker or mother, it has caused a lot of stress and anxiety for women.[39] Rather than accepting the dichotomy of work or motherhood assumed by traditional liberals, Hobart proposed a third option for women: work and motherhood.

Whether homework is a viable way to combine work and motherhood, however, depends on the conditions in the home under which both work and mothering occur. What appears a reasonable alternative for Kathy Hobart and others living in single family dwellings with employed husbands in fact opens the way for the continued exploitation of poorer, more desperate women. For many women, the self-sufficiency and alternative organization of work and home promised by homework is often illusionary. Clerical homeworkers in California, Wisconsin, and South Carolina have found that insurance companies periodically speed up their claims quotas, define homeworkers as "independent contractors" to avoid paying benefits, and force homeworkers to rent or purchase machines. For some, the opportunity to have more time for their families has also proven to be a myth. One California woman described how "her daughter would stand outside her workroom and ask, 'Mommy, are you going to be done tonight before I go to bed?' "[40]

Deregulation of homework also allows factory employers to overburden underpaid garment seamstresses with additional piecework to be done at home. As Sarah, an undocumented worker for more than a decade, testified at New York State hearings in April 1981, "The homeworkers never get a rest. They don't go home to their families. They go home to continue to work so they can feed their families and when they go to get paid, the boss has an excuse not to pay them and they have to wait until he feels like paying and sometimes not the amount that they thought they were going to get paid." For these immigrant women, who live mostly in New York, New Jersey, Miami, and Los Angeles, the family economy exists close to the edge of survival; internalized clocks, set by low piece rates, push them on. As one woman explained, she purchased her sewing machine because "I had no choice being that I'm a mother with children without a husband, in order to alleviate the cost of living"—though it took her two to three hours to sew a dress for which she received $1.30. Moreover, since the homeworker cannot predict exactly how long her bundle of piecework will take, she must sometimes turn to her children for help: "You have sort of a deadline and the child is brought in."[41]

Such women live lives reminiscent of an earlier generation of immigrant pants finishers, artificial flower makers, and embroiderers whose exploitation symbolized homework for reformers and unionists. Opponents of homework have these women in mind when they speak of the homeworker as a victim, "the most desperate, especially mothers with small children," "the most vulnerable," scared, poor workers "who don't know their rights" and need protection. At 1982 House hearings, Senator Daniel Patrick Moynihan (D-N.Y.) expressed the classical argument for protective legislation when he protrayed homework as a system for exploiting defenseless women, "locked up in a house with a month's supply of gloves . . . to sew at 20 cents an hour," who if they complain of underpayment face deportation. Moreover, like proponents of homework, he called on the language of rights, evoking the success of the New Deal's Frances Perkins who "got those women out of those sweatshops. She got them their rights."[42] However, whereas proponents referred to women's right to work, Moynihan referred to a very different notion of rights: women's right to be protected under the law from unfair labor practices.

Moynihan and other opponents of homework, like ILGWU's former president, Sol Chaikin, argue that the portrayal of homeworkers as middle-class women handcrafting while their toddlers play by the fire distorts "the real world." Class and race stratify homeworkers not only in terms of their material conditions but also in terms of their ability to see themselves as part of a single economic system. One Vermont woman expressed her resentment of "a regulation that the manufacturers and the union people feel that we need to protect the illegal alien," as if FLSA was intended to protect only immigrants.[43]

Opponents of homework, like their predecessors generations ago, also argue for justice and moral right, drawing on turn-of-the-century concerns for health and family welfare. One state AFL-CIO official noted: "How industrial homework, as it has forced women workers to labor for long hours for low pay, as it has forced mothers to 'subcontract' to their children to raise the household income, fosters a nurturing, loving home environment is beyond our belief." Another opponent relied on contemporary feminist ideas that state that "the laws have to apply to everyone, no matter where I live or what kind of a family I have." Hence, she concluded that because homework is particularly advantageous for women with children to care for, permitting it "would discriminate against those with older or no children."[44]

Advocates of women, in contrast, have rejected the portrait of the homeworker as victim even when they oppose homework generally. Grace Lyu-Volckhausen of the New York City Commission on the Status of Women, a consultant to Local 23-25, ILGWU, emphasized that homeworkers are skilled seamstresses whose self-image suffers from the lack of recognition given to their work. Representing the National Consumers' League and the Coalition of Labor Union Women, Ruth Jordan couched her testimony at the Washington hearings in the rhetoric of sisterhood. She spoke of a public policy based on women's values, the same "female difference" that her predecessors at the league had drawn on and that the Vermont knitters themselves associate with women: "I stress the caring part, because I think as women workers, we should be concerned with all aspects of nurturing. And part of the aspect is what is happening to our other sisters, whether they work in rural settings or in urban slums." She rejected any proposal that threatened to undermine national standards as pitting one group of "sisters" against another or that inhibited the ability of workers to organize, as homework historically has. For her, homework became a women's rights issue but not as defined by Senator Hatch: "It is more of a women's issue than anything else. Women already earn less than 59 percent of what men earn, and as in the knitwear case it is the women who are workers. They are denied the ability to upgrade their skills and economic well-being."[45] Jordan argued that homework rarely brings a living wage for women and their children, that the problem with homework was that employers, not women, benefited.

The Future of Homework

The debate over industrial homework in the 1980s emphasizes women's precarious position in the restructuring of the U.S. economy. Unable to find jobs that pay enough for them to afford child care, unable to find adequate child care even when they can afford it, women are resorting to homework. How can feminist arguments accommodate women's need for both wage labor and child care without reinforcing the gender stratification of labor or the ways in which class and race divide women?

The Vermont knitters' merger of home and workplace calls into question labor legislation that focuses only on the workplace, but it does not adequately challenge the home's place in the economy or of women within the home. Homeworkers are underpaid by their employers and continue to perform unpaid household labor for their families; for them, both parts of the double day take place in the home, which often leads to a continuous working "day." Their willingness to perpetuate these conditions encourages the view that *all* women are only secondary earners who need not have jobs that pay better and undercuts women's struggle in the workplace for flexible hours, better pay and benefits, and more control over the work process. Furthermore, combining home and work may conflict with other rights women should have in the home: the right to rest and leisure, the right to nurture and mother with dignity, the right to keep homes free from exploitative labor, whether waged or unwaged. Finally, homework discourages setting up alternative facilities for child care. Because the performance of piecework under deadlines or financial pressures leads women to tend but not necessarily care for their children, the presumed advantage of homework is an illusion for many women. By being both mothers and wage earners, they relieve men of responsibility for family labor and reinforce the notion that children should be cared for in the home by their own mothers.

If allowing homework is a poor option for women as a group, prohibiting it also fails to address the problem of women's need to perform both family labor and wage labor. We need to devise social alternatives that value the care of children but do not limit women to this activity. Some alternatives already exist. Black Americans, for example, have relied on extended kinship networks to care for children. European social democracies have devised family policies that allow mothers to stay home with small children and keep their seniority and other job rights. In the United States, proposed parental leave legislation is a first step toward dissolving the gendered identity of caretaking, although until women earn as much as men, it will be mostly women who, because they have less pay to lose by leaving their jobs, look after dependents. Single women still will have limited choices. Income transfer payments for caring for dependents could relieve women of the burden of wage earning but would do so at the cost of reinforcing the sexual division of labor unless they matched male wages so that some men might also choose to stay home. Unless implemented with other reforms—among them, accessible child care, elder care, and comparable worth legislation—such payments will not be adequate for many women to become independent. Moreover, only when nurturing is a primary value for men as it is for women will the gender stratification be broken that now crowds women into a few occupations, encourages part-time work, and leads to lower wages for women as a group. By transforming the power relations under which women work in the workplace and in the home, we can reorganize both the political and the gender economies.[46]

The solution of the knitters—workplace autonomy without financial independence—cannot benefit working women as a group. Control over time allocation does not compensate for lack of control over one's product or piece rates without benefits. Historically, homework has meant exploited labor, meager wages, and excessive hours. Theoretically, these conditions could be regulated, but no evidence suggests that the state could do so adequately in the future when it so consistently has failed in the past.[47]

The ILGWU has been monitoring labor department regulation of homework over the last few years in order to document its inadequacy and argue for the imposition of a new ban. The labor department, in turn, has proposed lifting the restrictions on the remaining six prohibited industries, an action that unions and many women's organizations oppose and that will be decided in the courts sometime in the late eighties. Meanwhile, the number of knitted outerwear employers resorting to homeworkers continues to increase, not only in rural regions and the Northeast but in New York City, Los Angeles, Miami, Chicago, and Philadelphia as well—a reminder that not all homeworkers will fit the profile of the Vermont women who sparked the protest. While many of the most prominent actors in the Vermont case are again knitting, Audrey Pudvah has moved on to form her own design firm. She creates patterns for her employees, who also work at home, to program with computers.[48]

Audrey Pudvah does not need a certificate because computer homework is legal, though the AFL-CIO has called for its prohibition. Though knitted outerwear is a small industry, telecommunications promises to use homeworkers even more extensively. Insurance, banking, and other industries in need of a cheap, flexible, clerical work force already are resorting to homeworkers.[49] The debate surrounding the old industrial homework prohibitions must therefore be seen as a prelude to a larger struggle over the shape and control of the American workplace, a struggle in which women's contribution to the reformulation of the gender system will play a crucial part.

NOTES

Research for this article was made possible by a fellowship from the National Endowment for the Humanities. I would like to thank the following people for their comments: Martha Fineman and the participants in the 1985 University of Wisconsin Feminism and Legal Theory Conference, "Women and Dependency"; Carol Stack, Karen Sacks, and the *Signs* editors; Cynthia Costello; and Nelson Lichtenstein.

1. Philip Shabecoff, "Dispute Rises on Working at Home for Pay," *New York Times,* March 10, 1981, A.

2. For the activities of the Right concerning homework during Ronald Reagan's first term, see Zillah Eisenstein, *Feminism and Sexual Equality: Crisis in Liberal America* (New York: Monthly Review Press, 1984).

3. Shabecoff, "Dispute Rises."

4. This analysis is based on extensive reading of the public record, including written comments and unpublished testimony, housed in the Division of Labor Standards, Office of Special Minimum Wage, 4th floor, Department of Labor, Washington, D.C. (hereafter referred to as DOL files). Donald Elisburg, telephone interview with author, December 22, 1984; *Daily Labor Report,* February 18, 1981, A-11–13, and July 14, 1981, F-21. For the original regulations, see U.S. Department of Labor, Employment Standards Administration, Wage and Hour Division, "Regulations, Part 530: Employment of Homeworkers in Certain Industries," Wage and Hour Publication no. 1026, rev. March 1980. See also Brief for the Appellees, International Ladies' Garment Workers' Union et al. v. Raymond J. Donovan et al., in the U.S. Court of Appeals for the District of Columbia Circuit (no. 82-2133), pp. 3–21; Brief for Appellants, ibid., pp. 4–33; *Daily Labor Report,* November 30, 1983, A-l, 9–10, and D-1 ff.; "Court Reinstates Federal Rules Affecting 'Industrial' Home Work," *New York Times,* November 30, 1983, A. For new regulations, see U.S. Department of Labor, Employment Standards Administration, Wage and Hour Division, 29 CFR Part 530, "Employment of Homeworkers in Certain Industries; Final Rule," *Federal Register,* v. 49, n. 215, pt. 2, Monday, November 5, 1984, 44262–44272.

5. For the feminist critique, see Judith Baer, *The Chains of Protection: The Judicial Response to Women's Labor Legislation* (Westport, Conn.: Greenwood Press, 1978).

6. For the various components of liberalism, see Eisenstein, *Feminism and Sexual Equality,* pp. 62–65, 83–113; for the rhetoric of sex equity, see testimony of Ruth Yudenfriend, Official Report of Proceedings before the Office of Administrative Law Judges of the U.S. Department of Labor, Docket no. FLSA, "In the Matter of: Public Hearing to Commence Labor Dept. Review of 'Homeworker Rules,' " Burlington, Vt., January 13, 1981, 26–33 (hereafter referred to as Burlington Hearings); Mark A. de Bernardo, "Statement on the Freedom of the Workplace Act (S. 2145) before the Subcommittee on Labor of the Senate Labor and Human Resources Committee for the Chamber of Commerce of the United States," Hearing before the Subcommittee on Labor of the Committee on Labor and Human Resources, U.S. Senate, 98th Cong., 2d sess., "Amending the Fair Labor Standards Act to Include Industrial Homework,"

February 9, 1984 (Washington, D.C.: Government Printing Office, 1984), p. 127 (hereafter referred to as Hatch Hearings).

7. Senator Orrin Hatch, remarks on "It's Your Business: Industrial Homework: Why Not?" transcript of program no. 231, tape date: January 31, 1984; air dates: February 4–5, 1984, p. 11. Available from U.S. Chamber of Commerce, Washington, D.C. 20262.

8. See, e.g., Jay Mazur, "Back to the Sweatshop," *New York Times,* September 6, 1986, A.

9. For regulation as a strategy to attain prohibition, see U.S. Department of Labor, Employment Standards Administration, Wage and Hour Division, "In the Matter of: Hearing on Proposed Amendments to Part 516 of Regulations with Respect to the Keeping of Special or Additional Records by Employers of Industrial Home Workers, in the United States and Puerto Rico," Washington, D.C. January 6, 1939, in DOL files.

10. See, e.g., Florence Kelley, *Some Ethical Gains through Legislation,* 2d ed. (New York: Macmillan, 1910); Eileen Boris, "The Quest for Labor Standards in the Era of Eleanor Roosevelt: The Case of Industrial Homework," *Wisconsin Women's Law Journal,* 2 (June 1986): pp. 53–74; Alice Kessler-Harris, "The Debate over Equality for Women in the Workplace: Recognizing Difference," *Women and Work: An Annual Review,* vol. 1, ed. Laurie Larwood, Ann H. Stronberg, and Barbara A. Gutek (Beverley Hills, Calif.: Sage Publications, 1985), pp. 141–61; on the male wage, see Heidi Hartmann, "Capitalism, Patriarchy, and Job Segregation by Sex," *Signs: Journal of Women in Culture and Society* 1, no. 3, pt. 2 (Spring 1976): 137–69.

11. For a profile of homeworkers in the past, see U.S. Department of Labor, Women's Bureau, *The Commercialization of the Home through Industrial Home Work* (Washington, D.C.: GPO, 1935); Jean Flexner and Mary Skinner, "A Study of Industrial Home Work in the Summer and Fall of 1934: A Preliminary Report to the National Recovery Administration" [1934] unpublished report, box 8387, Records of Homework Committee, Records of the National Recovery Administration, RG9, National Archives, Washington, D.C. (hereafter cited as NRA Homework Committee Papers), pp. 10–22; Laura C. Johnson with Robert E. Johnson, *The Seam Allowance: Industrial Home Sewing in Canada* (Toronto: Women's Press, 1982); Cynthia Daniels, "Between Home and Factory: Homeworkers of New York" in this volume, pp. 13–32; Julia Kirk Blackwelder, *Women of the Depression: Caste and Culture in San Antonio* (College Station: Texas A&M Press, 1983).

12. See, e.g., State of New York, Department of Labor, Bureau of Women in Industry, *Some Social and Economic Aspects of Homework,* Special Bulletin no. 158 (Albany, 1929); Mary Skinner, "Prohibition of Industrial Home Work in Selected Industries under the National Recovery Administration," Children's Bureau Publication no. 244 (Washington, D.C.: GPO, 1938), pp. 21–28.

13. Annie S. Daniel, "The Wreck of the Home: How Wearing Apparel Is Fashioned in the Tenements," *Charities* 14 (April 1, 1905): 628; Mary O'Reilly, "Sweat-Shop Life in Pennsylvania," Paper presented at the International As-

sociation of Factory Inspectors of North America, Ninth Annual Convention, (Cleveland: Forest City Printing House, 1985), pp. 68; for a full discussion of these discourses, see Eileen Boris, "Tenement Homework and the Reorganization of Immigrant Life" (Paper presented at the tenth biennial convention, National American Studies Association, San Diego, California, November 2, 1985).

14. Mary Skinner, "Industrial Home Work under the National Recovery Administration," Children's Bureau Publication no. 234 (Washington, D.C.: GPO, 1936), pp. 2–6; Ruth Shallcross, *Industrial Homework: An Analysis of Homework Regulation Here and Abroad* (New York: Industrial Affairs Publishing Co., 1939).

15. Eileen Boris, "Regulating Industrial Homework: The Triumph of 'Sacred Motherhood,'" *Journal of American History 71* (March 1985): 745–63; Mitchell v. Nutter, 161 F. Supp. 799 (April 28, 1958), for the legislative history of the FLSA; see also Brief for the Petitioner, Mitchell v. Whitaker House Cooperative, U.S. Supreme Court, October Term, 1960 (n. 274), pp. 20–45; U.S. Department of Labor, Employment Standards Administration, Wage and Hour Division (n. 9 above).

16. "Suggestions for Possible Use at Hearing on Conflicts in the Homework Provisions [Particularly relating to Pleating and Stitching Code]," n.d., attached to letter from Lucy Manning to Oscar W. Rosenzweig, November 19, 1934, box 8386, folder "Labor, U.S. Department of," NRA Homework Committee Papers.

17. [Mary Anderson], *Women at Work: The Autobiography of Mary Anderson as Told to Mary N. Winslow* (Minneapolis: University of Minnesota Press, 1951), p. 244.

18. O. H. Brinkerhoff, Central Square, Oswego Co., N.Y., February 16, 1935, to Franklin Delano Roosevelt, box 8385, folder "Industries (I-N)," NRA Homework Committee Papers.

19. For conditions in knitted outerwear, see U.S. Department of Labor, Wage and Hour Division, Research and Statistics Branch, "Current Status of Home Work in the Knitted Outerwear Industry," November 1941, pp. 4–33, and Findings and Opinion of the Administrator, "In the Matter of: The Recommendation of Industry Committee No. 32 for a Minimum Wage Rate in the Knitted Outerwear Industry and Industrial Home Work in the Knitted Outerwear Industry," March 30, 1942, pp. 13–20 ff., both in the Department of Labor Library, Washington, D.C.

20. For the legality of such rulings, see Gemsco v. Walling, 365 U.S. 244 (1945); Brief for the Petitioner, Mitchell v. Whitaker House Cooperative, pp. 40–43. The other prohibited industries were women's apparel, embroidery, jewelry, gloves and mittens, buttons and buckles, and handkerchiefs.

21. On resurgence, see Naomi Katz and David Kemnitzer, "Fast Forward: The Internationalization of Silicon Valley," in *Women, Men and the International Division of Labor,* ed. June Nash and Patricia Fernández-Kelly (Albany: State University of New York Press, 1983), pp. 332–45; Hardy Green and Elizabeth Weiner, "Bringing It All Back Home," *In These Times 5* (March

11–17, 1981): 8–9; State Senator Franz S. Leichter, "The Return of the Sweat-shop: A Call for State Action," October 1979, pt. 2, February 26, 1981, type-script, in author's possession; State of New York, "Report to the Governor and the Legislature on the Garment Manufacturing Industry and Industrial Homework, February 1982," unpublished report, Division of Labor Standards, New York State Department of Labor, Albany; "To amend the Fair Labor Standards Act of 1938 to facilitate industrial homework, including sewing, knitting, and craftmaking, and for other purposes," 98th Cong., 1st sess., 1984, S.2145; and *Daily Labor Report,* March 28, 1984, A-6–7, D-1–11, and No-vember 6, 1984, A-6. Eileen Boris, telephone interview with aide in Senator Hatch's office, December 1984.

22. For example, comments of Congressman George Miller and testimonies of Manny Eagle, Eugene Steinberg, Yale Garber, Samuel Blutter, Jerome B. Kauff, all of Federation of Apparel Manufacturers; Joseph Moore, Associated Garment Industries of St. Louis; Sol C. Chaikin, ILGWU; Ray Denison, AFL-CIO; State Senator Joseph Montoya of California, all in Committee on Edu-cation and Labor, House of Representatives, "The Reemergence of Sweatshops and the Enforcement of Wage and Hour Standards" (hereafter cited as "The Reemergence of Sweatshops"), 97th Cong., 1st and 2d sess. (Washington, D.C.: GPO, 1982); Frederick Simms *[sic],* testimony, State of New York, Department of Labor, "Public Hearing on Industrial Homework" (hereafter cited as N.Y. Hearing), transcript of proceedings, April 2, 1981, p. 97.

23. C. B. Vaughan, testimony, U.S. Department of Labor, "In the Matter of: A Public Hearing to Commence Labor Department Review of 'Home-worker Rules,' " February 17, 1981, Washington, D.C., p. 440 (hereafter cited as D.C. Hearings); Senate Concurrent Resolution no. 105 (Iowa 1984 Bills) (see also 1984 sess., House Joint Resolution no. 49, Virginia Bills); Joel Cher-ington, testimony, February 18, 1981, D.C. Hearings, pp. 66–67, all in DOL files (n. 4 above).

24. Michael Avakian and Edward F. Hughes, "Statement of the Center on National Labor Policy, Inc., in support of Proposed Rulemaking to Rescind Restriction on Homework in the Knitted Outerwear Industry," May 11, 1984, pp. 5, 9–10; for the knitters, Debra Waugh to William M. Otter, May 11, 1984. See also Beth Fitzammson, The Busy Bee, Newtown, Conn., to William M. Otter, Administrator, Wage and Hour Division, U.S. Department of Labor, April 23, 1984; a Mother Grandmother and Great Grandmother *[sic]* to Wil-liam Otter, Administrator, Wage and Hour Division, April 10, 1984; Pamela Morris, Gioia Couture, Inc., Akron, Ohio, to Otter, May 6, 1984, all in DOL files.

25. Senator Jeremiah Denton, comments, Hatch Hearings (n. 6 above), 76–77; Peter Germanis, "Why Not Let Americans Work at Home?" *Heritage Foundation Backgrounder,* 325 (January 30, 1984): 3, 6–7, 9; Avaiken and Hughes, "Statement . . . in support of Proposed Rulemaking."

26. Germanis, "Why Not Let Americans work at Home?" Orrin Hatch, "Women's Initiative," *Congressional Record—Senate,* 98th Cong., 1st sess., November 18, 1983, S-16981-2.

27. See the testimony of Gloria Gill, former chair of Governor's Commission on the Status of Women, Burlington Hearings (n. 6 above), January 14, 1981, p. 189; National Institute of Education, "Women in the Rural Economy: Employment and Self-Employment," Draft Report, DOL files.

28. Violet Jones, Box 322, Hardwick, Vt., to William M. Otter, n.d., and attached untitled paper; Mary Berard, R.F.D. L1, Box 3890, Oakland, Maine, to Otter, April 11, 1984; Mrs. Ellen Z. Lampner, 48 Orchard St., Randolph, Mass., to Otter, May 3, 1984, pp. 4–5, all in DOL files.

29. Linda Clutterbuck, R.F.D. L1 Box 1540, Norridgewock, Maine, to Otter, April 18, 1984; testimony of Audrey Pudvah and Peggy York, Burlington Hearings, January 14, 1981, pp. 232, 268; see exchange between Lazare Teper and a number of the Vermont women, D.C. Hearings, February 17, 1981, pp. 460–76.

30. Virginia Gray, testimony, Burlington Hearings, p. 249; Robin Frost, P.O. Box 62, Anson, Maine, to "Dear Sir," n.d.; see also, Linda Thomas, Wapella, Ill., to "Dear sir," April 21, 1984; Kathleen Berube, Mandala Farm, Starks, Maine, to Otter, April 21, 1984; Nancy A. Baillie, 139 Mattson Road, Boothwyn, Penn., to Raymond Donovan, May 3, 1984, all in DOL files. References to homeworkers as craftsworkers exist throughout the Burlington Hearings and in the Hatch Hearing as well.

31. For a discussion on this matter, see testimony of Roberta Orticerio, D.C. Hearings, February 18, 1981, pp. 121–29. For the actual work process, see Nancy Smith, Burlington Hearings, January 14, 1981, pp. 265–66.

32. Stowe Woolens Receipt and Order Sheet for Gene Gray, exhibit no. 21, Burlington Hearings, DOL files (n. 4 above); testimony of Peggy York, Burlington Hearings, January 14, 1981, pp. 268–71.

33. Testimony of Audrey Pudvah, Nancy Smith, Emma Pudvah, Christine Brown, Bonnie Merhier, and Virginia Gray, Burlington Hearings, January 14, 1981, pp. 232–66; Mrs. Jan Kuhn, Box 74, Johnson, Vermont, to Mr. Henry T. White, Jr., January 2, 1981, in "Exhibits, Public Hearing to Commence Labor Dept. Review of 'Homeworker Rules,'" DOL files.

34. Eisenstein *Feminism and Sexual Equality* Frances E. Olson, "The Family and the Market: A Study of Ideology and Legal Reform," *Harvard Law Review 96* (May 1983): 1497–1578.

35. Eileen Boris and Peter Bardaglio, "The Transformation of Patriarchy: The Historic Role of the State," in *Families, Politics and Public Policy: A Feminist Dialogue on Women and the State,* ed. Irene Diamond (New York: Longman, Inc., 1983), p. 82; the best summary of protective legislation is Ann Corinne Hill, "Protection of Women Workers and the Courts: A Legal Case History," *Feminist Studies 5* (Summer 1979): 247–73; Adkins v. Children's Hospital, 261 U.S. 525, 43 S.Ct. 394 (1923).

36. Testimony of Mary Clement, Hatch Hearings (n. 6 above), 73; for one example of the knitters' rejection of "protection," see Linda Guetti, Sunset Drive, Bennington, Vt., to Deputy Administrator, Wage and Hour Division, December 23, 1980, DOL files.

37. See Susan D. Becker, *The Origins of the Equal Rights Amendment: American Feminism between the Wars* (Westport, Conn.: Greenwood Press, 1981).

38. Mary Louise Norman, Nicely Knit—Denver, 1310 Clermont Street, Denver, Colo., to Otter, April 21, 1984; Martha A. Hall, 46 Main St., Yarmouth, Maine, to Otter, April 15, 1984; Wendie Ballinger, Special Stitches, 624 Westmoore, Oreana, Ill., to Otter, April 21, 1984, all in DOL files; William Fern, Division of Special Minimum Wage, Department of Labor, interview with author, Washington, D.C., June 10, 1985.

39. Testimony of Kathy Hobart, Burlington Hearings, January 14, 1981, p. 314; testimony of Kathy Hobart, D.C. Hearings (n. 23 above), February 17, 1981, pp. 490–91; see also her questioning of Gerald Coleman, officer of the United Hatters, Cap, and Millinery Workers International Union, and Alice Ruotolo, New Jersey Consumers' League, D.C. Hearings (n. 6 above), February 18, 1981, pp. 30–31, 53.

40. Philip Mattera, "High-Tech Cottage Industry: Home Computer Sweatshops," *Nation* 236, no. 13 (April 2, 1983): 390–92; Cynthia Costello, "The Office Homework Program at the Wisconsin Physicians Service Insurance Company," in this volume, pp. 000–00; Andrew Pollack, "Home-based Work Stirs Suit," in "Business Day," *New York Times,* May 26, 1986; "Statement of Roderick L. MacKenzie, Attorney, Sacramento, Ca., Representing Home-based Clerical Workers," in "Pros and Cons of Home-based Clerical Work," hearing before a subcommittee of the Committee on Government Operations, House of Representatives, 99th Cong., 2d sess., February 26, 1986 (Washington, D.C.: Government Printing Office, 1986), 68–82.

41. Testimony of Sarah, N.Y. Hearing (n. 22 above), 65–79, esp. 65–66; testimony of unnamed woman through an interpreter, New York Hearing, pp. 81–92. For conditions in Los Angeles and California, see Merle Linda Wolin, "Homework: The Alien's Secret Support System," pt. 4 of a 16-pt. series, *Los Angeles Herald Examiner,* January 18, 1981, and her testimony in "The Reemergence of Sweatshops" (n. 22 above), 169–79; and testimony of Joe Razo, D.C. Hearings, February 17, 1981, 408–20. For Miami, see testimony of Robert T. Rosenfeld, D.C. Hearings, February 17, 1981, pp. 342–45.

42. Jill Pollack, "Stamping Out New Sweatshops," *News, North Jersey,* September 8, 1981; Frederick Siems, "Sweatshop Close-up: Filth, Crowding and Child Labor Are the Norm," *Herald Journal* (Indiana), September 21, 1979, ILGWU clippings file; testimony of Alice Ruotolo, D.C. Hearings, February 18, 1981, pp. 39–40; "Proceedings of the Thirty-seventh Convention of the International Ladies' Garment Workers' Union, October 4, 1980," pp. 1–3, Exhibit 54, D.C. Hearings, DOL files (n. 4 above); "Statement of Hon. Daniel Patrick Moynihan, a U.S. Senator from the State of New York," in "The Reemergence of Sweatshops," 38–45.

43. Moynihan; and "Statement of Sol C. Chaikin," in "The Reemergence of Sweatshops," 66–73; testimony of Corinne Lunt, D.C. Hearings, February 17, 1981, p. 481.

44. "Prepared Statement of Amado H. Gallardo, California Labor Federation, AFL-CIO," in "Reemergence of Sweatshops," 200; testimony of Billie Ann Pilling, D.C. Hearings, February 18, 1981, pp. 99–100.

45. Testimony of Grace Lyu-Volckhausen, N.Y. Hearing, 106–14; testimony of Ruth Jordan, D.C. Hearings (n. 23 above), February 18, 1981, pp. 230–44, esp. 233–36; "Statement of Ruth Jordan, Member, Board of Directors, National Consumers' League," in "Reemergence of Sweatshops," 148.

46. Carol Stack. *All Our Kin: Strategies for Survival in a Black Community* (New York: Harper & Row, 1974); for the policies of European social democracies, see Sheila B. Kamerman, "Women, Children, and Poverty: Public Policies and Female-headed Families in Industrialized Countries," *Signs* 10 (Winter 1984): 249–71; Carolyn Teich Adams and Kathryn Teich, *Mothers at Work: Public Policies in the United States, Sweden, and China* (New York: Longman, Inc., 1980); for proposed U.S. legislation, see Nadine Taub, "Nurturing Leaves: A Public Policy of Private Caring," *Nation* 242 (May 31, 1986); 756–58; Susan Morse, "Careers: The Hill Debate on Time Off for Children," *Washington Post,* May 20, 1986, C. For an alternative organization of space, see Dolores Hayden, *Redesigning the American Home: The Future of Housing, Work, and Family Life* (New York: W. W. Norton & Co., 1984).

47. The possibility of regulating electronic homework is more promising, since programs already exist to monitor the number of keystrokes made by typists. For one discussion of this issue, see Donald Elisburg, "Legalities," in *Office Workstations in the Home,* ed. National Research Council (Washington, D.C.: National Academy Press, 1985), pp. 59–65.

48. Sol C. Chaikin, ILGWU, 1710 Broadway, N.Y., to Hon. Ford B. Ford, Undersecretary, U.S. Department of Labor, December 14, 1984, available from Shea & Gardner, 1800 Massachusetts Ave., N.W., Washington, D.C.; on certification program and recent developments, Eileen Boris, telephone interview with William Fern, 1986; on proposal to rescind remaining homework bans, see Kenneth B. Noble, "U.S. Weighs End to Ban on Factory Homework," *New York Times,* August 20, 1986, A; Eileen Boris, "A Woman's Place?" *Nation* 243 (October 18, 1986): 365–66.

49. On proposed new ban, "AFL-CIO Resolution on Computer Homework," in *Office Workstations in the Home.* pp. 152–53; on future trends, see Eileen Appelbaum, "Restructuring Work: Temporary, Part-Time and At Home Employment," in *Computer Chips and Paper Clips: Technology and Women's Employment,* ed. Heidi Hartmann (Washington, D.C.: National Academy Press, 1987), pp. 268–310; and Karen Sacks, "Out of the Frying Pan, into the Fire: Macroeconomic Trends and Women's Life Chances" (Paper presented at the conference on Women, Welfare, and Higher Education, Smith College, Northampton, Massachusetts, April 1985).

13

Home-Based Work: Labor's Choices

VIRGINIA duRIVAGE and DAVID JACOBS

In 1983, the International Ladies' Garment Workers' Union (ILGWU) took the Department of Labor to court to prevent the deregulation of industrial homework. While Reagan administration officials considered the long-established ban on low-wage production in the household to be obstructive of U.S. competitiveness, ILGWU activists and many others in the labor movement perceived homework as a threat to unionism and decent labor standards. In 1981, the Department of Labor had lifted the ban on home knitting for an eighteen-month period. In 1984, the forty-two year-old ban was lifted permanently. It appeared that administration officials were determined to promote homework as one solution to America's economic ills.[1]

As both industrial and clerical homework appear to grow, trade unionists seek to devise means to control their exploitative potential. Unionists are concerned about the impact of homework upon the conditions of organized workers, about the quality of the new jobs created, and about the prospects for new organizing. The campaign against homework provides an opportunity to defend the unorganized as well as protect union members. It may be, however, that homework represents only one dimension of a changing economy increasingly inhospitable to unionism and union standards in employment.[2] The purpose of this essay is to explore labor's struggle to develop an appropriate strategy toward homework.

Why Homework Is Often Exploitative

The appeal of homework is based on the perception of autonomy for those who choose it. Working at home appears to permit the worker to control her time, to choose her pace, to be free from direct supervision. A measure of autonomy is a reality for home-based entrepreneurs and professionals, whose home workplace reflects their affluence, their ownership of spacious homes with rooms to spare. However, for the clerical and industrial homeworkers, whose subordinate status is not altered by the language of "independent contracting," the reality is different.[3] Here, the employer appropriates a portion of the home and exercises indirect control. No compensation is paid for this appropriation of property. The economic security of the homeworker depends upon the accommodation of home life to the demands of the employer. The homeworker must balance employer demands and personal/family needs. If piece rates are paid, rather than an hourly wage, payment is contingent upon a succession of employer decisions, and homeworkers surrender their homes and time with no guarantee of return. In the case of industrial homework, worker health and safety are endangered by the use of toxic chemicals without adequate safeguards in the home.[4]

The labor movement is most concerned with the home-based clerical and manufacturing employee, who is particularly vulnerable to exploitation, rather than the home-based entrepreneur, manager, or professional. Despite the facile assumption that clerical work is relatively dignified and conforms to high standards as a form of employment, the potential for exploitation is the same in industrial and clerical homework.

The majority of homeworkers, industrial and clerical, are female. Whether a worker is processing insurance claims on her computer in the kitchen or stitching sweat suits in her living room, she is likely to earn less per hour and work fewer hours per week than employees inside the factory or office. She is likely to be paid piece rates, especially if she is classified as an independent contractor (despite her exclusive relationship to one employer).[5]

In 1980, female homeworkers, on average, earned subminimum hourly wages—$3.06—compared to women who worked outside the home and earned $4.02 an hour. Male home-based workers were paid, on average, $6.77 an hour compared to $8.20 paid to men who worked inside the plant or office. The Office of Technology Assessment reports that in 1980, 10 percent of persons who worked exclusively from home were officially poor compared to 6 percent of other workers.[6]

Given that employers often do not pay homeworkers benefits and that they may evade the payment of social security and other taxes through the fiction of independent contracting, it should be clear that the homework option is a means to cut labor costs. Employers seldom choose the homework option for altruistic reasons, to accommodate employee needs. While cost-reduction need not be pursued in ways so damaging to employee interests, homeworkers individually do not have the power to compel fair treatment by employers.[7]

Homework and Broader Economic Trends: Marginalization

Much to the concern of trade unionists, homework is one dimension of a growing marginal workforce in the United States. Part-time jobs now constitute more than one-fifth of total U.S. employment; six million Americans are working in part-time jobs because full-time work is unavailable. The temporary services industry is the third fastest growing industry in the economy today. According to Audrey Freedman of the Conference Board, more than twenty-eight million workers—a quarter of the nation's work force—comprise the "contingent work force."[8]

Desperate to drive up productivity in a stagnating economy, businesses are automating offices and factories, laying off workers, hiring greater numbers of part-time and temporary workers, and contracting out work on a regular basis. Employer discretion in retrenchment and restructuring staffing increasingly takes precedence over the classical management goal of a well-trained, committed work force. The newly hired part-time and temporary workers are predominately female, receive low wages, and lack fringe benefits and job security.[9]

Many homeworkers belong to the growing category of contract workers. While home-based clerical workers may be directly hired by an employer, they may also work for a business service that contracts to do the work for a firm and then subcontracts or distributes it among a number of home-based clerical workers. Subcontracting has increased in popularity as an employment practice which reduces labor costs, particularly in unionized firms where other cost-cutting work schedules—like part-time and temporary employment—may be better regulated by union contract.[10]

In 1986 the Bureau of National Affairs surveyed 442 companies on the use of temporary employees and subcontractors. Nearly every employer interviewed reported an increased use of flexible staffing arrangements between 1980 and 1985. Sixty-three percent of respondents claimed that they contracted out work (for example, cleaning, clerical, and production services) to firms or individuals outside of the responding company. In unionized firms, 77 percent reported they contracted out work compared to 61 percent of nonunionized companies.[11]

Since 1981, subcontracting costs in the federal government have increased from $15 billion to $53 billion. In contrast to this, the federal payroll for permanent workers in 1986 was $51 billion. More money is spent by the federal government for contract labor such as custodial work and clerical tasks than for all regular federal employees.[12]

The growth of subcontracting and other types of contingent work exacerbates the problem of declining living standards of American working families. From 1973 to 1985, real average weekly and hourly earnings for individuals dropped by 14.4 percent and 10.1 percent respectively. Current average weekly wages are equivalent to those being earned in 1962, nearly twenty-five years ago.[13] And despite the increased work efforts of American women and the decreased size of family households, real family income in the U.S. declined 6.2 percent between 1978 and 1984.[14]

Lousy Options: Why Workers Take These Jobs

High unemployment rates, reduced family incomes, and spiraling divorce rates compel many women in two-parent and one-parent families to seek work. The lack of a national policy on child care, combined with the genuine desire on the part of many working families to better balance work and family responsibilities, have created a labor market drawn to such options as homework.[15] In her study of home-based workers, Kathleen Christensen found that the majority of homeworkers sought to earn extra money for the family without jeopardizing the primary relationship with their children.[16]

Industrial homeworkers in the past were motivated by similar desires. The need to supplement inadequate earnings of spouses while caring for children was a major factor including women to take industrial work into their homes. Yet, during the Depression years a consensus emerged within labor and government that homework posed too great a social and economic hardship for the majority of working families. The notion that jobs should provide a decent standard of living for families inspired the abolishment of certain types of homework from 1933 to 1935 and again from 1942 until recent years.[17] Today, the partial deregulation of homework and the growth of low-wage service-sector employment have eroded the concept of the family wage. The current reality is that families require more than one breadwinner, and many family members are being compelled by economic necessity to accept home-based work. To the extent that economic policies, social legislation, and collective bargaining intervene to improve employment options and child care will workers have genuine choices about homework versus work in the office.[18]

The Obstacles to Organizing Homeworkers

Employers recognize that reliance on homework is a powerful anti-union tool. Historically, workers have been most inclined to organize in situations in which their proximity to one another and frequent interaction permitted the development of a sense of collective identity. Homeworkers have almost no opportunity to discuss their grievances as a group and assess the possible advantages of organizing. Their isolation and dispersion render organizing almost impossible.

Not surprisingly, a New York State Assembly panel reported recently that homework is illustrative of "anti-union attitudes among employers in New York State." Among its recommendations to improve labor-management relations was state refusal to legalize "some types of work at home, a tactic used by some employers to get around unions."[19]

Anti-union employers may also introduce homework in the midst of a campaign to organize traditional office or factory workers. Susan Adams, business representative for the United Food and Commercial Workers (UFCW) Local 1444 in Madison, Wisconsin, argues that the Wisconsin Physicians Service (a hospital insurance firm) hired 120 to 140 part-time homeworkers in response to union organizing efforts at the company. The action was prompted by a protracted battle to negotiate a first contract between the company and Local 1444.[20]

As Cynthia Costello has shown, managers at the Wisconsin Physicians Service were motivated to hire homeworkers as a way to circumvent the union and create a permanent strike-breaking force. One former supervisor said plainly, "The thought was if it comes down to striking, they can send everything out to the homeworkers." The service also added 400 part-time workers to its night shift in an effort to maximize its flexibility with employees outside the bargaining unit. The union has repeatedly sought without success to win the right to represent homeworkers and part-time workers or to prevent their hire through bargaining and NLRB procedures.[21]

Employers who seek to hire homeworkers are almost certainly pursuing the lower costs associated with nonunion status. Given current NLRB policy as well as the anti-union mood of the public, the homework strategy is likely to cripple efforts to organize these workers. Moreover, the availability of homework as an option for employers both weakens the position of organized employees, who must fight to retain their jobs, and retards new organization of traditional employees. In the case of clerical homeworkers, the absence of much precedent for the unionization of any clericals further depresses prospects. The leadership of the International Ladies' Garment Workers' argues that the unionization of industrial homeworkers would be futile because no union could monitor the enforcement of contracts in dispersed home work sites. In this context, it is not surprising that many unions would prefer that homework be largely banned.[22]

Labor's Choices: Bans and Other Forms of Control

Because many women and men are now seeking alternatives to full-time work in the office as a strategy to better balance work and family, the trade union movement must identify ways to satisfy its members' diverse concerns while at the same time maintaining effective controls to avoid worker exploitation. In this context, homework poses a problem. Homework appears to provide an attractive option to many, but the history of homework is replete with exploitation, and efforts to regulate it (rather than ban it) have failed.

In the 1870s, union cigar makers were threatened by the rise of highly exploitative, nonunion tenement factories in which cigar manufacturers rented rooms for the use of their employees as both workplaces and residences. In 1877, with the support of the Cigar Makers International Union, the tenement workers struck their employers. They won neither union recognition nor improved wages and conditions. Union cigar makers grew convinced that in order to preserve their gains in traditional factories they must seek the elimination of tenement work. In this they were supported by many employers opposed to what they deemed the unfair competition of tenement work and by social reformers appalled by the tragedy of tenement life. But when they won a legislative ban, the New York Supreme Court struck it down, calling it interference with a man's right to do what he pleased in his own home.[23]

Reformers sought to regulate homework on the federal and state levels. Federal regulation began in 1933 when the National Recovery Administration issued the Codes of Fair Competition, which prohibited homework in almost one hundred industries with reasonable success. In 1935, when the Supreme Court invalidated the National Industrial Recovery Act, federal restrictions on homework were no longer in force. That same year, New York State developed a model regulatory system featuring certification and record-keeping requirements for employers hiring homeworkers. In the mid-thirties, the Amalgamated Clothing Workers of America worked closely with state officials to obtain homework prohibitions in men's and boys' clothing and men's neckties.[24]

The Fair Labor Standards Act (FLSA), passed in 1938, made a new effort to regulate homework on the federal level. The Department of Labor required employers to maintain records of homeworkers' hours and wages. Employees were to enter information about the terms of their work in employer-provided guidebooks. Despite these efforts, labor department hearings between 1941 and 1943 revealed a pattern of employer violation of homework regulations which seemed to extinguish any hopes that the regulatory approach was workable. Industrial homework appeared to threaten the intent of the Fair Labor Standards Act to establish minimum wages and maximum hours by guaranteeing freedom from effective regulation to a potentially significant share of manufacturing. The Department of Labor then chose to prohibit homework altogether in seven industries: women's apparel, knitted outerwear, embroideries, buttons and buckles, gloves and mittens, handkerchiefs, and jewelry. With the support of organized labor, amendments to the FLSA in 1949 incorporated these provisions into federal law.[25]

Thus, unionists have considerable experience with which to evaluate alternative approaches to homework. Because of the apparent obstacles to industrial homework regulation, unionists were almost universally outraged by the Reagan administration's deregulation of knitted outerwear homework in 1981. The administration intended to eliminate prohibitions on industrial homework in the remaining six industries by the summer of 1987. While the Department of Labor now requires industry employers to be certified, following an adverse ruling by the District of Columbia Court of Appeals in the ILGWU suit, there is no evidence that regulation is effective. Only fifty-five of the hundred of employers who use homeworkers have registered with the department, and only thirty-five have been investigated to confirm compliance with regulations. Of those investigated, 77 percent were found to be in violation of record-keeping rules.[26]

The inherent difficulty in regulating homework is compounded by the Reagan administration's refusal to adequately fund FLSA enforcement. While the workload of the department's Wage and Hour Division has increased, the number of compliance officers enforcing FLSA provisions decreased from 1098 to 895 between 1980 and 1984; the number of investigations dropped by 16 percent.[27]

Most unions strongly support an effective ban on industrial homework. They have sharply criticized the Reagan administration's moves in this area. Some unions question the degree to which they should focus on bans, at least in the case of clerical and computer homework, and propose instead initiatives in bargaining that would create a non-exploitative homework alternative.

The International Ladies' Garment Workers' Union has, of course, played a crucial role in the campaign against industrial homework. It should be noted that ILGWU seeks to organize immigrant workers, despite linguistic barriers and the precarious status of the undocumented. Union leaders express concern about the particular vulnerability of immigrants, who may be afraid to assert their rights for fear of termination, to homework exploitation. While ILGWU is prepared to undertake the arduous task of unionizing aliens, the leadership finds organizing homeworkers to be impractical, for which reason they favor a homework ban as the best means of protecting immigrants.[28]

The Amalgamated Clothing and Textile Workers (ACTWU), Service Employees International Union (SEIU), and the AFL-CIO itself are among the other labor organizations which have lobbied strenuously against administration plans to deregulate industrial homework. All represent workers in industries which would be affected by deregulation. The International Jewelry Workers Union recently merged with SEIU, increasing the saliency of the issue of industrial homework for the latter.[29] (Labor does not ignore special worker needs; ACTWU President Jack Sheinkman has indicated that unionists do not oppose government programs that permit the handicapped to perform homework under limited circumstances, as is the case in Gloversville, New York.[30])

In 1983, at its fifteenth constitutional convention, the AFL-CIO adopted a resolution on clerical homework that called for "an early ban on computer homework by the Department of Labor." SEIU, which has a growing clerical division of over 120,000 members, has likewise called on the department to prohibit computer homework. The union's 1984 resolution to this effect was preceded by a 1982 statement by the union's executive board, which concluded that "because enforcement of wage, hours, and safety standards in the home is absolutely impossible, we call for an early ban on computer homework by the Department of Labor as a measure of protection for those workers entering the market for the fastest growing occupation in the U.S.[31]

In a series of resolutions on technological change adopted at the union's 1986 convention, the Office and Professional Employees International Union (OPEIU) included a ban on electronic homework. The delegates pledged that local unions would pursue safeguards for workers at the bargaining table through legislation including a "ban on monitoring, machine-paced work, and electronic homework.[32]

The AFL-CIO, SEIU, and OPEIU proposals for an outright ban on electronic homework stem from the belief that collective bargaining and government regulation are incapable of eliminating exploitation in clerical as well as industrial home-based work. Unions like SEIU and OPEIU, which seek to organize clericals, worry that homework threatens their efforts to protect clericals in the office by providing a low-wage, nonunion alternative.

In contrast, the Newspaper Guild and the American Federation of State, County, and Municipal Employees (AFSCME) hope to win controls on homework so that employee options can be maximized without increased exploitation. In the case of the guild, newspaper reporters are more likely to work at home than are clerical workers. The union has been reluctant to oppose the practice because of the number of reporters who express a preference for alternative working arrangements. Instead, the union has sought information on such homework practices as working overtime without pay and other health and safety violations, in order to protect reporters from exploitation. At the same time, the union is concerned that the business practices of some advertising companies, using remote computers to directly transmit classified ads, threaten to displace lower-skilled office workers.[33]

At the guild's annual convention in 1985, the union passed a bargaining recommendation that instructed locals to "seek full information regarding employees' use of personal or remote computers in the service of the employer and the use of tie-in with the employer's computer by free lancers, news sources, advertisers, and the like."[34]

Similarly, the Coalition of Labor Union Women (CLUW) resolved at its 1986 convention to seek more information on the exploitative features of clerical homework. Convention delegates opposed lifting the ban on industrial homework and agreed to undertake a campaign to educate members on the exploitative nature of clerical homework.[35]

AFSCME, which represents a substantial proportion of all clerical employees in the public sector, has passed resolutions on computer homework at both its 1984 and 1986 international conventions. The first resolution opposed the unilateral imposition of homework by management but did spell out the terms under which a homework program could be negotiated:

> No employee shall be assigned home-based work without agreement of the local union. Employer provides all necessary equipment, modifications to phone lines, etc. . . . The cost of long distance phone use will be at the employer's expense, as well as reasonable travel costs. Work rules and standards shall be the same as those performing similar tasks at work. Vacancies shall be filled through contractual procedures. Em-

ployer pays U.S. mail service to employees by local union. No piece work.[36]

AFSCME's willingness to negotiate homework agreements is the result of a successful pilot project for home-based workers between AFSCME District 24 and the University of Wisconsin Hospital. Peak demands in medical transcription work and a shortage of physical office space encouraged the hospital administration to contract out word processing. Partly due to worker interest, the union proposed a homework experiment as a way to decrease subcontracting and expand AFSCME's bargaining unit. The hospital benefited in its ability to expand staffing levels without adding costly office space. Labor and management negotiated the terms of the pilot project, and both parties were involved in monitoring standards. Initially three workers volunteered for the program. Homeworkers remained members of the bargaining unit, receiving the same pay, benefits, and promotional opportunities as in-house workers. The union kept contact with these workers via an electronic switchboard and weekly meetings at the office.[37] At the 1986 convention, AFSCME called for a ban on computer homework until comprehensive labor standards were established and effectively enforced by the U.S. Department of Labor. However, in the absence of meaningful regulation and in recognition of worker interest in homework options, AFSCME resolved that collective bargaining was the only approach that could assure labor protection for home-based work:

> The only forum through which labor standards can be assured, and through which actual experiences with computer homework will be open to full review and evaluation by all parties, is the forum of collective bargaining. Locals that negotiate over computer homework are encouraged to insist at a minimum that any agreement provide: a trial period; an option for either party to discontinue computer homework; and protections against unrealistic work standards, excessive stress, and economic exploitation.[38]

The success of AFSCME's experiment with homework suggests that homework may be a viable option if unions are involved in the decision to implement such a program, if homework is voluntary, if labor and management negotiate every feature of the program, and if strong contract language exists clearly stating the terms and conditions of such work. However, where management is aggressively seeking to weaken a union, as was the case with the Wisconsin Physicians Service, and is diverting work to homeworkers as an anti-union strategy, AFSCME's model "problem solving" becomes irrelevant.

Legislative Approaches

AFSCME's approach to limiting the exploitive character of homework so as to provide a new employment option for its members is an attractive bargaining strategy. However, it is unlikely that the problem of homework can be resolved more generally in the near future by organizing and collective bargaining. The organized proportion of the work force is currently under 20 percent and prospects for a new wave of organizing are poor.[39] Unionizing homeworkers would be particularly difficult. Labor is likely to continue to rely primarily on statutory approaches to control homework.

Since the 1930s, labor unions have repeatedly chosen to abandon elements of voluntarism—that is, the principle that collective bargaining is the only meaningful route to the improvement of workers' conditions. Voluntarist orthodoxy led unions to oppose unemployment insurance and other legislative remedies as likely to weaken demand for unionism and collective bargaining. The severity of the Great Depression produced a conversion on this issue, and unions came to support the Wagner Act, the Fair Labor Standards Act, and other such legislative initiatives. In February of 1987 the AFL-CIO executive council endorsed legislation to guarantee workers protection against termination without cause. Most unions now agree that the protection of unorganized workers requires new public policy.[40]

Homework is so serious a problem that unions have been inclined to reject voluntarism on this issue as well. The goal must be to provide statutory protection for workers without discouraging organizing and collective bargaining. If labor is identified with lobbying on behalf of disadvantaged groups of homeworkers, it should redound to labor's benefit. However, homework remains a problematic issue, and unions must avoid being cast as reactionary in their efforts to restrict homework. For this reason, unions must develop new legislative proposals only after relevant issues have been discussed with other interested organizations.[41] Labor should explicitly seek agreement with women's groups, employee associations, and professional groups on the outline of proposed legislation. Indeed, the ILGWU has pursued such an approach in its campaign against homework deregulation. Such legislation might re-establish the ban on industrial homework, limit the legal definition of independent contractor status, require extensive company services to support the homeworker where this option remains legal, and even mandate the formation of worker committees (with consultation rights) to monitor FLSA observance. (Such worker committees would be of the sort required by law in many enterprises in Canada and Western Europe, providing a mechanism through which employees, selected by their peers, can communicate their concerns to employers.[42]) The interorganizational deliberations to produce such a policy proposal should increase the likelihood that women and other constituencies will see labor as an ally rather than as a special interest and improve prospects for success. Moreover, the dialogue may provide a climate in which union organizing once again attains the status of a broad social movement.[43]

NOTES

1. Cynthia B. Costello, *Home-Based Employment: Implications for Working Women* (Washington, D.C.: Women's Research and Education Institute, 1987), pp. 8–9.

2. Bureau of National Affairs, *The Changing Workplace: New Directions in Staffing and Scheduling,* (Washington, D.C.: BNA, 1986).

3. See Kathleen Christensen "Home-based Clerical Work: No Simple Truth, No Single Reality," in this volume, pp. 183–97.

4. Representative Austin J. Murphy, Chair, Subcommittee on Labor Standards, opening statement, *Oversight Hearings on the Department of Labor's Proposal to Lift the Ban on Industrial Homework,* hearings before the Subcommittee on Labor Standards, Committee on Education and Labor, U.S. House of Representatives, 99th Cong., September 16 and 23, 1986 (Washington, D.C.: 1987), pp. 3–5.

5. Francis W. Horvath, "Work at Home: New Findings from the Current Population Survey," *Monthly Labor Review* 109 (November 1986): 31–35.

6. U.S. Congress, Office of Technology Assessment, *Automation of America's Offices* (Washington, D.C.: 1985).

7. Representative Austin J. Murphy, opening statement, *Oversight Hearings,* pp. 3–5.

8. Bureau of National Affairs, *The Changing Workplace.*

9. Eileen Appelbaum, "Reconstructing Work: Temporary, Part-Time, and At-Home Employment," in *Computer Chips and Paper Clips: Technology and Women's Employment,* ed. Heidi I. Hartmann, 2 vols. (Washington, D.C.: National Academy Press, 1987), 2:268–310.

10. Virginia duRivage, *Working on the Margins* (Cleveland, Ohio: Working Women Educational Fund, 1986).

11. Bureau of National Affairs, *The Changing Workplace.*

12. John Harris, assistant to the president, American Federation of Government Employees, interview with author, February 1987.

13. Larry Mishel, *The Polarization of America* (Washington, D.C.: AFL-CIO Industrial Union Department, 1986).

14. Frank S. Levy and Richard C. Michel, "The Economic Future of the Baby Boom," commissioned paper, Joint Economic Committee, U.S. Congress, 99th Cong. (Washington, D.C.: Joint Economic Committee, 1985).

15. Costello, *Home-Based Employment,* p. 13.

16. Kathleen E. Christensen, "No Simple Truth."

17. Eileen Boris, "Regulating Industrial Homework: The Triumph of 'Sacred Motherhood,'" *Journal of American History* 71 (March 1985): 745–63.

18. Eileen Boris, prepared statement, *Oversight Hearings,* pp. 211–21.

19. "Anti-Union View Reported among Employees in NY State," *New York Times,* February 17, 1985, I-58.

20. Susan Adams, business representative, UAW Local 1444, Madison, Wisconsin, interview with author, March 1987.

21. Cynthia B. Costello, "The Clerical Homework Program at the Wisconsin Physicians Service Insurance Corporation," in this volume, pp. 198–214.

22. Dennis Chamot, "Ban Work at Home: It Exploits Workers," *USA Today,* March 28, 1986; Jay Mazur, testimony, *Oversight Hearings,* p. 71.

23. Dorothee Schneider, "The New York Cigarmakers Strike of 1877," *Labor History* 26 (Summer 1985): 325–52; *In Re Jacobs* (98 NY 98).

24. Costello, *Home-Based Employment,* pp. 4–5; Industrial Commissioner, New York State Department of Labor, *Matter of Proposed Order Prohibiting Industrial Homework in the Men's Clothing Industry: Public Hearing Before the Industrial Commissioner,* January 29, 1936 (New York: N.Y. State Department of Labor, 1936).

25. *Ibid.*

26. Jay Mazur, testimony, *Oversight Hearings,* pp. 47–73.

27. Representative Austin J. Murphy, opening statement, *Oversight Hearings,* p. 4.

28. Jay Mazur, testimony, *Oversight Hearings,* pp. 71–72.

29. Jack Sheinkman, testimony, Lane Kirkland and Service Employees International Union, prepared statements, *Oversight Hearings,* pp. 147–60, 163–68, 242–54.

30. Jack Sheinkman, testimony, *Oversight Hearings,* p. 160.

31. Dennis Chamot and John L. Zalusky, "Use and Misuse of Workstations at Home," in *Office Workstations in the Home,* ed. National Research Council, (Washington, D.C.: National Academy Press, 1985), pp. 76–84.

32. OPEIU policy statements, 1986 convention, *White Collar* 420 (July - August - September 1986): 6.

33. David Eisen, director of research and information, Newspaper Guild, interview with author, February 1987.

34. Bargaining recommendations, Newspaper Guild 1985 convention.

35. "Homework Resolution," resolutions passed at the 1986 CLUW convention.

36. "Resolution on Computer Homework—Bargaining Proposal," 26th AFSCME International Convention, San Francisco, 1984.

37. Kevin Murphy, former research economist with AFSCME, interview with author, February 1987; "Hospital Medical Record Department Home-Based Work Station Pilot Study," AFSCME Council 24, Madison, Wisconsin, 1986.

38. "Resolution on Computer Homework," AFSCME 27th International Convention, Chicago, 1986.

39. AFL-CIO, Committee on the Evolution of Work, *The Changing Situation of Workers and Their Unions* (Washington, D.C.: AFL-CIO, 1985).

40. AFL-CIO Executive Council, "Employment or Will," resolution adopted February 1987.

41. See David C. Jacobs, "UAW and the Committee for National Health Insurance: The Contours of Social Unionism," in *Advances in Industrial and Labor Relations,* vol. 4, ed. David Lewin, David B. Lipsky, and Donna R. Sockell (Greenwich, Conn., JAI Press, 1987), pp. 119–40.

42. See Roy J. Adams, "Should Works Councils Be Used as Industrial Relations Policy?," *Monthly Labor Review* 108 (July 1985): 25–29.

43. See Michael Piore, "Unions and Politics," in *The Shrinking Perimeter: Unionism and Labor Relations in the Manufacturing Sector,* ed. Hervey Juris and Myron Roomkin (Lexington, Mass.: Lexington Books, 1980), pp. 173–86.

14

Locating Homework in an Analysis of the Ideological and Material Constraints on Women's Paid Work

SHEILA ALLEN

The study of homework under conditions of late twentieth-century capitalism raises in acute form the limitation of social theories regarding women and work. In general it has been assumed that in industrialized societies men work and women care for families. It is not surprising, therefore, that industrial sociology ignored or treated as an exceptional case the paid work of women. Its conceptual frameworks ensured that women's work, paid and unpaid, fell outside the normal perceptions of how structures and processes operated. Nowhere has the effect of male-dominated social science been more obvious that in the lack of understanding and explanation or even adequate description of homework.

Homework—that is, waged work carried out largely, but not exclusively, by women in their domestic premises—falls outside the sociology of the family and household, outside the sociology of work and industry, and outside theories of the development of capitalism as an economic and political system. The kind of sociological theory developed to explain the nature and consequences of industrialization, in which the separation of home and work became a taken-for-granted assumption, has distorted the sociology of work and the sociology of the family and obscured the relations of women to productive and reproductive labor.

It is one of the strengths of current feminist scholarship that it has called for and begun to undertake a re-examination of areas which have become locked into virtually self-contained disciplines. By asking and exploring questions which cross over the conventional boundaries erected in so much academic social science, feminists have begun to provide the possibilities for developing theories adequate to the task before it. It is, however, much easier to criticize the deficiencies of a social science concerned only with half the population (and frequently only portions of that half) than to overcome them. For it is not only in social science that women are ignored or marginalized. We live in societies in which women are subordinated as social persons. Their activities are marginalized, continuously and consistently, by language, by ideologies, and by material conditions. Unequal gender relations result in an inadequate social science. The cultural struggle to improve social science and the political struggle to reduce gender inequalities are related. The former will not be gained without the latter.

Homework is hidden, both as a form of production and as a form of paid work. The persistent invisibility of much of women's economic activity is not specific to homework but is institutionalized through the ideological separation of home and work. It does not appear in the formal state measures of economic production or economic participation and is generally ignored in economic modeling. In Britain, it was thought to have disappeared in the early decades of this century, until it was rediscovered in the early 1970s. The analysis of its relation to contemporary economies is in its infancy. Its existence is now acknowledged in many parts of Europe, North America, Australia, and the Third World. The supposition that there is an increase in homeworking derives from a denial of how widespread it has been throughout the industrial period.[1]

The development of discrete categories of work and workers, consequent on material and ideological changes in the nineteenth century, made the association of women and work normatively unaccepted and unacceptable. The very definitions of work changed, so that most commonly work was equated with full-time, regular, paid employment. This provided a basis to escape from any serious consideration of the work women do, whether paid or unpaid, and the conditions under which it is done. According to this conceptualization, which has lasted well into the third quarter of the twentieth century, unpaid work becomes nonwork and the links between women and paid work, where recognized, take on a conditional form. This varies with the social and economic structures of households, familial ideologies, and the structures and processes involved in the demands for labor. It is possible to specify the conditions which both separate women from and integrate them into different forms of work in contemporary Western societies. These conditions include (1) kinship networks, particularly relations with husbands, fathers, children, elderly parents and parents-in-law, and sick or handicapped relatives; (2) authority structures, especially those of the state and religious bodies in determining the obligations of wives and mothers; and (3) paid work for men, its availability, organization, appropriateness, and rewards.

Who Does Homework?

The dominant view that industrialization brought a separation of home and work with the male as the breadwinner and the female isolated in the home bearing and rearing children is, of course, a gross oversimplification, but its influence is pervasive. Equally, the view that this sexual division of labor takes place within a nuclear family unit of a conjugal pair with dependent children dominates both the social science literature and common-sense views of the world. These perspectives together not only ignore the statistical realities of household composition and women's economic activity but also obscure the most important aspects of the relations between production and reproduction, as these constrain women.

Though given relatively little attention the economic advantages of homework as a form of production to those who supply it—contractors or entrepreneurs—constitute a significant part of the explanation of why homeworking persists.[2] The explanation of who does homework and why relates to how women's paid labor, both inside and outside the home, is organized according to priorities set by others.

Evidence gathered in the early 1970s in Britain and elsewhere shows homework to be characterized by low pay and poor conditions, with all the inconvenience associated with using one's home as a work place and in some cases with danger to health and safety.[3] In the mid 1980s scholars and the press gave attention to "new" homeworking, which often was portrayed as being different—offering better pay and conditions and carried out by more highly educated women. In fact, the pay is lower, relative to that paid for the same work done outside the home, and the conditions likewise poorer. The characteristics of "new" technology homeworkers are important in so far as they demonstrate that highly skilled and educated women are integrated into paid labor according to priorities set by others. The most common explanation of why people do homework is that women needing to earn an income and also carrying domestic responsibilities—for young children in particular, but also for the elderly, the sick and handicapped, and for those who go out to work—find this the only or most convenient form of paid work available. These explanations take for granted that domestic responsibilities are the concern of women alone and do not explore further. The argument is then frequently extended to trace homeworking to the preferences of housewives wishing to earn pin-money in their spare time. In my own research I investigated these explanations in interviews with ninety homeworkers and a dozen ex-homeworkers. The subsequent analysis conceptualizes the structuring of domestic constraints in the more general context of women's work paid and unpaid, inside and outside the home, in order to specify the ways in which ideological and material factors conditioned their lives. One of the most important elements was that of the ideology of women both as marginal to the labor force and as economic providers in their households.

The sexual division of labor is not a division between male breadwinners and female housewives or domestic laborers. The importance of this distorted conceptualization of the division of labor is the ideological force it carries. The sexual division of labor is, on the one hand, between women as unpaid workers within the household and the relative freedom of men from such work and on the other, the differential bases on which women and men are integrated into the system of production.

The constraints on women to engage in paid work are as strong as those which condition men. The difference between them arises from an ideology which declares that women are primarily wives and mothers and that men are supporters of families. This ideology puts women in a position of construed dependency, so that they are required to shoulder simultaneously all the time-consuming, laborious, caring work of reproduction and their paid work as well. Therefore, the sexually segregated labor market both reflects and causes the limited options open to women. This is particularly evident in the case of homeworking.

In order to appreciate homeworkers' actual position within the labor process, we need to understand what the domestic sphere means for women and, in particular, the work obligations which women experience within it. Only through confronting the diverse obligations which women experience can we comprehend their conditions as homeworkers and relate these to women's working lives more generally. The notion of homeworkers' autonomy in paid work holds sway because of powerful associations made between ideas of home, privacy, and freedom from work constraints imposed by "the rude, commercial, aggressive world."[4] If we look closely at their situation, we find something quite different.

Only three of the ninety homeworkers used their pay primarily for "extras," which they defined as Christmas presents, holidays, cosmetics, cigarettes, and husband's car expenses. The expenditure pattern of the others indicates that homeworking pay is not pin-money but an essential contribution to household expenses, such as food, heating, lighting, rent or mortgage repayments, and children's shoes and clothes. Without it there would be hardship for most households.

Material subsistence was the overriding reason given for engaging in homework.[5] Intertwined with this was a desire for some modicum of independence from the male partner or from the state. "He has all the say when there is only his wage," summarizes the attitude of many of the homeworkers. Women without a male partner described in graphic detail the humiliation and harassment they received at the hands of state officials and their need and wish to avoid the stigma associated with accepting state money. One woman, for instance, supported herself and two children by working fifty-five hours a week at two part-time jobs in addition to her homeworking. She also took care of other children for pay. In *total* she earned $ 117 a week, well below the low pay limit. Since she falls outside all the definitions of economic activity, her paid work went unrecorded in official statistics. She is not an ordinary worker in any of the dominant constructions of a worker, though her hours are longer than most. She typifies the working patterns of women more clearly than either the theories of social scientists or definitions of governmental agencies.

Constructing Marginality

Homeworkers are characterized as something different from ordinary workers. Variations and elaborations on this theme can be found in many statements from official bodies. For instance, the Department of Employment officials asserted that homework belongs to another labor market, that it "is done by people who would not otherwise be in the ordinary labour force and therefore are not going in any way to be directly affected by the unemployment rate of an area."[6] This assertion is bolstered by the fact that in interviews and testimony employers do not discuss the many advantages this form of production has for them but rather talk about women *choosing* to do homework, its *freedom* from industrial discipline, and the flexibility it offers the women, because of "no set hours," the ability to arrange their work to suit their own convenience, and the saving of time and traveling.[7]

In general official bodies like the Arbitration and Conciliation Advisory Service (ACAS), the Wages Inspectorate, and the Health and Safety Commission do not view homeworkers as ordinary workers, and often see them as performing below the standards of ordinary workers and thus as receiving wages commensurate with their skill and effort.[8] The Department of Employment, which since 1978 has had a Homeworking Unit with resources for relevant research far beyond that of any individual researcher, maintained that "homeworkers are clearly a minority group within the labour force and probably a minority among those who work at and from home, but it has been suggested that they are an exploited or deprived minority which deserves further attention."[9]

The ideological construction of homeworkers as a minority group in the labor force begs all the questions about the recording of labor force activity. On the most conservative estimates homeworkers equal the number of coal miners, those employed by British Rail, and they outnumber academics by at least ten to one. The Department of Employment approach since 1981 is not to deny homeworking but to include within it all those working at or from home regardless of their contracts or conditions of employment.[10] The plastic bag packer, the laid-off executive starting up his own business, the hand knitter, the garage proprietor, the child minder, the builder, and the freelance photographer, script-writer, or novelist are treated as though they are equivalent. Such mystification denies all social-scientific analyses of work and employment and indeed denies even common sense understandings. These constructions make those which a minority of homeworkers use to describe their work as "just a bit extra" or "a job on the side for housewives" pale into insignificance.

Analytically such constructions are open to serious questioning. For the most part they exhibit little appreciation of the causes and conditions of domestic production and fail to differentiate the labor supply in terms of the variety of contractual arrangements. They demonstrate the failure of the theoretical and empirical work on women and waged work, and on unregulated and casualized work, to make any serious impact on official conceptions and techniques of data collection.

The majority of homeworkers we interviewed were well aware of their poor pay and conditions and of the level of skill and performance required of them. Virtually all had external labour market experience with which to make these comparisons. The official views about them and their paid work are seriously at odds with the social realities of homework.[11]

Who Controls Homeworking?

To turn labor into labor for profit requires a system of control.[12] To discipline and reward the work force, and to supervise and evaluate its performance, entails authority over it. The attempt to exercise this authority may be more or less hidden, more or less subtle, more or less successful. Control of the pace and intensity of work and the quality of output is in many cases exercised directly, through close supervision, or technically, through the design of machinery and work processes which demand a certain way of working and which leave the actual producers with little or no discretion over how they perform their jobs. This applies to both in-workers and homeworkers.

An example of control in new technology is the way in which the productivity of many workers is tracked by keystrokes per hour. A North American off-shore data processing firm illustrates this: "When a worker turns on a machine, she must sign on with her identification number. . . . if she goes for a break, she must turn off the machine. . . . Some think they are being smart and fooling us by leaving the machine on when they go to the bathroom, but we can tell when they do this, because their recorded productivity level drops since they've been gone from their terminal."[13]

Direct supervision and subordination of the worker to a machine are only two of a range of mechanisms through which the employer exercises control. In homework, as in the office or factory, it is not the worker but the supplier who organizes control. Autonomy for the homeworker is more apparent than real.

The Work Task

Homeworkers are not independent contractors trading on their own account. The supplier purchases the materials and sells the product. The homeworker does not design or choose her work tasks. Most homeworking is in fact characterized by a division of labor in which production subdivides into discrete, standardized tasks using standardized components, leaving the homeworker with discretion over only the most trivial aspects. In the production of greetings cards, for instance, one set of homeworkers makes the decorations, another group attaches them to the cards, and yet another boxes the finished product. The last homeworker acts as the quality controller who can and must refuse payment to the others if the work is not of the required standard. Similarly, the homeworker who stitches together the ends of fan belts or glues together lampshade pieces has no control over her work tasks. Any possibility of originality or skill has been organized out of the work.

Some homeworkers do complete the whole product and rely on craft skills. Handknitters are one of the best examples. They are skilled workers who knit whole garments, usually for high-class outlets. Before they are accepted as homeworkers, they must prove their skill. Once they become homeworkers, they work with materials supplied by the employer to a design and size specified by him or her. The high-class fashion market depends heavily on homeworking, using highly skilled women, working to strict deadlines and paid menial wages. Machinists who complete whole products, making dresses, blouses, trousers, and leisure wear, do so from cut-out pieces under instructions from the supplier. The popular view that machinists earn extra money "on the side" by using some of the materials supplied to make and sell clothes is in fact not possible under this system.[14]

Output: Payment and Organization

Payment by results establishes an immediate connection between payment and pieces produced. It is the chief mechanism through which suppliers control output and maintain or increase the intensity of work. Homework is almost invariably piece work, not only in manufacturing but among clerical workers.[15] Computer programmers are sometimes paid hourly wages, but their employers have both the financial resources and the technology to monitor the pace of their work with extreme accuracy.[16] In our research all the homeworkers received piece-work rates which determined their hours and intensity of work.[17] In homeworking, piece work operates more successfully than in factory or office, for in the situation known as "sweating," piece rates can be pushed down almost indefinitely, making it necessary for homeworkers to work excessively long hours and to ask the help of family labor to make up their earnings or to meet deadlines. Not only is there no basic wage, but the absence of a standard working day or week means that suppliers do not need to establish a national hourly, daily, or weekly wage from which to calculate piece rates.

Under such conditions the worker comes to see piece-work earnings as the result of her individual effort and so becomes "a willing accomplice to his or her exploitation."[18] Ideologically constrained from seeing herself as a regular worker earning a regular wage, the homeworker comes to regard her earnings as deriving from the additional tasks and effort she takes on by choice. It is because homeworkers are characterized as housewives and irregular earners, supported by a male wage, that the exploitation to which she is subjected by piece work can be ignored so consistently in depictions of the homeworker's autonomy or flexible work load.

Additionally, when the labor force is employed under casualized conditions and is largely unorganized, suppliers have no need to consider collective action from their workers. In consequence the ideological force of piece work, as a system of payment, is reflected in conflicting assessments by homeworkers themselves. For example, one homeworker packed greetings cards for three hours a night, seven days a week. Her earnings were so low that even though her husband helped her most nights they earned only $25.50 to $34 a week between them for forty-two hours work. Not surprisingly, she said that she was "permanently tired," but she went on to say "This is my own fault; I needn't take all the work I do." In fact when the greetings cards work finished, she had to take another homeworking job packing rubbish bags for even less pay.

But homeworkers also recognize that the low piece rates make long hours essential. "To earn anything worthwhile," one comments, "you'd have to chain yourself to the envelopes." Many recognize the peculiar meaning of choice in this context. As one put it: "It was up to the worker to say how many boxes she wanted delivered to her in any week, so I suppose there was an average order, but often I'd order ten boxes and only complete seven. Nobody complained; it was up to me just what amount of work I'd do. But then the less I did the less I got paid, so the incentive was there to do more."

Piece-work earnings depend on being able to build up speed and accuracy with a consistent product. But homeworkers are asked to do anything within a broadly agreed range of products and level of skill. They may experience changes in the product from week to week, but the pay is not adjusted to reflect the difficulties and time necessary to complete different products. The supplier's control over earnings through the allocation of work is shown, moreover, by the commonly recognized practice of rewarding some homeworkers with work carrying higher piece rates. This happens most frequently with the most skilled workers. Nevertheless others, often those known to be the most needy, are given only the lowest rates. The homeworker is dependent on the employer for the type of work supplied, regardless of the effect on her earnings, so a hand-knitter, working thirty hours per week in 1981, could report "Earned $8.50 a week on average - occasionally I had thicker wool and earned about $10.20 a week."

The supplier sets not only the amount of work and rate of pay but the times for the delivery of materials and the collection of finished work. Homeworkers therefore work to tight deadlines, leaving little scope for adjusting their hours to suit themselves. For 90 percent of those we interviewed, work was delivered and collected by the supplier, in some cases with such frequency that the management of the work flow is reminiscent of factory employment. Weekly supply and collection of work was most common, but for over 15 percent it was more than once a week and in two cases more than once a day. One supplier made two deliveries each Friday, so that the homeworker would have "enough" work over the weekend. One homeworker observed, "You can't wash your hair or take the dog for a walk in case you miss the work." The relation between homeworker and supplier is in reality very one-sided. By controlling the work, the supplier leaves the homeworker with little or no autonomy in relation to her paid work.

Nonwage Obligations and the Working Day

Other limitations on autonomy in setting hours and pace of work arise from within the household. Along with other women, homeworkers experience controls on the use of their labor which men rarely experience. In self-employment men often seek advantages like the capacity to set their own hours and pace of work or to exchange time spent on leisure or family life for a higher income or more rewarding work.[19] Such possibilities for women are limited by the sexual division of labor within the home.

The freedom to set one's hours "to suit oneself," to fit paid work around housework and child care, is believed to distinguish homework from other kinds of paid employment and is seen as one of the advantages of homework. People retain an image of the homeworker popping out to do the shopping in a convenient moment, stopping work to run a load of washing, to get the children's tea, or to comfort a crying baby, and then picking up work where she left off. Or the homeworker is thought to get down to work when the family is busy with other things. Close attention to the real conditions of women's work, paid and unpaid, suggest that this whole scenario, with its assumptions of convenient moments and orderly routine, is misleading. It smacks more of some imagined domestic idyll than of the harassed coping strategies with which most women are familiar. Since homeworkers work the same number of hours, paid and unpaid, as women going out to work, they face most of the same problems, but added difficulties, distinctive to doing paid work at home, compound these.

Homeworkers' own accounts provide striking evidence that the working day is tightly structured by the constant demands of paid work and unpaid domestic labor. This is true not simply exceptionally, as when children are ill, but as the normal condition of work.[20] The combination of homeworking, housekeeping, child care, and in some cases other paid work means that every moment is occupied. One woman reported:

> I get the kids off to school, then do the washing and clean round for ten o'clock when the work is delivered. I work through until lunchtime,

stop for a sandwich, and continue until four in the afternoon. About six, after tea and clearing it up, I work another hour, get the youngest off to bed, start again about eight and work until eleven at night. Sometimes I stop work at about nine and get up early the following morning so it will be ready at ten in the morning, when the delivery comes. My day varies according to what crops up—some days the youngest goes to the speech therapist—and how fast I can do a certain job. I am faster at each job as I go along. But it always has to be done by 10 A.M. the next day.

Indeed in many respects homeworking is more onerous than going out to work. This is partly because there is no spatial separation between paid and unpaid work. Homeworking is "always on your mind, always there." As homeworkers recognize, "You do not come home from work and leave it behind you." Moreover, while those going out to work are allowed breaks, the homeworker's day is so dominated by simultaneous demands on her labor that a break in one kind of work is used to get on with another. As few homeworkers have a separate place to work, they are unable to leave their work set up. Three-quarters of our sample worked in the kitchen or living room and had to clear work away to prepare and serve meals or to make room for children to play, and then set up again, all in their "own" time.

Studies demonstrate that the domestic labor of women going out to work is rarely reduced or shared with other household members, but household routines may be adjusted to some extent. Meals may be served earlier or later or consist of different foods, or the house may be left untidy and cleaned in long hours put in at the weekend.[21] In contrast, the homeworker's family still expect the services of a full-time housewife, including, for instance, the preparation of a cooked dinner in the middle of the day.[22]

Likewise, despite the claims of some suppliers, homework is not done casually, in front of the television set, nor picked up and put down in odd moments.[23] While there may be a few opportunities for adjustment of the particular hours in which homework is done, these are limited by the suppliers' control of the amount of work and deadlines. In West Yorkshire the majority did homework for between eleven to thirty hours a week, and twelve for more than forty hours a week. Over a third worked in the evenings, as well as during the day, and nearly as many worked at the weekend. This was in addition to the time put into unpaid domestic labour. The reality is that homeworking permits the worker to go on working until she drops. Her working day extends into unsocial hours, evening and night work, and her working week into a full seven days.

Nor is homework as readily combined with the care of young children as is usually supposed. Homeworkers recognize that despite being at home they are unable to give their children their full attention:

> It took attention away from the three-year-old if I did only 250 boxes a week. Five hundred, and I neglected home, children, husband.

> I have to work very hard to earn a worthwhile wage and can't look after my children properly.

It is evident that there is little about homeworking which is convenient for the worker. Homeworking points up the situation shared by many, perhaps most, women workers—that of fitting their unpaid labor around the demands of employers. For instance, part-time work outside the home is frequently portrayed as convenient for women with domestic responsibilities. In practice, however, women are hired to cover periods of high customer demand or to keep machinery running during breaks in the work of full-time employees, however inconvenient such hours may be for them or their families.[24]

Personal Constraints: Husband's Control and Expectations

The more general ideological and material constraints under which homeworkers sell their labor are experienced as controls within their personal lives: "My husband says I *should* be here for the kids if they're ill and I *have* to take them to and from school in case of accidents. Also he doesn't want me to meet other men or women who'd put ideas in my head" (emphasis added).

In West Yorkshire husbands did not directly exploit or appropriate women's labor as homeworkers. None, including those from ethnic minorities, were employed by their husbands or other male kin, and only a few gave over their wages to a man. However, the husband frequently makes the decision which leads to homework rather than going out to work. Over half of the women said that their families expected them to stay at home rather than go out to work. They saw the husband's opinion as crucial in most cases, since they expressed definite preferences about whether wives should work outside the home or not.

Men and women justified their views through a number of rationales. In some cases it was that "a woman's place" was in the home and he was the breadwinner. For instance, "My husband feels he should support the family financially. He likes me to stay at home. My husband is willing to work longer hours to discourage me going out to work." More usually, however, the husband's preference was expressed in terms of the wife's obligations to their children: "My husband objects to me not looking after our child." "He would not like the idea of a childminder." "My youngest child has asthma and I'm expected to be here in case he's ill." Husbands also had a high expectation that a wife should fit in with his needs and routine and his definition of a satisfactory family life or acceptable standards of housekeeping. In explaining why they did homework, women made comments such as, "My husband is away a lot so he wants me to be at home on the days he has off; . . . because sometimes he finishes work at 3 P.M. and expects me to be in when he comes home. He likes me at home although he wouldn't force me to. He likes me to be at home when he gets in from work. He doesn't like coming in to an empty house; my husband likes meals ready when he gets home."

With some notable exceptions, both husband and wife accepted that it was the husband's right to determine the use of the wife's labor. Even those husbands who were said to have no preference were given this right: "My husband does not prevent me going out to work. I have to think of the children—so I decided." Moreover, many home-workers whose opinion differed from their husbands' still gave way, feeling this to be part of their marital bargain: "He thinks that women should be in the home. He is a male chauvinist pig, but I let him get away with a lot because he treats me well."

In some cases the couple saw housekeeping and child care as a full-time job which left no room for the wife to undertake paid employment: "I have a full-time job at home. I don't want to go out to work, as there is enough to do at home." Homework to them was invisible as work and a source of income. By colluding in the definition of being a full-time housewife, paid work becomes the wife's "choice" of how she uses her "free" time. The significance of her paid homework labor is denied and her earnings barely acknowledged: "My husband still insists that we don't need my homework money, but he's glad of the extra really."

While some men object only to work outside the home and are willing to help with homework ("He helped to get more done; he wanted a little extra money and hated my outside cleaning job"), others resent homeworking. Some condemned the fact that suppliers were getting away with paying wages so far below average: "He complains about the poor pay and thinks I'm a fool 'cos I'm frightened to ask for more."[25] Others expressed dissatisfaction in terms of the mess or inconvenience: "He likes us to relax at night." One woman summarized the views of many that homework was "too badly paid to be worth the upset to the family."

While many husbands expect a wife at home as an integral part of married life, others do not care so long as their own needs are met and the children looked after. In general, taken-for-granted ideological expectations about the sexual division of labour are so effective that explicit controls need never emerge. However, though in most instances the women did homework to provide crucial financial support, the men ignored the material and ideological constraints which forced their wives into this exploitative labour.

Organizing for Change

The reasons why women do paid labor in the home and the conditions under which they do it cannot be understood by theoretical approaches which separate home and work. It is the interrelation of reproductive and productive labour which is central. This interrelation constitutes a major social and economic contradiction represented ideologically and materially in the sexual division of labor in the home and the labor market.

In the 1980s unemployment and the deployment of new technologies have concentrated attention on ways of earning a living outside the factory or office. Many promote the ideas of self-employment, working at home, and flexible labor strategies as new, glamorous solutions. The evidence about homeworking indicates that an unprotected, nominally self-employed, individually segregated, highly flexible, and systematically controlled female labor force has few, if any, benefits and many disadvantages for the workers. Far from resolving the contradiction of productive and reproductive labor, the proposed solutions compound them further.

Many have looked toward improving the lot of homeworkers; in Britain trade unions and women's groups have attempted to come to grips with specific manifestations of homework within the context of late capitalism. None has been as successful in organising casualised homeworkers as the Self-Employed Women's Association in the Indian State of Gujerat. There, a trade union organizer of some twenty years standing overcame immense opposition and managed to attract local and international support to help found in 1972 an organization for the lowest-paid women workers: "The experts refer to them as unorganised, informal, marginal, unregulated, peripheral, residual. These are negative terms which give them an inferior and insignificant position in the whole economy, whereas in reality they contribute enormously to the economy. . . . To give them positive status and to draw positive attention to them we call them self-employed workers."[26]

The Self-Employed Women's Association is a challenge to all those who maintain that homeworkers cannot be organised. It has brought together in one organization women rag pickers, waste-paper collectors, and vegetable or second-hand-clothes sellers as well as homeworkers in textiles, cane and leather work, and, above all, in the cigarette making industries (*bidi* workers) to fight for better wages and conditions and to obtain fair contracts from the state government. It combines trade union action with development strategies. A women's bank has been established, a co-operative program for training as well as production in rural areas is under way, and facilities for legal aid, health and maternity care, and education are provided.[27] Though its 30,000 members represent only a drop in the ocean of India's estimated 8.8 million workers in household industries (in itself a gross underestimation), by successfully reaching formerly unorganised workers SEWA has lessons for all those concerned to improve the position of homeworkers.[28]

Until very recently trade unions, in Britain and elsewhere, have argued that homeworking should not exist and their hostility to it has extended to homeworkers. Whereas in the United States unions in some trades, such as cigar making and textiles, campaigned vigorously and successfully to make homeworking illegal, in Britain trade unions for the most part ignored homeworkers and concentrated on improving conditions for factory and office workers.[29] They recognised the threat posed by unorganised workers in undercutting wages and worsening conditions. Casualised workers, such as homeworkers, were seen in this way, and so long as they remain unorganised were deemed to be unorganisable.

Stripping away the many layers of the ideological constructions which separate home and work and reinforce the low waged work of women has been left, in the main, to women in the labor movement, supported on occasions by women politicians and researchers. Historically, their part in organizing against sweated labor, in shops, factories, and in homework, was one of the most important chapters not only in securing legislation which created trades boards and minimum wages but also, if only briefly, in forcing some recognition of the realities of women's working lives.[30]

In the past few years we have seen a resurgence of these same concerns: from the 1950s onwards, growth of part-time work for women resulting from labor shortages and employer-led demand; in the 1960s and 1970s, legal changes for employee protection, strengthened for women by the Equal Pay and Sex Discrimination legislation. Although the 1980s have brought many reversals, some gains are evident, not least the heightened awareness among women trade unionists of the many forms of low-paid work and poor conditions experienced by women. This has helped to bring about a changed policy toward homeworkers.[31]

After the failure in 1979 and 1981 to obtain legal protection for homeworkers, similar to that for other employees in Britain, many of the campaigning groups came together to establish a National Group on Homeworking to facilitate organization among homeworkers and to press for change. Many local groups had already succeeded in influencing local councils to recognize workers' problems associated with homeworking and some were persuaded to provide financial help or to amend local regulations, but the few who looked toward controlling suppliers were unable to do so because of the lack of adequate regulations or appropriate sanctions.[32]

In fact the pressures toward deregulation of labor increased markedly from 1980 and the political emphasis switched to unregulated enterprise. Similar pressures developed in the United States.[33] Although in Norway and West Germany the present law affords better protection for homeworkers, and the need for legal protection is well documented in many societies, the present political climate is antipathetic to both improvements in the law or its effective implementation.[34] The International Labour Office has given some attention to homeworking, but there are as yet no guidelines, let alone instruments, proposed for member states to consider.[35] Some of the changes necessary are particular to an individual industry, locality, or society, but many are relevant to all societies.

For instance, the official national and international definitions of economic activity need revising to record the participation of women, so that the patterns and amounts of their paid work can be revealed and realistically assessed. This would require a radical overhaul of most social and economic statistics. Social insurance, social security, and tax legislation must be reformed so that women, independent of their marital status, are not disadvantaged compared to men. Adequate facilities for child care and for the care of the sick, handicapped, and elderly and a recognition of, and appropriate provision for, the education and training needs of those currently excluded from all but the lowest-paid work with poor conditions are essential for those who presently undertake unpaid reproductive work.

On the more specific question of homeworking, in most societies legislation guaranteeing employee status is the necessary first step for all other improvements for homeworkers. Both full-time and part-time workers should receive employee benefits and legally enforceable minimum wages and conditions The effective implementation of such changes would require the registration of all those using homeworking labor and a close monitoring of their practices.[36]

There has been an advance in the recognition of the pervasive, exploitative, and international character of homeworking in the last few years. Since without radical changes in the power relations within households and between capital and labor it will continue and possibly increase, the need for effective control to provide decent working conditions and reasonable standards of living is as great as it was at the end of the nineteenth century. It presents a crucial challenge to all who seek such improvements, but particularly to socialist-feminists.

A close analysis of homeworking demonstrates, in a particularly stark way, the theoretical and methodological issues crucial to understanding women's integration into productive labor. Fortunately, much recent work has focused on retrieving evidence of every-day working lives and reconceptualizing the relations of women and work. This work must be incorporated into theory and research in order to avoid repeating the inadequacies of earlier theorizations about work. With regard to practical policies, it is not sufficient to describe or itemise diversities. It is necessary to draw out the commonalities of women as wives, mothers, and workers, specifying the exploitative relations which enmesh them, and to devise effective means of implementing change.

NOTES

I wish to acknowledge the support for the initial research financed by the E.S.R.C. and the University of Bradford. My special thanks are due to the homeworkers who gave up their precious time to answer questions and to many others with whom I have discussed the issues, notably Sahba Husain, Julia Graham, Cyndi Daniels, Martha Fowlkes, and Carol Wolkowitz. This papers draws on several previously published papers either directly or indirectly. These are listed in the references with the exception of Allen and Wolkowitz, "The Control of Women's Labour: The Case of Homeworking," which appeared in *Feminist Review*, no. 22 (1986).

I began to research homeworking in 1978. The interviews with homeworkers, ex-homeworkers, suppliers, and "middlemen" in West Yorkshire took place in the early 1980s.

For readers unfamiliar with the agencies referred to, the U.S. parallels are:
ACAS = National Labor Relations Board
Department of Employment = Department of Labor

Wages Inspectorate = Division of the Dept. of Labor
Health and Safety Commission = Division of the Dept. of Labor
TUC = AFL/CIO

1. Sheila Allen and Carol Wolkowitz, *Homeworking, Myths and Realities* (London: Macmillan, 1987).

2. *Ibid.* and Kathy Wray, "The Demand for Labour in a Textile Local Labour Market with Particular Reference to Twilight Workers and Homeworkers," (Ph.D. thesis, University of Loughborough, 1985).

3. Brian Bolton, *An End to Homeworking?* Fabian Society, Tract no. 436 (London, 1975); Simon Crine, *The Hidden Army* (London Low Pay Unit, 1979); Trades Union Congress, *A Statement on Homeworking* (London: Trades Union Congress, 1978).

4. Diana Leonard Barker and Sheila Allen, eds., *Dependence and Exploitation in Work and Marriage* (London: Longman, 1976), p.1.

5. Sheila Allen, "Production and Reproduction: The Lives of Women Homeworkers," *The Sociological Review* 31, no. 4 (November 1983): 649–65. Dollar amounts are in 1981 equivalents.

6. House of Commons, Select Committee on Employment, *Homeworking,* Minutes of Evidence, 24 February, para. 47, (London: HMSO, 1981).

7. House of Commons, Select Committee on Employment, *Homeworking,* CBI Wages Councils (Employers') Consultative Committee Memorandum, 7 April, para. 11 (London: HMSO, 1981).

8. House of Commons, Select Committee on Employment, *Homeworking.*

9. Arnold Cragg and Tim Dawson, *Qualitative Research among Homeworkers,* Research Paper no. 21 (London: Department of Employment, 1981).

10. Catherine Hakim, "Employers' Use of Homework, Outwork and Freelances," *Employment Gazette* 92, no.4 (April 1984): 144–50.

11. Sheila Allen, "Invisible Threads," in *Women in the Informal Sector,* ed. K. Young and C. Moser, *Institute of Development Studies Bulletin,* Special Issue, 12, no 3 (1981): 41–47 Sheila Allen, "Domestic Production and Organising for Change," *Economic and Industrial Democracy* 3, no. 4 (1982): 381–411.

12. Paul Thompson, *The Nature of Work: An Introduction to Debates on the Labour Process* (London: Macmillan, 1983).

13. Anne Posthuma, "High Tech Job Wars," unpublished paper, n.d.

14. cf. Beatrix Campbell, "Lining Their Pockets," *Time Out,* July 13–19, 1978.

15. Marie Brown, *Sweated Labour: A Study of Homework,* Pamphlet no. 1, (London: Low Pay Unit, 1974); Cragg and Dawson, *Qualitative Research among Homeworkers;* Crine, *The Hidden Army;* Catherine Hakim, "Homeworking: Some New Evidence," *Employment Gazette* 80, no. 10 (1980): 1105–9; Hakim, "Employers' Use of Homework," David Jordan, *The Wages of Fear,* Bulletin no. 20, (London: Low Pay Unit 1978).

16. Ursula Huws, "New Technology Homeworkers," *Employment Gazette,* January 1984; Ursula Huws, *The New Homeworkers: New Technology and the*

Changing Location of White Collar Work, Pamphlet no. 28 (London: Low Pay Unit, 1984).

17. Sheila Allen, *Homeworking in the West Yorkshire Connurbation: S.S.R.C. Final Report,* September 1981; Allen "Invisible Threads"; Allen, "Production and Reproduction."

18. Harry Braverman, *Labour and Monopoly Capital: The Degradation of Work in the Twentieth Century* (New York: Monthly Review Press, 1974, p. 62

19. Richard Scase and Robert Goffee, *The Entrepreneurial Middle Class* (London: Croom Helm, 1982).

20. Cragg and Dawson, *Qualitative Research among Homeworkers.*

21. Heidi I. Hartmann, "The Family as the Locus of Gender, Class and Political Struggle: The Example of Housework," *Signs,* 6, no. 3 (Spring 1981): 366–94; Pauline Hunt, *Gender and Class Consciousness* (London: Macmillan, 1980); M. Meissner et. al., "No Exit for Wives: Sexual Division of Labour and the Cumulation of Household Demands," *Canadian Review of Sociology and Anthropology* 12, no. 4 (1975): 424–39.

22. Sheila Allen, "The Labour Process and Working at Home," *Social Scientist* (New Delhi) 13, nos. 10–11 (1985): 86–94.

23. Jill Rubery and Frank Wilkinson, "Outwork and Segmented Labour Markets," in *The Dynamics of Labour Market Segmentation,* ed. F. Wilkinson (London: Academic Press, 1981).

24. Angela Coyle, *Redundant Women,* (London: Women's Press, 1984); O. Robinson and J. Wallace, "Growth and Utilisation of Part-time Labour in Great Britain," *Employment Gazette* 92, no. 9 (1984): 391–97.

25. See also Sue Sharpe, *Double Identity: The Lives of Working Mothers* (Harmondsworth: Penguin, 1984).

26. Ela Bhatt, "Address at the Thirteenth World Congress of The I.C.F.T.U., Oslo, June 23–30," in *We, The Self Employed* (Ahmedabad, India: SEWA, 1983), p. 12

27. Anila R. Dholakia, "Rural Women in White Revolution" (Paper presented to the UNICEF seminar on women's dairy co-operatives, Ahmedabad, India, May 1984); R. Jhabvala, "The Home-Based Workers," in *We, The Self-Employed.*

28. Ela Bhatt, "The Invisibility of Home-Based Work: The Case of Piece Rate Workers in India," Paper presented to the Women and the Household Conference, New Delhi, 1985.

29. Sheila Allen, "Domestic Production and Organising for Change."

30. Sarah Boston, *Women Workers and the Trade Union Movement* (London: Davis Poynter, 1980); Gail Braybon, *Women Workers in the First World War* (London: Croom Helm, 1981); Barbara Drake, *Women in Trade Unions* (London: Virago Press, 1984; original edition, Labour Research Department 1920); Ada Nield Chew, *The Life and Writings of a Working Woman* (London: Virago Press, 1982).

31. Trades Union Congress, *Homeworking: A TUC Statement* (London: Trades Union Congress, 1985).

32. Liz Bissett and Ursula Huws, *Sweated Labour: Homeworking in Britain Today,* Pamphlet no. 33 (London: Low Pay Unit, 1985); Mary Hopkins, "Homeworking Campaigns, Dilemmas and Possibilities in Working with a Fragmented Community," (M.A. diss., University of Warwick (Leicester Outwork Campaign), 1982); Leicester Outwork Campaign, *Annual Report 1984–5,* 1985

33. "Colorado Legislature Passes Pro-Homework Resolution," *Telecommuting Review,* September, 1985

34. Allen and Wolkowitz, *Homeworking;* U. Baxi, "State, Seths and Shiksha: The Saga of Satteora" (Paper presented at the Women and the Household Conference, New Delhi, 1985; Laura Johnson with Robert E. Johnson, *The Seam Allowance: Industrial Home Sewing in Canada* (Toronto: Women's Press, 1982); Margaret Owen, "Legal and Policy Issues Relating to Homebased Producers" (Paper presented at the Women and the Household Conference, New Delhi, 1985); Martha Roldan, "Industrial Outworking: Struggles for the Reproduction of Working Class Families and Gender Subordination" in *Beyond Employment,* ed. N. Redclift and E. Mingione (Oxford: Basil Blackwell, 1985).

35. Margaret Owen, "Rationale for an International Instrument to Protect the Home-based Producers," unpublished paper, n.d.

36. See Allen and Wolkowitz, *Homeworking,* for a detailed discussion.

Notes on Contributors

Sheila Allen, professor of sociology at the University of Bradford in England, is the former chair of the British Sociological Association. She is the co-author, with Carol Wolkowitz, of *Homeworking: Myths and Realities* (Basingstoke, England: Macmillan Education, 1987). Her research and writing have focused on race and ethnic relations, the sociology of work and employment, and gender. Currently she is researching women in business.

Betty A. Beach, associate professor of early childhood education at the University of Maine at Farmington, is investigating preschool children's perceptions of parental work. She is the author of the forthcoming *Integrating Work and Family Life: The Homeworking Family* (State University of New York Press) and articles in such journals as *Journal of Contemporary Ethnography, Illinois Teacher,* and *Family Relations: Journal of Applied Child and Family Studies.*

Susan Porter Benson, associate professor of history at the University of Missouri-Columbia, earlier taught at Bristol Community College in Fall River, Massachusetts, and worked on the *Treads* program of the Amalgamated Clothing and Textile Workers Union. She is the author of *Counter Cultures: Saleswomen, Managers, and Customers in American Department Stores, 1890–1940* (University of Illinois Press, 1986) and co-editor, with Stephen Brier and Roy Rosenzweig of *Presenting the Past: Critical Perspectives on History and the Public* (Temple University Press, 1986). Her current research focuses on class, gender, and consumption.

Julia Kirk Blackwelder is professor of history and chair of the History Department at the University of North Carolina, Charlotte, where she formerly directed Women's Studies. She is the author of *Women of the Depression: Caste and Culture in San Antonio, 1929–1939* (Texas A&M Press, 1984) and numerous articles in southern history.

Eileen Boris, assistant professor of history at Howard University, was a fellow at the Woodrow Wilson International Center for Scholars during 1988–89, where she worked on a history of industrial homework and its regulation in the United States. She is the author of *Art and Labor: Ruskin, Morris, and the Craftsman Ideal in America* (Temple University Press, 1986). Her articles have appeared in the *Journal of American History, Signs, Wisconsin Women's Law Journal,* the *Nation,* and other publications.

Kathleen Christensen is director of the National Project on Home-based Work and associate professor of Environmental Psychology at the Graduate School and University Center, City University of New York. She is the author of *Women and Home-based Work: The Unspoken Contract* (Henry Holt & Co., 1988) and the editor of *The New Era of Home-based Work: Directions and Policies* (Westview Press, 1988). Her extensive writings have focused on women and work, recently on the consequences of contingent work arrangements for women.

Cynthia B. Costello, who holds a Ph.D. in sociology from the University of Wisconsin-Madison, is coordinator of the Employment and Voluntarism Program at the Villers Foundation, Washington, D.C. Formerly a research fellow at the Russell Sage Foundation and study director, Committee on Women's Employment and Related Social Issues, National Research Council, National Academy of Sciences, she recently has completed a manuscript, entitled *"We're Worth It!" Women, Work, and Organizing.*

Jamie Faricellia Dangler is a graduate student in sociology at the State University of New York at Binghamton, where she is finishing a dissertation on industrial homework in Central New York State and has been an active member of the research working group on world labor at the Fernand Braudel Center. Her previous publications include "Industrial Homework in the Modern World-Economy," *Contemporary Crises* 10 (1986).

Cynthia R. Daniels is a research associate with the Family, Work, and Social Policy Program at the Stone Center, Wellesley College. She is also the women's occupational health coordinator for the Massachusetts Department of Public Health, where she directs the Working Women's Health Project. She currently is researching the impact of "fetal protection policies" on women working in the high-tech industry.

Virginia duRivage is a member of the professional staff of the Select Committee on Children, Youth and Families of the House of Representatives, U.S. Congress. Formerly she was the associate research director of 9 to 5, the National Association of Working Women.

M. Patricia Fernández-Kelly is an associate professor of sociology and a research scientist at the Institute for Policy Studies at the Johns Hopkins University. She is the author of *For We Are Sold, I and My People: Women and Industry in Mexico's Frontier* (State University of New York Press, 1983) and has published extensively on questions regarding international development, women's employment in export processing zones, and the informal economy. With filmmaker Lorraine Gray, she co-produced *Women on the Global Assembly Line,* which was awarded an Emmy by the National Academy of Television Arts and Sciences in 1987.

Anna M. García is a research associate at the Center for U.S.-Mexican Studies at the University of California at San Diego. She has participated in several projects focusing on the health of Mexican immigrants and their access to public services. Her current work focuses on the impact of immigration reform upon the employment patterns of California businesses. She has co-authored several articles with M. Patricia Fernández-Kelly.

David Jacobs is assistant professor of management at Kogod College of Business Administration, American University, where he specializes in union decision making in the larger economic context. His articles have appeared in *Labor Law Journal, Advances in Industrial and Labor Relations, ILR Report,* and other scholarly journals.

Margrethe H. Olson, associate professor in the Graduate School of Business at New York University, is director of the Center for Research on Information Systems. She was chair of the 1984 panel on telecommunicating for the National Academy of Sciences and has evaluated homework experiments for major corporations, like Control Data. She is the editor of the forthcoming book *Technological Support for Work Group Collaboration* (Erlbaum) and the author of numerous articles on telecommuting as an organizational work option.

Hilary Silver is assistant professor of sociology and urban studies at Brown University. Her work includes articles on the service industries, constraints on women's time, welfare states, urban economic development and housing, and a forthcoming book, *The New Urban Inequality.* She currently is writing on the spatial and ideological separation of home and work.

Index